PHYSICAL AND HEALTH EDUCATION

PHYSICAL AND HEALTH EDUCATION

Arul Jothi
M.Sc., M.Ed.
Principal, Arcot Sri Mahalakshmi Women's Teacher Training Institute,
Villapakkam, Vellore Dist.-632521 T.N.

Dr. D.L. Balaji
B.Com., M.A., M.Phil., D.Lit.
Correspondent, Arcot Sri Mahalakshmi Educational Institutions,
Villapakkam, Vellore Dist.-632521 T.N.

Dr. Jagdish Prasad Sharma
Reader, Teachers Training College,
Patna

CENTRUM PRESS
NEW DELHI-110002 (INDIA)

CENTRUM PRESS

H.O.: 4360/4, Ansari Road, Daryaganj,
New Delhi-110 002 (India)
Ph.: 23278000, 23261597

B.O.: No. 1015, Ist Main Road, BSK IIIrd Stage
IIIrd Phase, IIIrd Block,
Bangalore - 560 085 (India)
Tel.: 080-41723429
Visit us at: www.centrumpress.com

Physical and Health Education

First Edition, 2009

PRINTED IN INDIA

Printed at Balaji Offset, Delhi

Contents

Preface

At this day and age the unity of mind and body is a widely recognised and accepted fact and the totality of life is universally emphasised. It has become commonplace to say that we have to live a healthy life and that, without health, we cannot achieve or retain anything accomplished. If we are to build bodies that are ready to become fitter instruments for the new work of transformation, health should not merely be defined as just the absence of disease or infirmity. It should be a powerful tool that gives us the ability to sustain adaptive effort ('adaptive' in the sense of a progressive overloading of the system) and use it to imply body power, vitality and ability to resist fatigue.

It is now a known fact within the scientific community worldwide - and also in the world of coaching - that even if one wishes to develop only one aspect of any formation, one cannot ignore the whole. So it is with the body: it is like an orchestra, each part integrating and working in unison with the other parts. The Integral Yoga emphasises the need for integral development of all levels of the being. Our aim should be to develop our physical capacities and attributes to their perfection through a consciously chosen programme. The notion of perfection implies a harmonious and complete development. Just as we train the young mind through studies of various subjects (e.g. language, mathematics, arts, history, science etc.), so also the body needs development and training in a comprehensive, varied programme that covers all different parts of the physical being.

In most educational systems, physical education is a course in the curriculum which utilizes the learning medium of large-muscle activities in a play or movement exploration setting. It aims to equip students with the knowledge, skills, capacities, and values along with the enthusiasm to maintain a healthy lifestyle into adulthood, regardless of their physical abilities. The book makes an in-depth investigation into aims of general and physical education; programme, promotion and methods of physical education in schools. This book is a unique presentation of physical and health education and will be useful for teachers, students, historians, health and fitness consultants and general readers. This book is unique because it focuses solely on the physical education teaching process—the skills and techniques that successful teachers use to make their classes more interesting and developmentally appropriate.

— *Dr. Jagdish Prasad Sharma*

UNIT-I

Introduction to Physical Education

Physical Education: Meaning, Definition, Aims and Objectives

In most educational systems, physical education (P.E.) class, (also known as Phys Ed, or Gym) is a course taken in lower, middle, and high school that utilizes learning in the cognitive, affective and psychomotor domains in a play or movement exploration setting. The term physical education is most commonly used in this way; however, this denotes they have *participated* in the subject area rather than *studied* it." Physical education (PE) is the interdisciplinary study of all areas of science relating to the transmission of physical knowledge and skills to an individual or a group, the application of these skills, and their results.

The primary aims of physical education have varied, based on the needs of the time and place. Most modern schools' goal is to provide students with knowledge, skills, capacities, values, and the enthusiasm to maintain a healthy lifestyle into adulthood. Activities included in the programme are designed to promote physical fitness, to develop motor skills, to instill knowledge and understanding of rules, concepts, and strategies. Students learn to either work as part of a team, or as individuals, in a wide variety of competitive activities. Due to the relative decrease in physical activity among American kids and teenagers in recent years, some schools also require physical education as a way to promote weight loss in students. The promotion of weight loss can also be harmful in mental ways so it is not always the best way of teaching. In all states in the United States, physical education is offered to students from grades K through 12. Illinois is the only state that requires physical education in all schools (even private schools) for all grade levels. However some activities, such as JROTC and marching band, are acceptable substitutes for physical education as a class. Most states do require physical education from 6th through 9th grades and offer "elective" physical education classes from 10th through 12th grades.

International P.E.

In the United States, the physical education curriculum is designed to allow school pupils a full range of modern opportunities, dozens of sports and hundreds of carefully reviewed drills and excercises, including exposure to the education with the use of pedometer, GPS, and heart rate monitors, as well as state-of-the-art excercise machines in the upper grades. Some martial arts classes, like wrestling in the United States, and Pencak Silat in France and Malaysia, are taught to teach children self-defense and to feel good about themselves..

The physical education curriculum is designed to allow students to experience at least a minimum exposure to the following categories of activities: aquatics, conditioning activities, gymnastics, individual/dual sports, team sports, rhythms, and dance. Students are encouraged to continue to explore those activities in which they have a primary interest by effectively managing their community resources. In these areas, a planned sequence of learning experiences is designed to support a progression of student development. This allows kids through 6th grade to be introduced to sports, fitness, and teamwork in order to be better prepared for the middle and high school age. Even though to most gym is a total waste of time and is very unsanitary, In 1975, the United States House of Representatives voted to require school physical education classes include both genders. Some high school and some middle school PE classes are single-sex. Requiring individuals to participate in physical education activities, such as dodgeball, flag football, and other competitive sports. This remains a controversial subject because of the social impact these games have on young children.

In Singapore, pupils from primary school through junior colleges are required to have 2 hours of PE every school week, except during examination seasons. Pupils are able to play games like football, badminton, 'captain's ball' and basketball during most sessions. Unorthodox sports such as tchoukball, fencing and skateboarding are occasionally played. In more prestigious secondary schools and in junior colleges, sports such as golf, tennis, shooting, squash are played. A compulsory fitness exam, NAPFA, is conducted in every school once every year to assess the physical fitness of the pupils. Pupils are given a series of fitness tests (Pull-ups/ Inclined pull-ups for girls, standing broad jump, sit-ups, sit-and-reach and 1.2 km for secondary/2.4 km for junior colleges run). Students are graded by gold, silver, bronze and fail. NAPFA for Year 2 males in junior colleges serves as an indicator for an additional 2 months in the country's compulsory national service if they attain bronze or fail.

In Scotland, pupils are expected to do two periods of PE in first year, one in second year and two in third and fourth year. In fifth and sixth year, PE is voluntary.

In the Philippines, some schools have integrated martial arts training into their Physical Education cirriculum.

In England, pupils are expected to do two hours of PE a week in Year 7, 8 and 9 and at least 1 in year 10 and 11.

In Wales, pupils are expected to do only one hour of PE per fortnight.

In Nepal, physical education is poor and poorly organized because the educational system has only been recently established and is still adjusting to recent changes and updates. Nepal has not gone very far in the sector of education because the educational history of Nepal is very short. Before 1951, Nepal was under a monarchy. The monarchy did not wish to provide education to the citizens as it did not want them to be educated and therefore politically aware. Institution of democracy did not result in a modern educational system; what education there was was little better. After 10 years of democracy the country again plunged into an autocratic monarchy. In 1990 democracy was restored and the education sector started to flourish. Since then, Physical Education became part of the school curriculum. At the primary level (1-5), some minor and local games are now taught, like hide and seek and some athletic based local events.

In lower secondary level (6-8), the students are taught general concepts on major games like football, volleyball, basket ball, Kho-Kho and Kabaddi. They also learn some athletics like 100m race 1004m relay race and some other minor and lead up games. In class Nine and ten it is an optional subject where they specialize in some games like volleyball, basketball, handball, cricket, Kho Kho Kabaddi, Badminton, table tennis and some athletics are also taught. In college it is taught in the education stream. Even though it is included in school curriculum, Nepal is not able to produce any worthwhile products of games and sports for reasons ranging from poverty to decentralized government.

Meaning and Definition of Physical Education

Physical Education is the process by which changes in the individual are bought about through movements experiences. Physical Education aims not only at physical development but is also concerned with education of the whole person through physical activities.

It would not be wrong if we say that Physical education is the play-way method of education.

Various Definitions of Physical Education are:

1. Barrow defined Physical Education as an education of and through human movement where many of educational objectives are achieved by means of big muscle activities involving sports, games, gymnastic, dance and exercise.
2. According to Webster's Dictionary Physical education is a part of education which gives instructions in the

development and care of the body randing from simple callisthenic exercises to a course of study providing training in hygiene, gymnastics and the performance and management of athletics games.

3. Jackson R. Sharman points out that physical education is that part of education which takes place through activities, which involves the motor mechanism of human body which results in an individual's formulating behaviour patterns.
4. Charles A. Bucher defines physical education, an integral part of total education process, is a field of endeavour which has as its aim the development of physically, mentally, emotionally and socially fit citizens through the medium of physical activities which have been selected with a view to realizing these outcomes."
5. Central Advisory Board of physical Education and Recreation defines Physical education as an education through physical activities for the development of total personality of the child to its fullness and perfection in body, mind and spirit.

Aim and Approach of the Curriculum

The aim of physical education is to enable all students to enhance their quality of life through active living. The Physical Education 11 and 12 curriculum builds on and expands the curriculum developed for Kindergarten to Grade 10.

Physical Education 11 and 12 provides opportunities for students to experience a variety of recreational pursuits, career interests, and activities that promote lifelong, healthy living. Students focus their learning in areas of personal interest and participate in activities that promote social interaction, community responsibility, and skill development.

In Physical Education 11 and 12, teachers work with students to develop programmes to meet student needs and interests. Programmes are structured so that the duration, intensity, and frequency of activities motivate students to meet their individual goals. Students participate in a balance of activities from the movement categories.

Framework of the Physical Education Curriculum

The Physical Education 11 and 12 curriculum focusses on promoting healthy attitudes and regular physical activity as important parts of each student's lifestyle. It emphasizes analysing and improving physical competence, maintaining personal fitness, developing effective leadership and sports-management skills, and planning for careers.

In senior physical education programmes, students:

- apply the concepts of a balanced, healthy lifestyle to design programmes for themselves and others
- apply the elements of movement and knowledge of fitness to improve personal functional levels of competence in a variety of activities and environments
- demonstrate an appreciation of the needs of various groups and adapt activities for them
- recognize an activity's impact on the environment
- integrate safety practices and the prevention and management of sports injuries in a variety of physical activities and environments
- apply knowledge and skills from certification programmes
- model and apply leadership skills and positive personal qualities in volunteer work and physical activities at school and in the community

Linking Past and Current Physical Education Curricula

As in the past, the present curriculum focusses on the unique and significant contributions of physical education in the development of every student. The previous curriculum (1987) organized important goal statements under three domains: affective (attitude), cognitive (knowledge), and psychomotor (skills). The prescribed learning outcomes of the new curriculum are grouped under three curriculum organizers: Active Living, Movement, and Personal and Social Responsibility. In each organizer, the prescribed learning outcomes incorporate learning from the three domains. In addition, the previous curriculum provided seven movement categories, while the new curriculum has only three.

Nature and Scope of Physical Education, Exercise Science, and Sport:

- What is "contemporary physical education?"
- How do different areas of physical education relate to the field overall?
- What is the importance of creating your personal philosophy of physical education, exercise science, and sport?

Goals for Physical Educators"

- Access to physical education and sport for all, regardless of: age, gender, race, ethnicity, sexual orientation, disability status, income, educational level, geographic location and ability.
- Prevent disease and positively contribute to health and well-being of all participants.

Expansion of Physical Education, Exercise Science, and Sport:

- Moved from the traditional school setting to:
- Community
- Home
- Worksite
- Commercial & Medical Settings
- Corporations

Who says Physical Activity is Good?

- National Reports:
- "Physical Activity and Health: A Report of the Surgeon General"
- "Healthy People 2010"
- "Promoting Better Health for Young People through Physical Activity and Sports"

Our Physical Activity Challenge:

Improve Participation of Populations with Low Rates of Physical Activity:

Current Participation Patterns:

- Women are generally less active than men at all ages.
- African Americans and Hispanics are generally less active than whites.
- People with low incomes are typically not as active as those with high incomes.
- People with less education are generally not as active as those with higher levels of education.
- Adults in the Northeast and South tend to be less active than adults in the North Central and Western States
- People with disabilities are less physically active than people without disabilities.
- Participation in physical activity declines with age. By age 75, one in 3 men and one in two women engage in no physical activity.

U.S. Department of Health and Human Services. Healthy People 2010: Understanding and Improving Health. Washington, DC: U.S. Government Printing Office, November, 2000.

Definitions: Physical Education

- Physical education....
- An educational process that uses physical activity as a means to help people acquire skills, fitness, knowledge, and attitudes that contribute to their optimal development and well-being.
- Contributes to the development of the whole person.
- Education
- An on-going process that occurs throughout our lifespan.

Definitions: Exercise Science

- Exercise Science...
- The scientific analysis of exercise or physical activity through theories from many different disciplines such as biology, biochemistry, physics, and psychology.

Definitions: Sports

- Organized competitive activities governed by rules that standardize the competition and conditions so individuals can compete fairly.
- Competition against oneself or opponent(s).
- Strategy and skill play a significant role in the determination of the outcome.

Definition: Athletics

- Highly organized, competitive sports
- Skillful participants

The Field (More than a Playing Surface!)

- Field.... "a combination of a well-established discipline and one or more professions that deliver a social service and are focused on common goals." (Corbin)
- Discipline ..."organized body of knowledge embraced in a formal course of learning." (Henry)

Physical Education, Exercise Science and Sport: The Profession

- Profession...
- An occupation requiring specialized training in an intellectual field of study that is dedicated to the betterment of society through service to others.
- Some examples of professional organizations:

Organizing the Profession

- With developing technologies, knowledge, and methods of inquiry from other disciplines in the 1960s, physical education, exercise science, and sport broadened its horizons to incorporate the fields of psychology and sociology.
- The result:12 subdisciplines

Sub-disciplines

- Exercise physiology
- Sports medicine

- Sport biomechanics
- Sport philosophy
- Sport history
- Sport psychology
- Motor development
- Motor learning
- Sport sociology
- Sport pedagogy
- Adapted physical activity
- Sport management

Exercise Physiology

- Impact of exercise and physical activity on the human body.
- Short-and long-term adaptations of the various systems of the body.
- Effects of physical activity and exercise on the health status of different populations.
- ACSM:

Sports Medicine

- Medical relationship between physical activity, sports-related injuries, and the human body.
- Prevention-the design of conditioning programmes, fitting of protective equipment, and counseling regarding proper nutrition.
- Treatment and rehabilitation-the assessment of injuries, administration of first aid, design and implementation of rehabilitation programme and treatment.

Sport Biomechanics

- Applies the methods of physics to the study of human motion and the motion of sport objects.
- Study the effects of force on the body and sport objects.
- Mechanical analysis of activities (production of power, leverage, and stability)
- Analysis of effectiveness and efficiency of movements

Sport Philosophy

- Study of the nature of reality and values of movement for all participants.
- Debate critical issues, beliefs, and values relative to physical education and sport (i.e. What is the relationship between the mind and the body?).
- Influences thoughts, actions, and decisions in our professional endeavors and personal lives.

Sport History

- Critical examination of the past with a focus on events, people, and trends that influenced the direction of the field.
- The "who, what, when, where, how, and why of sport" is examined within the social context of the time.
- Looking into the past provides greater understanding of present events and insight with respect to the future.

  NASSH: North American Society for Sport History publishes the Journal of Sport History.

Sport and Exercise Psychology

- Uses principles from psychology to study human behavior in sport to enhance performance.
- *Sport Areas:* achievement motivation, arousal regulation, goal setting, self-confidence, leadership, and team cohesion
- *Exercise Areas:* exercise addiction, adherence, motivation, and satisfaction

Sport and Exercise Psychology

- Sport areas:
- achievement motivation
- arousal regulation
- goal setting
- self-confidence
- leadership
- team cohesion

- Exercise areas:
- exercise addiction
- adherence to exercise
- motivation
- satisfaction
- Uses principles from psychology to study human behavior in sport to enhance performance.

Motor Development

- Interaction of genetic and environmental influences on movement and lifespan motor development.
- Use theories of development to design appropriate movement experiences for people of all ages and abilities.

Motor Learning

- Study of factors that influence an individual's acquisition and performance of skills, such as practice, experience, use of reinforcement, and condition of learning environment.
- Progression through stages of learning from a beginner to a highly skilled performer.

Sport Sociology

- Study of the role of sport in society.
- "What is the influence of society on sport?"
- "What is the influence of sport on society?"

Center for the Study of Sport in Society at Northeastern University publishes the Journal of Sport and Social Issues.

Sport Pedagogy

- Study of teaching and learning.
- Creation of effective learning environments, instructional strategies, outcome assessment, and relationship of instructional process to learning.
- Development of effective practitioners through the analysis of the behaviors of teachers/coaches and students/athletes.

Adapted Physical Activity

- Providing individual programmes and services that encourage participation to the fullest extent by those with disabilities.

Sport Management

- Encompasses the managerial aspects of sport and sport enterprise.
- Facility and personnel management, budgeting, promotion of events, media relations, and programming. The Journal of Sport Management is the official journal of the North American Society for Sport Management (NASSM).

A New Name for the Field

- Physical Education-traditional, but too narrow; does not reflect the expanding nature of the field.
- Kinesiology-study of human movement, but the public is not familiar with the term.
- Exercise and Sport Science-reflects the broad emphasis of the field and easy to understand.
- Physical Education and Sport-traditional, familiar, and includes sport as a vital part.
- No common agreement as to the name of the field, but there is a growing central focus: Physical Activity.

Allied Fields

- Health:
- Health Instruction
- Health Services
- Environmental Health
- Recreation
- Dance

These fields share many purposes with physical education, exercise science, and sport, but the content of the subject matter and methods to reach their goals are different.

Definition of Terms

- *Health:* A state of positive well-being associated with freedom from disease or illness.
- *Wellness:* A state of positive biological and psychological well-being that encompasses a sense of well-being and quality of life.

Definition of Terms

- *Holistic Health:T*the physical, mental, emotional, spiritual, social, environmental, and genetic factors' influence on an individual's life. (similar to wellness)
- *Quality of Life:* overall sense of well-being that has a different meaning for each individual.

Definition of Terms

- *Physical Activity:* any bodily movement produced by the contraction of the skeletal muscles that increases energy expenditure above the baseline level.
- *Exercise:* physical activity that is planned, structured, and repetitive with the purpose of developing, improving, or maintaining physical fitness.

Definition of Terms

- Physical Fitness: the ability to perform daily tasks with vigor and without undue fatigue, and with sufficient energy to engage in leisure-time pursuits, to meet unforeseen emergencies, and the vitality to perform at one's fullest capacity.
- Health-related and Performance-related physical fitness: what are the components of each?

Physical Fitness

- Health-related Fitness
- Cardiovascular endurance
- Body composition
- Flexibility
- Muscular endurance
- Muscular strength

- Performance-related Fitness
- Agility
- Speed
- Coordination
- Power
- Reaction time
- Balance

Philosophy

- "The love of wisdom" (Greek)
- A set of beliefs relating to a particular field.
- A system of values by which one lives and works.
- Helps individuals address the problems that confront them through the use of critical thinking, logical analysis, and reflective appraisal.

Branches of Philosophy

- Metaphysics-the ultimate nature of reality; what is real and exists.
- Epistemology-the nature of knowledge
- Logic-Examines ideas in an orderly manner and systematic way.
- Axiology-the nature of values
- Ethics: issues of right and wrong, responsibility, and standards of conduct.
- Aesthetics: the nature of beauty and art.

General Philosophies

- *Idealism:* The mind interprets events and creates reality; truth and values are absolute and universally shared.
- *Realism:* The physical world is the real world and it is governed by nature; science reveals the truth.
- *Pragmatism:* Reality and truth is determined by an individual's life experiences.
- *Naturalism:* Reality and life are governed by the laws of nature; the individual is more important than the society.

- *Existentialism:* Reality is based on human existence; individual experiences determine what is true.
- *Humanism:* Development of the full potential of each individual. Emphasized meeting the needs individuals' needs.

Philosophical Approaches

- "Education of the Physical"
- Focus on fitness development and acquisition of skills; the development of the body.
- "Education through the Physical"
- Focus on the development of the total person: Social, Emotional, Intellectual, and Physical development.

Sport Philosophy

- Study of the true meanings and actions of sport and how sport contributes to our lives.
- Eclectic philosophy of education (1875-1950)
- Comparative Systems Approach (1950-1965)
- Disciplinary Approach (1965-present)
- Sport philosophy offers us guidance in addressing inequities in physical activity opportunities experienced by underserved populations.

Why Develop Your Own Philosophy?

- Assists in the development and clarification of beliefs and values that guide your behaviors.
- Aids in decision-making.
- Helps determine goals, objectives, and methods of instruction and evaluation used in physical education programmes

Education in India : Sports and Physical Fitness

If a career in sports and physical fitnsess holds your fancy, there are three main options you can choose from. Pursue the sport or game on a full time basis generally with sponsorship from an employer/promoter Become a trainer/instructor/coach for a game or sporting event.

Finally use the experience acquired over years as a sportsperson to work in a related field, such as, sports journalism, sports goods manufacture/marketing or as commentator. To be a sports person one needs to be physically fit, energetic and enthusiastic. If aspiring to become a trainer or manager, a graduate degree in physical education can be pursued after Class XII (any stream with physical education).

Personality Traits

- Sports persons are required to be energetic, enthusiastic and physically fit.
- All professionals in this field must be absolutely committed to the profession and the game.
- Coaches and instructors have several years of experience and training.
- Patience, perseverance and a sporting spirit are required to excel.
- In allied areas of work, communication and business skills are gaining importance and value.
- A sportsperson's work needs psychomotor and physical conditioning.

Courses/Training

Courses:

1. Class XII-any subject with physical education
2. Graduate degree in Physical education; Postgraduate degree in Physical education. Jobs as Physical education trainers/ educators/therapists/coaches.
3. Graduation in Physical Education followed by Post graduation for Trainers and Managers
4. Graduation/ Post graduation in Physical Education and B.Phy.Ed for teachers.

Admission Procedure: Sports can be pursued at any age, hence the trajectory gives information on the schemes for promoting talent. Sports talent can be spotted at the school level. The Sports Authority of India has been constituted at the National level to encourage and develop acumen in sports. SAI has State level branches to organise, manage and conduct a host of schemes intended to promote sports facilities and assistance for the talented. Sports Authority of India (SAI) is responsible for training coaches, R&D in sports, physical education, R&D in physical education, sports promotion, nurturing talent, and training of athletes.

1. *Age 9-12 National Sports Talent Scheme:* Talent in swimming, athletics, gymnastics as well as ball and net games which include tennis, hockey, basketball, table tennis, football, volleyball, badminton and wrestling are supported under this scheme. Students in the 9 to 12 age can qualify tests conducted by the Sports Authority. The tests check general and specific physical skills required for each of the disciplines. Selected students undergo sports training along with school education in one of the SAI sponsored schools. The sponsorship includes all expenditures including tuition fee, boarding, lodging, incidental expenditures, sports kits maintenance allowances, medical facilities, travel etc. Coaches provide the necessary training to students selected under this scheme, conduct evaluation tests and maintain performance records.
2. *Age 16-20 years Students:* Can benefit from the Hostel scheme in sponsored institutions. Special Area Games Schemes operate for identifying and nurturing talent from all regions in the country.
3. *Army:* Regimental training centres have schools where students with sporting talent from neighbouring areas are enrolled. Education, training in sports, and military training completes the curriculum.
4. *Scholarships at Colleges/universities:* Students participating in national championships, inter-university tournaments are eligible for the Sports Talent Scholarship awarded by the Government of India, Department of Youth Affairs and Sports. Candidates are selected on the basis of merit, ascertained by a duly constituted Selection Committee.

5. *Private Sponsorships:* SAI has six regional sports centres. Coaching facilities in popular sports such as badminton, tennis, hockey and cricket are provided. The facilities provided are of international standards. Special Sports Academies/Federations provide similar facilities. These are often privately sponsored and sportspersons with proven talent are supported by these academies.

Physical Fitness

General Fitness: In a more general meaning, physical fitness is a general state of good somatic health and abilities.

A handicapped person may nevertheless be physically fit. Fitness helps them to compensate disability.

Physical fitness is usually a result of regular physical activity, e.g., physical exercise, and proper nutrition.

Cardio is a type of fitness designed to improve cardiovascular strength.

Task-oriented Fitness

A person may be said to be physically fit to perform a particular task with a reasonable efficiency, for example, fit for military service.

Military-style

In recent years, Military-style fitness training programmes have become increasingly popular among civilians. Courses are available all over the US and Europe.

They are usually taught by ex-military personnel. Very often the instructors held highly regarded positions within various military organizations. Often times the instructors were formerly Drill instructors, Special Forces Operatives or held otherwise distinguished positions.

These courses always have some common elements. They often focus on military style calisthenics and group runs. The courses are often held very early in the morning and will meet in almost any weather. Students can expect push-ups, sit-ups, pullups, and jumping jacks, as well as more obscure drills such as flutter kicks, sun worshippers and flares. Almost invariably a workout will include short runs while longer runs are more scheduled. Special forces are renowned for their level of fitness and intensity of their workouts.

Importance of Physical Fitness

Research polls shows that people today are turn out to be more health centered. As a result, people are becoming more concerned in making fitness exercise an integral part of their life-style. This article will introduce you to the importance of physical fitness. You will discover all about exercise and its benefits and will also learn how to make a personal exercise programme that is safe, reasonable, effective, and, most important, rewarding and enjoyable. For years everybody has identified that regular exercise together with good nutrition is good for their health. The trick is how to construct sound exercise habits and a balanced diet into your busy schedule. The pressure of modern times order that you develop and maintain a fit, trim and fully functioning body. Being active and physically fit improves your self-expression and self-esteem. This is the importance of Physical Fitness.

Long ago, health meant only absence of disease. At present, we have a much broader viewpoint and consider physical fitness to be the main component of total health. The modern life-style promotes unfitness due to its technological advances have eradicated much fitness producing physical exertion from everyday activities. Everyday activities, even for the laborer, no longer sufficiently stimulate the heart, lungs, and muscles to create physiological benefits. Society, particularly the corporate world, is beginning to appreciate the importance of health promotion and the role of exercise in developing and sustaining good health habits.

Being physically fit connotes living at your fullest physical potential. Physical fitness is the capacity of the heart, blood vessels, lungs, and muscles to function at optimal efficiency. It gives a basis for living a full and satisfying life style. The essential health components of physical fitness are cardio-respiratory endurance, strength, muscular endurance, flexibility, and body composition. To be physically fit requires effort, but exercise does not have to be punishing to help you develop and maintain physical fitness. Regular and vigorous exercise of the total body is an essential ingredient of muscular and circulatory fitness-the key to good health and well being. Lack of exercise is starts to show its consequence. An increase of body fatness, a loss of muscle tone, and a poor breathing capacity are some of the evident signs of physiological deterioration.

Now that inactivity has been known as a danger to physiological well being, some authorities have suggested that exercise may be the cheapest preventative medicine in the world. Researchers in medicine, nutrition, psychology, physiology, and physical education agree that exercise, properly executed, is essential for sustaining functional physical fitness. No responsible health educator will ever suggest that exercise is a universal remedy. But it is obvious that, just as we need food, rest and sleep, we need daily exercise for the maintenance of our physical capacities. Physical fitness is not an end in itself but a way to an end. It offers the basis for optimal physiological health and provides us the ability to enjoy a full life. You must make use of energy to gain energy. In other words, normal stimulation of the total body through vigorous exercise give off increased strength and endurance, characteristics associated with good health.

Wesley Virgin simply cannot be described nor defined. Instead, he must be experienced. The remarkable combination of his personal style and his message does something to people that cannot be captured in a text de scription. The power that is behind his extraordinary affect on people is not found just in what he enables them to learn, but in what he makes them feel.

Scope of Physical Education

Effective human functioning depends upon optimum physical development and health. Education for physical development and health provides students with the knowledge and attitudes to achieve healthful living throughout their lives and to acquire physical fitness, coordination and leisure skills. To help all students learn, develop, and apply the skills needed for daily participation in personal fitness and lifetime activities which contribute to a healthy lifestyle.

Scope:

A. Aerobics/cross training
B. Aquatics
C. Archery
D. Badminton
E. Basketball
F. Conditioning/Weight Training/Skill and Body
G. Field Hockey
H. Floor Hockey
I. Football
J. Golf
K. Gymnastics and Tumbling
L. Lacrosse
M. Lifetime
N. Low Organizational Games
O. Manipulative Skills
P. Physical Fitness Testing
Q. Physical Management
R. Recreational Games
S. Rhythmics and Dance
T. Roller Skating
U. Self Defense
V. Soccer
W. Softball
X. Team Handball
Y. Tennis
Z. Track and Field
AA. Volleyball
BB. Wrestling
CC. Heart Adventure

Foundation of Physical Education

Preschool educators must provide children with developmentally appropriate motor skill instruction in an effort to build a foundation for successful participation in later childhood and adult physical activities. A developmentally appropriate curriculum for preschool children provides experiences which encourage development in the psychomotor, affective, and cognitive areas. If any of these areas has been neglected in the past, it is perhaps the psychomotor area. Historically, early childhood educational programmes have focused more on academic readiness skills and less on motor skill instruction. Physical education should be comprehensive and should address all of the national standards. Concepts of physical education addressed in standard two should provide the foundation. One of the most significant questions that all educators face is "what specific knowledge, skills, and experiences do high school graduates need in order to live high quality lives in the 21st century?"

Physical Fitness: Meaning, Definition, Components and Benefits

Physical fitness refers to the ability to function as healthy human beings with energy and alertness in all daily activities. There are many places to learn about fitness, but the most common resources are easily found and can be used by anyone.

These resources include libraries, the Internet, a physical fitness instructor, or a health teacher. Libraries contain vast amounts of information about health in general and physical fitness in particular. Libraries have medical journals, magazines, and many books that can inform people about the ways to become fit and to maintain their fitness levels. Information sources can provide information about the physical and psychological benefits of being fit, as well as the benefits for a persons self-esteem and emotions. Libraries also may offer an opportunity to obtain audio and video materials that can provide the same types of information as magazines or books. Libraries also give low-income people a chance to see fitness materials that they may not readily have.

The Internet represents an excellent source of information about physical fitness. It is like a combination of many articles, books, libraries, and information from other people. If a search is performed on the word fitness using one of the popular search engines on the Internet, a list of many, many resources will be returned.

Search engines generally provide their lists in terms of the relevance of the material to the initial questions, so users should keep that in mind and ask relevant questions. With any search engine, the first few pages will provide the most useful links to information about the topic. Using a search engine, individuals can find information about local fitness centers and instructors in their area who offer specialized, one-to-one fitness training programmes.

Local schools are also good sources of information. A schools physical education instructors and health teachers represent valuable sources of fitness information. They understand and are educated about the major issues related to physical fitness. Their expertise can help individuals find other reliable sources of fitness data. Many articles that are found may not always be totally accurate, so having the ability to ask teachers and health instructors specific questions is very useful to those interested in pursuing a physical fitness routine.

Additionally, the federal government publishes lots of information about fitness issues in the United States from a variety of perspectives. The United States Department of Agriculture, which is responsible for setting the daily recommended allowances of various vitamins and other food substances for human consumption, collects and provides information about fitness alternatives, the status of fitness in the country, and how well Americans participate in fitness programmes.

The local fitness center also has considerable information to share about the subject of physical fitness. These centers may provide posted information or current magazines that address the most current fitness questions. The centers often let people observe fitness programmes in action as well.

Definition of Physical Fitness

The Definition of Physical Fitness is Relative: Definition of Physical Fitness is AgelessWhen you think of physical fitness you may think of athletic feats such as Lance Armstrong riding endlessly through the Swiss Alps.

Maybe you think of professional football players sprinting past their competition? You may even think of bodybuilders flexing their ripped muscles on stage.

What about the contortionists performing on stage bending their bodies as far as they can bend?

What about someone who is confined to a wheel chair? Do you think physical fitness means the same thing to them as it dos to you or a professional athlete?

The Point is, Physical Fitness Vastly Differs from Person to Person

What you consider physically fit others may not. You may be proud of your 7 minute mile, but professional track stars would think it is slow. You may feel tremendously proud for your 200 pound bench press but a professional powerlifter would not be so happy.

Athletic feats are part of physical fitness but there is far more reasons why physical fitness is important. It is best to look at physical fitness as a hierarchy to attempt an accurate general definition.

Definition of Physical Fitness

Base Level: The base level of the physical fitness pyramid highlights the primary reason why physical fitness is important. This level of physical fitness directly relates to quality of life. A physically fit body has less chance of acute health problems and chronic disease.

The base level of physical fitness represents your ability to efficiently perform the anaerobic and aerobic activities of daily living (ADLs) which exist in your environment on a daily basis in addition to novel tasks which may arise during day to day living.

Mid Level: Only after your body has grown accustomed to the the base level of physical fitness you can advance to the mid level. The middle level of the pyramid is about adaptation and improvement.

Most people remain at the mid level for their entire lifetime as they adapt and progress only to regress and start the process over and over again.

In order to improve mid level physical fitness it is important to have a balanced exercise programme. Exercise selection should focus on all 5 components of fitness.

Top Level: Very few are able to reach the top level of the physical fitness hierarchy. Elite athletes often spend their entire lifetime aiming to reach the very top level.

The top level of physical fitness tends to mesh physiology and psychology. In order to reach the top level of physical fitness one must reach their full potential.

5 Components of Physical Fitness

Why are the Five Components of Physical Fitness Important?

Remember High School P.E. Class?

If you have searched for the 5 components of physical fitness and are reading this there is a great chance that you first heard about the five basic components of physical fitness many years ago.

Your parents and teachers told you to get off the couch, out of the house and exercise because it's good for you. Exercise is good for, but in order to get the most out of you should lead a balanced exercise programme and that is where the main components of physical fitness come in.

An Effective Long-Term Exercise Programme is a Balanced Exercise Programme

The following should be considered important health related fitness components because if you improve on all five components you are likely to stay healthier, happier and live longer with a balanced exercise programme.

You can look at the five components of physical fitness as a marker of true fitness. You are only as strong as your weakest link and if you are weak at any of the following five components you should work at them to be considered a balanced, physically fit person.

Cardiovascular Endurance Cardiovascular Endurance

What is Cardiovascular Endurance?

Cardiovascular, which is synonymous with cardiopulmonary exercise or "Cardio" is aerobic physical activities that last longer than 90 seconds.

To understand the terminology you should know, cardio = heart, vascular = related to blood vessels, and pulmonary = related to the lungs.

Cardiovascular or cardiopulmonary endurance is your physical ability to maintain aerobic exercise for prolonged periods of time.

Physiologically, cardiovascular endurance deals with the efficiency of your body's (heart, lunges and vascular system) ability to transfer oxygen rich blood to your working muscles during activities that last longer than 90 seconds.

Why is Cardiovascular Endurance Important?

Cardiovascular endurance is very important because the more cardiovascular flt you arc, the healthier your lungs, heart and vascular system is. While exercising this may be obvlous to you but there is more.

If you demonstrate high levels of cardiovascular endurance during exercise you also have more efficient heart, lungs and vascular system while at rest which takes up the bulk of your time.

This means less stress is put on your heart and lungs around the clock which enables you to avoid illness and live a long healthy life. Many argue that cardiovascular endurance is the most important of the 5 components to physical fitness.

Muscular Strength Weight Training

What is Muscular Strength?

Muscular strength is the amount of force your muscle can exert against resistance for short duration, anaerobic (without oxygen) activities. Resistance includes external objects such as free weights or household objects as well as your own body weight. Physiologically, muscular strength it is the ability to your body to supply ATP (Adenosine Tri-Phosphate or muscle energy) to your muscle fibers for concentric, eccentric and isometric contractions in short times, which range from 0 to around 15 seconds.

Why is Muscular Strength Important?

While muscular strength may be subjective, the primary reason why muscular strength is important is your efficiency at Activities of Daily Living (ADLs). ADLs one of the most important reasons why being proficient at all 5 components of physical fitness are important. At the very least, to be physically fit for in the muscular strength department, you should demonstrate the basic muscular strength needed to efficiently your ADLs. While ADLs vary from person to person, you can also consider activities such as push-ups, pull-ups and carrying heavy objects as ADLs.

Even though each of the 5 components of fitness depends on one another, poor muscular strength can also effect aerobic fitness and muscular endurance negatively.

Physical Exercises VideoWeight Training Exercise Videos

You can use all forms of resistance training to increase your muscular strength. If your strength is your weakest of the 5 components of physical fitness you need to start weight training.

Muscular Endurance Physical Fitness Component 3. Muscular Endurance

What is Muscular Endurance?

While muscular strength deals with short duration muscle contractions muscle endurance deals with sustained muscle contractions and other anaerobic activities lasting less than about 90 seconds.

Why is Muscular Endurance Important?

Muscular endurance is the bridge between muscular strength and cardiovascular endurance. In order to be cardiovascularly fit, you must demonstrate muscular endurance.

Physiologically while muscle strength deals primarily with type II, fast twitch muscle fibers, muscular endurance deals with primarily type I, slow twitch muscle fibers. Your body contains both but only anaerobic exercises which last longer than around 15 seconds and less than 90 seconds strengthen your type I muscle fibers.

Sets and Reps

Learn all about how your resistance training workouts can best improve each of the 5 components of physical fitness through different exercise selection, sets, reps, weight training volume and training splits.

FlexibilityFlexlbilily Physical Fitness Component

What is Flexibility?

Flexibility is the range of motion possible for each of your joints or groups of joints.

Why is Flexibility Important?

To some degree, your flexibility determines how efficiently your muscles are. Increased flexibility has also been associated with decreased risk of acute and chronic (overuse) injuries.

Poor flexibility can directly effect cardiovascular endurance, muscle strength and muscular endurance. Physiologically flexibility can include extra-muscular (range of motion at a joint) and intramuscular factors such as hypertonicity (knots) within the muscles themselves.

Posture Problems

Learn in detail why flexibility is very important for your muscle balance which can effect all 5 components of physical fitness.

Body CompositionBody Composition is one of the 5 Basic Components

Why is Body Composition?

Body composition is the percentage of your body's tissues which you exhibit. The easiest way to look at body composition is with a 2 compartment analysis which estimates the amount of body fat you have with lean body mass which includes muscle, bone, water, and organs. It takes expensive equipment for a 3 compartment analysis which isolates bone mass which can also be considered an important part of body composition.

Why is Body Composition Important?

You could say body composition depends on the other components of physical fitness.

Having a poor body composition has many negative physical and psychological effects such as increased chance of a host of chronic diseases and depression. As mentioned previously, improper exercise habits and choices can not only lead to being overweight and obesity, but decreased bone mass associated with osteopenia and osteoporosis.

Body Fat Measurement

If you want to know you are physically fit according to the 5 components of physical fitness you should learn about the cheap and effective ways to estimate your body composition.

Fat Loss Information Fat Loss

If you think you have a high body composition you can click on your body type and estimate your lean body mass as well as fat mass. From this data you can find out how much fat you should lose to accomplish your weight loss goals.

Which of the 5 Basic Components of Fitness is the Most Important?

You are Only as Physically Fit as your Weakest Link

If you have not got the point of the whole article, you cannot rank one of the health related components of physical fitness over the other. All 5 components of physical fitness are interdependent upon each other.

If you are very strong but cannot jog a mile without getting out of breath, you need to focus more on your aerobic exercise. If you are very lean and cardiovascularly fit but you cannot touch your toes you need to work on your flexibility and so on.

Health Benefits of Physical Fitness

Regular activity has a number of proven, positive health effects, especially on heart health. Vigorous exercise strengthens the heart as a pump, making it a larger, more efficient muscle. Even moderate activity can boost HDL ('good') cholesterol, aid the circulatory system, and lower blood pressure and blood fats. All these effects translate into reduced risk for heart disease, heart attack, and stroke.

Fitness Basics

- Benefits
- Why Warm Up?
- Approaches
- Tips & Hints

Exercise can also offer other benefits, including strengthened muscles, increased flexibility, and stronger bones, which can help ward off the bone-thinning condition called osteoporosis.

Regular activity also promises mental-health benefits, like relieving stress and anxiety. It can help you sleep better and renew your energy. If exercise could be bottled, it would be a best-selling potion at the local pharmacy.

Activity is for Everyone

Virtually everyone can get health benefits from activity. But every few years, surveys confirm the well-known fact that most people aren't active enough. Unfortunately, we pay for it. The American Heart Association attributes about 250,000 deaths a year in the US-about 12 percent of total deaths-to lack of regular physical activity.

The reasons for inactivity aren't hard to figure out. Most of us have jobs where we sit most of the time, so chances are limited to be physically active at work. We also rely heavily on modern, labour-saving devices-cars, appliances, and power tools-to spare us manual effort.

But there's another reason why many people, especially the overweight, avoid activity. Check out the firm, supple bodies shown exercising on television or on magazine covers. They give the impression that exercise is sweaty, strenuous work best reserved for the young, super-fit, and athletic. But the latest research is proving that picture false: Benefits can be gained even from low-intensity activity, like gardening.

Activity and Weight Management

If you burn more calories than you consume, then you'll shed pounds. For every extra 3,500 calories you spend, you'll drop one pound. Do strenuous exercise, and you'll burn calories in a hurry. And you can burn the same number of calories with gentler activity: You just have to do it longer and/or more often.

If you're not familiar with the number of calories burned during exercise, you may be discouraged when you first learn about it. For instance, if you weigh 150 pounds and go on a brisk, 1-mile walk for 20 minutes, you'll expend about 100 calories, considerably short of the 3,500 calories needed to drop a pound.

But such efforts add up. If you expend an extra 300 calories a day through activity and reduce your dietary intake another 200 calories, then by the end of a week, you'll have a calorie deficit of 3,500, comparable to a one-pound weight loss. This is precisely the kind of gradual success that experts recommend for long-term weight management.

Exercise also has other body-slimming effects. It builds muscle and displaces fat. A given volume of muscle weighs more than the same bulk of fat. So your bathroom scale may not record dramatic changes, but your clothes will be looser, and you'll have a trimmer body shape.

Because exercise builds muscle, it may also help counter a problem caused by dieting. When you reduce calories, your body metabolism may slack off and burn calories more slowly.

This makes further weight loss more difficult. But some research suggests regular activity helps correct this slowdown and makes it easier to keep shedding pounds.

How Activity Affects Calorie Needs?

The more active you are, the more calories you'll burn, which can help with weight loss. And exercise also promotes fat loss and builds muscle. This, in turn, increases your body's metabolic rate, the rate at which you burn calories, even after you've finished exercising.

Weight loss by reducing your calorie intake without activity can have just the opposite effect: It can cause your body to break down muscle, which ultimately lowers your metabolic rate and makes losing weight even harder.

The problem of reducing your calorie intake without exercise is compounded when people go off their diets. Because they've lost muscle, they tend to regain their weight quickly and then some.

A better approach is to increase activity, which builds muscle, at the same time that you're cutting back on excess calories from food. Physical activity can also reduce stress and regulate your appetite, making it easier to curb the urge to overeat.

The amount of energy needed for any activity, whether it's raking leaves or playing a computer game, depends on three factors: your muscle mass, your body weight, and the activity itself. The larger the muscle mass and heavier the body part being moved, the more calories you use. The duration, frequency, and intensity of exercise also count.

UNIT-II

Olympic Games, Laying of 400 Meters Track, Basic Skills and Rules of Few Games

Olympics—Ancient and Modern Olympics

Olympics the Official Olympic Flag

Created by Pierre de Coubertin in 1914, the Olympic flag contains five interconnected rings on a white background. The five rings symbolize the five significant continents and are interconnected to symbolize the friendship to be gained from these international competitions. The rings, from left to right, are blue, yellow, black, green, and red. The colours were chosen because at least one of them appeared on the flag of every country in the world. The Olympic flag was first flown during the 1920 Olympic Games.

The Olympic Motto: In 1921, Pierre de Coubertin, founder of the modern Olympic Games, borrowed a Latin phrase from his friend, Father Henri Didon, for the Olympic motto: Citius, Altius, Fortius ("Swifter, Higher, Stronger").

The Olympic Oath

Pierre de Coubertin wrote an oath for the athletes to recite at each Olympic Games. During the opening ceremonies, one athlete recites the oath on behalf of all the athletes. Belgian fencer Victor Boin first took the Olympic oath during the 1920

Olympic Games. The Olympic Oath states, "In the name of all competitors, I promise that we shall take part in these Olympic Games, respecting and abiding by the rules that govern them, in the true spirit of sportsmanship, for the glory of sport and the honour of our teams."

The Olympic Creed

Pierre de Coubertin got the idea for this phrase from a speech given by Bishop Ethelbert Talbot at a service for Olympic champions during the 1908 Olympic Games. The Olympic Creed reads: "The most important thing in the Olympic Games is not to win but to take part, just as the most important thing in life is not the triumph but the struggle. The essential thing is not to have conquered but to have fought well."

The Olympic Flame

The Olympic flame is a practice continued from the ancient Olympic Games. In Olympia (Greece), a flame was ignited by the sun and then kept burning until the closing of the Olympic Games. The flame first appeared in the modern Olympics at the 1928 Olympic Games in Amsterdam. The flame itself represents a number of things, including purity and the endeavor for perfection. In 1936, the chairman of the organizing committee for the 1936 Olympic Games, Carl Diem, suggested what is now the modern Olympic Torch relay. Women wearing ancient-style robes and using a curved mirror and the sunlight the Olympic flame at the ancient site of Olympia. The Olympic Torch is then passed from runner to runner from the ancient site of Olympia to the Olympic stadium in the hosting city. The flame is then kept alight until the Games have concluded. The Olympic Torch relay represents a continuation from the ancient Olympic Games to the modern Olympics.

The Olympic Hymn

Spyros Samaras composed the Olympic Hymn, played when the Olympic Flag is raised, and the words added by Kostis Palamas. The Olympic Hymn was first played at the 1896 Olympic Games in Athens but wasn't declared the official hymn by the IOC until 1957.

Real Gold Medals

The last Olympic gold medals that were made entirely out of gold were awarded in 1912.

The Medals

The Olympic medals are designed especially for each individual Olympic Games by the host city‘s organizing committee. Each medal must be at least three millimeters thick and 60 millimeters in diameter. Also, the gold and silver Olympic medals must be made out of 92.5 percent silver, with the gold medal covered in six grams of gold.

The First Opening Ceremonies

The first opening ceremonies were held during the 1908 Olympic Games in London.

Opening Ceremony Procession Order

During the opening ceremony of the Olympic Games, the Greek team, followed by all the other teams in alphabetical order (in the language of the hosting country), except for the last team, which is always the team of the hosting country, always leads the procession of athletes.

A City, Not a Country

When choosing locations for the Olympic Games, the IOC specifically gives the honour of holding the Games to a city rather than a country.

First Modern Champion

James B. Connolly (United States), winner of the hop, step, and jump (the first final event in the 1896 Olympics), was the first Olympic champion of the modern Olympic Games.

The Exact Length of a Marathon

During the first several modern Olympics, the marathon was always an approximate distance. In 1908, the British royal family requested that the marathon start at the Windsor Castle so that the royal children could witness its start. The distance from the Windsor Castle to the Olympic Stadium was 42,195 meters (or 26 miles and 385 yards). In 1924, this distance became the standardized length of a marathon.

Women

Women were first allowed to participate in 1900 at the second modern Olympic Games.

Winter Games Begun

The winter Olympic Games were first held in 1924, beginning a tradition of holding them a few months earlier and in a different city than the summer Olympic Games. Beginning in 1994, the winter Olympic Games were held in completely different years (two years apart) than the summer Games.

Cancelled Games

Because of World War I and World War II, there were no Olympic Games in 1916, 1940, or 1944. Tennis Banned.

Tennis was played at the Olympics until 1924, then re constituted in 1988.

Walt Disney

In 1960, the Winter Olympic Games were held in Squaw Valley, California (United States).

In order to impress the spectators, Walt Disney was head of the committee that organized the opening day ceremonies. The 1960 Winter Games Opening Ceremony was filled with high school choirs and bands, releasing of thousands of balloons, fireworks, ice statues, releasing of 2,000 white doves, and national flags dropped by parachute.

Russia Not Present

Though Russia had sent a few athletes to compete in the 1908 and 1912 Olympic Games, they did not compete again until the 1952 Games.

Motor Boating

Motor boating was an official sport at the 1908 Olympics.

Polo, an Olympic Sport

Polo was played at the Olympics in 1900, 1908, 1920, 1924, and 1936.

Stadium

The first recorded ancient Olympic Games were held in 776 BCE with only one event-the stade. The stade was a unit of measurement (about 600 feet) that also became the name of the footrace because it was the distance run. Since the track for the stade (race) was a stade (length), the location of the race became the stadium.

Counting Olympiads

An Olympiad is a period of four successive years. The Olympic Games celebrate each Olympiad. For the modern Olympic Games, the first Olympiad celebration was in 1896. Every four years celebrates another Olympiad; thus, even the Games that were cancelled (1916, 1940, and 1944) count as Olympiads. The 2004 Olympic Games in Athens was called the Games of the XXVIII Olympiad.

Gymnasium

The word "gymnasium" comes from the Greek root "gymnos" meaning nude; the literal meaning of "gymnasium" is "school for naked exercise." Athletes in the ancient Olympic Games would participate in the nude.

Ancient Olympics

The first ancient Olympic Games can be traced back to 776 B.C and were celebrated until 393 A.D, according to historical records. The Games continued for twelve centuries and were dedicated to Olympian gods. Olympia became the site of these historic ancient games that sowed the seeds for the most coveted sporting international event of modern times, the Modern Olympics. The site of the Ancient Olympics is located in the western part of Peloponnese. According to Greek mythology, Peloponnese is the island of Pelops, the founder of the Olympic Games. Olympia, Greece is the sanctuary site for the ancient Greek gods. The central part of Olympia was dominated by the majestic temple of Zeus. The ancient games enjoyed a secular tradition and aimed at securing good relations between the cities of Greece and showing physical qualities and evolution of the performances accomplished by the youth. The Olympic Games were held in four years intervals at the ancient stadium in Olympia that could accommodate more than 40,000 spectators. The surrounding areas around the ancient Olympic stadium were continuously developed until the 4th century BC and were used as training grounds for athletes or to serve as homes for the Olympic judges.

The Ancient Olympics were not international in the modern sense of the term as they allowed only free men who spoke Greek to participate in the Games. The games none the less had a slight international spirit as they included participants from other Greek city-states. The Olympic Games originally consisted of just one competing event, the 'stadion' or 'stade' race. It was a short race covering the distance of 180 or 240 meters or the length of the stadium. It was only gradually that modifications were done in the stade race and other sporting events were also introduced. Other running events that were included in the Ancient Olympics were 'dolichos', which was similar to modern day marathon event; 'diaulos' or two stade race and 'hoplitodromos' in which the athlete wore the heavy armor partially or fully, carried a shield and was additionally equipped with greaves or a helmet. The other popular events that were added to ancient games were boxing, chariot racing, wrestling, pankration (similar to martial arts) and pentathlon that consisted of long jump, stadion, wrestling, javelin throw and discus throw.

In the ancient Olympics, married women were not allowed to participate in any way. However unmarried women could watch the Olympic Games. The ancient Olympic Games though did not allow female participants; an exception was made at the Herean Games, staged every four years to honour Hera, wife of Zeus, allowing female athletes to participate in the games. Kyniska, daughter of King Archidamos of Sparta, was the first woman to be listed as an Olympic victor in Antiquity. The events were judged by the 'Herald', a Hellanodikis (Greek

Judge). The Olympic victors in ancient times received their awards immediately after the competition. The Herald after announcing the name of the victor placed a palm branch in his hands. Red ribbons were tied on his head and hands to symbolize his victory. The official award ceremony that took place on the last day of the Games was a proud day for the victor. From the elevated vestibule of the temple of Zeus, the Herald announced the name of the winner, his father's name and the name of his homeland. The winner was finally honored with the Herald placing the sacred olive tree wreath or 'kotinos' on the winner's head.

Ancient to Modern Olympics

Ancient Olympics has a history dating as long back as 776 BC. These games originally linked to the religious festivals of the cult of Zeus, were dedicated to the Olympian Gods. The games were held in Olympia located in the western part of the Peloponnese, 145 km west of Athens, Greece, and comprised of only a few events where any male youngster from the various cities of Greece could participate to show off their physical qualities.

Olympia the ancient city of worship with its magnificent and elaborate shrines had a stadium which could accommodate 40,000 spectators. The games were first held here in 776 BC and continued to be played every four years for nearly 1200 years. Corebus, a cook from Elis is known as the very first Olympic champion in history by winning a run of approximately 192 metres. Stadion running, discus and Javelin were some of the early athletic events of that era. The victors received their first award of a palm branch from a Hellanodikis (Greek judge) soon after the competitions. The official award ceremony were held on the last day at the venue of the temple of Zeus and after announcing the winners, they were awarded with the sacred olive tree wreath (Kotinos) placed on their heads. Red ribbons were tied on the winners head and hands as a mark of victory.

But in 393 CE, the ancient Olympic games came to a halt when the Roman emperor Theodosius I, abolished the Games.

The games stay put until in 1890, a young Frenchmen named Pierre de Coubertin organized and founded a sports organization, Union des Societes Francaises de Sports Athletiques (USFSA). Two years later, Coubertin first put forward his idea to revive the Olympic Games. Although initially his proposal did not invoke an interest, his persistence won when in 1894, at a meeting of the Union des Sports Athletiques with 79 delegates representing nine countries, the delegates voted unanimously for the Olympic Games.

It was also decided to have Coubertin construct an international committee to organize the Games. This committee became the International Olympic Committee (IOC; Comite Internationale Olympique) and Demetrious Vikelas from Greece was selected to be its first president. Demetrios Vikelas and Evangelos Zappas were among those who made efforts for the revival of Olympic games. Thus the Olympic Games revived after around 1500 years, was held in Panathenaic stadium in Athens in the first week of April 1896 and came to be known as the Modern Olympic games. Since then, this game has boon held enthusiastically every four years in different participating countries and acts as a medium for encouraging cordial relationships between the countries.

Modern Olympics

The Modern Olympic Games were founded in the year 1894 by Baron Pierre de Coubertin, who was a French educationist and sought to promote international harmony and understanding through sporting competition. The great French man strongly believed in the Olympic ideal that even enemies could be united in sporting competition. The first Modern Olympics were finally held in 1896 and attracted athletes from fourteen nations of the world. At the first Modern Olympic Games in 1896 that were held in the place of birth of the philosophy of Olympism, Greece, the largest delegates came from the Greece, Germany, France and Great Britain.

The interest in reviving the ancient Olympic Games as an international event grew in the mid-nineteenth century. It was during this time that the ruins of ancient Olympia were excavated by German Archaeologists. Coubertin in 1890 founded the Union des Societes Francaises de Sports Athletiques (USFSA), a French sports organization. Two years later in a historic meeting of Union des Societes Francaises de Sports Athletiques on November 25, 1892 in Paris, Coubertin suggested the revival of the Olympic Games. Head strong about reviving the games, he arranged for a conference with 79 delegates representing nine countries in 1894. The delegates unanimously voted for hosting the first Modern summer Olympic Games in 1896.

Held in Athens in 1896, the first Modern Olympic Games were the biggest international sports event staged in the times. The international multi-sporting event hence began from the place of birth of the Olympics and came to be sub-divided as Summer and Winter Olympic Games. The first Summer Olympics as we know it were organized in 1896 but the Winter Olympics began from the year 1924 and were held in Chamonix, France. The International Olympic Committee (IOC) is the organization that organizes the Olympic Games. The International Olympic Committee was created by Pierre de Coubertin and Demetrios Vikelas on June 23, 1894. The Games are the exclusive property of the IOC, which has the last word on any issue related to the Games. The modern Olympic Games are organized through a partnership between the IOC and the Organizing Committee for the Olympic Games (OCOG). Women also found an entry into the Modern Olympic Games, though not in the first games but in 1900. Since then, women have been regularly showing their sporting prowess in the Games.

Coubertin and the IOC believed in the noble thought that the Games should be a means to promote harmony between the nations of the world. Keeping this in mind, they decided to host the games in different nations across the globe. As a consequence, the second modern Olympic Games were held in Paris, France in 1900. The modern Olympic Games, which started with merely fourteen nations participating in the sporting event now has over 200 nations across the globe as participants of the modern Olympic Games. 203 countries will be sending their athletes to participate in the Beijing Olympic

2008. The modern Olympic Games too have had gone through difficult times. The Games were begun to encourage international peace and harmony, however in 1980, the United States of America did not participate in the Moscow Olympic Games. USSR followed suit, when the Olympic Games were held in Los Angeles, USA. In a shocking incident in Munich in 1972, 11 athletes were killed by terrorists. Later in 1996 a bomb attack during the games killed two people in Atlanta. The Olympic Games despite the trying times have been a great link between nations and people of different faiths, culture and backgrounds.

Olympic Torch

The torch relay marks the opening of the Olympic celebration. The Olympic Flame from the ancient games was re-introduced during the 1928, Amsterdam Olympic Games. In the modern Olympic Games, Torch Relay was revived during the Berlin Olympics in 1936. Torch relay, however, originated way too before the 1936 Olympic Games. In ancient Greece, torch relay races begun as religious rituals at night. However soon it turned into a popular athletic sports event. In an altar dedicated to Goddess Hestia, sacred flames were always lit in Olympia. Every time prior to the Modern Olympic Games, the sacred flame is lit by the head priestess in Olympia, Athens and then is transferred to the torch of the first runner finally resulting in the journey of the Torch Relay beginning.

The Torch Relay in modern times, however, has not regained everything that was followed in ancient Greece. The Torch Relay in modern times is a non-competitive replication of the ancient Flame Relay. The Torch Relay however marks the symbolic celebration of the Olympic Games. 1936, Berlin Olympics saw the introduction of Torch Relay, when a lighted torch from Olympia was carried to the site of the Berlin Olympic Games. The modern Olympic flame is lit at the site where the temple of Goddess Hera, wife of Zeus used to stand. The lighted torch was carried from Olympia to the site of the Games in 1936, passing through seven countries – Greece, Bulgaria, Hungary, Yugoslavia, Czechoslovakia, Austria and Germany.

The first runner of the Olympic Torch was young athlete Konstantinos Kondylis.

The Olympic Torch Relay ends on the day of the opening ceremony in the main stadium of the Games. The choice of the athlete, who lights the flame in the Olympic Stadium, is enjoyed by the host nation. Usually a popular and great sportsperson enjoys the honour to light the flame in the cauldron of the stadium. The Olympic Torch today has become a great symbol of peace between the continents of the world. The Olympic Torch since the inception of the torch relay in the Modern Olympic Games has traveled across almost all the nations that participate in the Summer and Winter Olympic Games. In 1960 Rome Olympics, the Olympic Torch Relay was televised for the first time. In 2000 Sydney Olympics, the Olympic Flame made its underwater journey in the Great Barrier Reef. Also, for the first time in the history of the Games, the distance traveled during the relay was very high. The 2008 Beijing Olympic Torch Relay however now enjoys the record of maximum travel during any Olympic Relay in the history of modern games.

The Beijing Olympic torch has been specially designed keeping in mind the characteristics of the Chinese people. The torch embodies the concepts of Green Olympics, People's Olympics and High-tech Olympics. Made of aluminum, the torch is 72 centimeters high and weighs 985 grams. The Beijing Olympics Torch flame was lit on March 24, 2008 at the temple of Goddess Hera in Olympia, Greece. The torch relay will finally conclude on August 8th, 2008 after the Olympic Flame reaches the Beijing National Stadium, marking the opening ceremony of the Beijing Olympic Games. The 2008 Beijing Olympic Games Torch Relay has however caused much stir world over this time, making the Olympic torch a symbol of either support or protest for and against the People's Republic of China. The mobilization of Army by the Chinese authorities in Tibet and the violent incidents in the state has invited much criticism over Human rights violation and Beijing hosting the Olympic Games. The Torch Relay saw protests in many cities along the route. The protest was especially noticeable in USA and many European countries such as Britain and France. In Asia, the torch relay was carried out amidst high security. In later segments of the relay, large-scale counter protests by overseas Chinese became prevalent. Apart from the protests the relay had several firsts to its credit. The 2008 Beijing Olympics Torch Relay will cover the longest distance (137,000 km) of any Olympic torch relay since the tradition begun in 1936 Berlin Olympics. The relay also included an ascent with the flame to the top of Mount Everest, with people from different ethnic origins in China, carrying the flame to the highest peak of the world.

Olympic Flag

The Olympic flag has the emblem: "The Olympic flag [...] has a white background, with five interlaced rings in the centre: blue, yellow, black, green and red [...] This design is symbolic; it represents the five continents of the world, united by Olympism, while the six colours are those that appear on all the national flags of the world at the present time." (1931) Toxtes choisis II.

Use of the Olympic Flag

An Olympic flag is raised during the opening ceremonies of each Olympic Games, and lowered during the closing ceremonies. A second flag is used for the Olympic Oath. Special flags are kept in the city halls of cities organizing the Olympic Games. At the closing ceremonies of each Olympic Games, the mayor of the city that organized the Games returns the flag to the president of thc IOC, who then passes it on to the mayor of the next city to host the Olympic Games. (This ceremony is known as the "Antwerp Ceremony" because it started there). There are three such flags, differing from all other copies in that they have a Five-colored fringe around the flag, and are tied with five colored ribbons to a flagstaff.

Specific Flags

Antwerp Flag: Was presented to the IOC at the 1920 Summer Olympics by the city of Antwerp, Belgium, and at the Closing Ceremony of the 1984 Los Angeles Olympic Games, was passed on to the next organizing city of the Summer Olympics until the Games of Seoul 1988 when it was retired. The Antwerp Flag is now on display at the Olympic Museum in Lausanne, Switzerland.

Seoul Flag: Was presented to the IOC at the 1988 Summer Olympics by the city of Seoul, South Korea, and is passed on to the next organizing city of the Summer Olympics.

Marathon Race

Men Marathon: The marathon has been in Olympics since its own inception in modern days and it has been part of all summer games after that. Usually, in the Olympics, the women's marathon is organized as the midway point of the games, while the men's marathon is organized in the last days of the event. The distance of the marathon race at the Olympics has varied in the early years, before being set at 42,195 m in 1924.

Rules and Regulations

As for all athletics events, rules and regulations for marathon too have been set by International Association of Athletics Federations or IAAF. Basic rules set by the IAAF for the marathon are given as under.

- The beginning and finishing points of the marathon race must be visibly marked.
- Even if an athlete is off the course with permission from the judge, he has to be under constant supervision of the judge, so that he might not try any unscrupulous means to win the race.
- All the sections of the race have to be well-marked.
- A sprinter will have to leave the race on the direction of an official medical staff.
- All marathon events in the Olympics have to be organized on roads. Athletes cannot participate in the event on soft land.
- Athlete will not be awarded any point until he reaches the finishing point.
- The runners should be made aware of the distance they are required to run.

- The athletes can have refreshment only at the designated places.
- Any athlete is not permitted to leave the road without permission of a judge.

Performers

Super performers in Marathon race in Olympics are Spiridon Louis, Michel Theato, Thomas J. Hicks, Johnny Hayes, Kenneth McArthur, Hannes Kolehmainen, Waldemar Cierpinski, Carlos Lopes, Gelindo Bordin, Hwang Young-Cho, Josia Thugwane, Gezahegne Abera, Albin Stenroos, Boughera El Ouafi, Juan Carlos Zabala, Sohn Kee-chung, Delfo Cabrera, Emil Zátopek, Alain Mimoun, Abebe Bikila, Mamo Wolde, Frank Shorter, and Stefano Baldini.

Women Marathon

The marathon is the longest distance in the athletics. The official distance for the Marathon in the Olympics is 42.195 kilometers or 26 miles 385 yards. The event is run as a road race. Women athletes from all over the world have participated enthusiastically in the marathon for women in Olympics.

Debut in Olympics

Marathon Women was introduced in the Olympics at the 1984 Los Angeles Summer Games. Thereafter, the event has been the feature of all summer Olympics.

Rules and Regulations

As for all athletics events, rules and regulations for marathon too have been set by International Association of Athletics Federations or IAAF. Basic rules set by the IAAF for the marathon are given as under.

- Marathon athletes are not allowed to run on soft land. The event has to be organized on metalled roads.
- For convenience of the athletes, the starting and finishing points of the marathon should be properly marked.
- An athlete has to reach the finishing point for getting any credit.

- Organizers have to well-mark the different stages of the race.
- Any sprinter is bound to leave the race if directed by an official medical staff.
- Refreshment stations have been specified for the athletes where they can have refreshments. They are not allowed to take refreshments in any other places.
- The athletes should be informed in advance about the distance and route they have to run.
- A marathon athlete cannot leave the road without prior permission of a judge. And if he comes out of the course, he has to be under constant supervision of the judge so that he might not take a short route for the finishing point.

Top Performers

Athletes who have performed will in the Marathon Olympics for Women are Paula RadcliffeValentina Yegorova, Mizuki Noguchi, Naoko Takahashi, Fatuma Roba, Deena Kastor, Rosa Mota, Joan Benoit, Catherine Ndereba, Lidia Simon, Yuko Arimori, Lisa Martin, Grete Waitz, and Joyce Chepchumba.

The Distance of the Marathon Race in Olympics

What is the distance of the Marathon Race in Olympics?

Responses

The marathon race distance is 42.195 kms or 26 miles 385 yards. The race marathon is named after the legend of Greek soldier Pheidippides who ran the distance between Marathon to Athens to announce the victory against persians in the Battle of Marathon. The distance of marathon was not constant until 1921. Now it is standardized to 42.195 kms.

Good Work Vyshnavi

The marathon is a long-distance foot race with an official distance of 42.195 kilometers (26 miles 385 yards) that is usually run as a road race. The event is named after the fabled run of the Greek soldier Pheidippides, a messenger from the Battle of Marathon to Athens. The historical accuracy of this legend is in doubt, contradicted by accounts given by Herodotus, in particular.

The marathon was one of the original modern Olympic events in 1896, though the distance did not become standardized until 1921. More than 800 marathons are contested throughout the world each year, with the vast majority of competitors being recreational athletes. Larger marathons can have tens of thousands of participants.

Year	*Distance (kilometres) Distance (miles)*
1896	40 24.85
1900	40.26 25.02
1904	40 24.85
1906	41.86 26.01
1908	42.195 26.22
1912	40.2 24.98
1920	42.75 26.56
1924	onward 42.195 26.22

Laying of 400 Meters Track with Stagger

The length of the inside lane is usually either 400 meters or 1/4 mile. All lanes on a running track share a common finish line. For events longer than 110 meters or so, each lane's starting line is a little ahead of the one to the left of it. This difference is known as stagger and the actual stagger distance is the difference between the event length and the distance around the track for that lane in that event. The stagger is greater for a 400 meter event than a 200 meter event because the longer event uses the whole circumference of the track while the shorter event only uses half. Almost all tracks are measured using the inside lane, but some are measured using a different lane. Want to know the length of a track from a different lane? (Remember races are usually staggered to give all entrants the same distance) If the track is a 1/4 miles track (inside lane measurement) and the lanes are 42" wide (a common width) then one lap in lane 4 will be .262 miles and one lap in lane 8 will be .279 miles.

400 meter sprint for men is run on an outside track. The length of the inside lane of the track is exactly 400 meter. Michael Johnson of USA is the most famous athlete of 400 meter race for men.

Debut in Olympics

400 meter sprint for men has been in Olympics since its beginning in 1896. Thereafter, the event has been the part of every Olympics.

Dominating Country

In 400 meter race for men, the United States of America or USA has played the dominating part. Athletes from the USA have been the winners of most 400 meter track events in the Olympics.

Rules

Rules governing 400 meter sprint for men have been specified by International Association of Athletics Federations or IAAF. All tracks and fields events in the Olympics are conducted as per the guidelines of the IAAF. Here are some basic rules for 400 meter sprint for men events.

- The length and width of every lane in the track should not be more or less than specified by the IAAF.
- If the participants are more than, preliminary heat events are held. Top ten of the heat events qualify for the next round.
- The maximum radius for the outside lane of the track is 50 meter.
- IAAF disallows stepping on the inner line of the track.
- Any athlete who has failed to reach the finishing line is not given any credit.
- A standard automatic timing device allowed by the IAAF must be used for measurement of time.

- Any athlete who steps once outside the track boundary is not allowed to rejoin the race.
- Athletes are allowed to run with spiked shoes.

Great Athletes

Participating in the Olympics, great athletes have earned the name for themselves and their country. These are Roger Black, Lee Evans, Otis Davis, Michael Johnson, Alberto Juantorena, Danny Everett, Michael Larrabee, Steve Lewis, Larry James, Alvin Harrison, Wyndham Halswelle, Archie Williams, Eric Liddell, Jeremy Wariner, Butch Reynolds, Quincy Watts, Jerome Young, Alonzo Babers, Viktor Markin, and Vincent Matthews.

Basic Skills and Rules—Volleyball

Volleyball is an Olympic team sport in which two teams of 6 active players are separated by a net. Each team tries to score points by grounding a ball on the other team's court under organized rules. This article focuses on competitive indoor volleyball; numerous other variations of volleyball have developed, most notably the Olympic spin-off sport beach volleyball.

Play proceeds as follows: a player on one of the teams begins a rally by attempting to serve the ball (tossing or releasing it and then hitting it with a hand or arm), from behind the back boundary line of the court, over the net and into the receiving team's court. The receiving team must not let the ball touch their court; they may touch the ball as many as three times, typically using the first two touches to set up for an attack, an attempt to direct the ball back over the net in such a way that the serving team is unable to prevent it from touching their court. The rally continues in the same manner, with each team allowed as many as three consecutive touches, until either (1): a team makes a kill, grounding the ball on the opponent's court, thus winning the rally; or (2): a team commits a fault, thus losing the rally. The team that wins the rally is awarded a point, and serves the ball to start the next rally. The complete rules are extensive; a few of the most common faults include:

- causing the ball to touch the ground outside the opponents' court or without first passing over the net;
- catching and throwing the ball;
- double hit: two consecutive contacts with the ball made by the same player;
- four consecutive contacts with the ball made by the same team.

The ball is usually played with the hands or arms, but players can legally strike or push (short contact) the ball with any part of the body.

A number of consistent techniques have evolved in volleyball, including spiking and blocking (because these plays are made above the top of the net the vertical jump is an athletic skill emphasized in the sport) as well as passing, setting, and specialized player positions and offensive and defensive structures.

History

Origin of Volleyball: On February 9, 1895, in Holyoke, Massachusetts (USA), William G Morgan, a YMCA physical education director, created a new game called Mintonette as a pastime to be played preferably indoors and by any number of players. The game took some of its characteristics from tennis and handball. Another indoor sport, basketball, was catching on in the area, having been invented just ten miles (sixteen kilometers) away in the city of Springfield, Massachusetts, only four years before. Mintonette was designed to be an indoor sport less rough than basketball for older members of the YMCA, while still requiring a bit of athletic effort.

The first rules, written down by William G Morgan, called for a net 6 ft 6 in (1.98 m) high, a 25×50 ft (7.6×15.2 m) court, and any number of players. A match was composed of nine innings with three serves for each team in each inning, and no limit to the number of ball contacts for each team before sending the ball to the opponents' court. In case of a serving error, a second try was allowed. Hitting the ball into the net was considered a foul (with loss of the point or a side-out)—except in the case of the first-try serve.

After an observer, Alfred Halstead, noticed the volleying nature of the game at its first exhibition match in 1896, played at the International YMCA Training School (now called Springfield College), the game quickly became known as volleyball (it was originally spelled as two words: "volley ball"). Volleyball rules were slightly modified by the International YMCA Training School and the game spread around the country to various YMCAs.

Refinements and Later Developments

The first official ball used in volleyball is disputed; some sources say that Spalding created the first official ball in 1896, while others claim it was created in 1900. The rules have evolved over time; In Philippines by 1916, the skill and power of the set and spike had been introduced, and four years later a "three hits" rule and a rule against hitting from the back row were established. In 1917, the game was changed from 21 to 15 points. In 1919, about 16,000 volleyballs were distributed by the American Expeditionary Forces to their troops and allies, which sparked the growth of volleyball in new countries.

The first country outside the United States to adopt volleyball was Canada in 1900. An international federation, the Federation Internationale de Volleyball (FIVB), was founded in 1947, and the first World Championships were held in 1949 for men and 1952 for women. The sport is now popular in Brazil, in Europe (where especially Italy, the Netherlands, and countries from Eastern Europe have been major forces since the late 1980s), in Russia, and in other countries including China and the rest of Asia, as well in as the United States.

Beach volleyball, a variation of the game played on sand and with only two players per team, became a FIVB-endorsed variation in 1987 and was added to the Olympic programme at the 1996 Summer Olympics.

Volleyball in the Olympics

The history of Olympic volleyball can be traced back to the 1924 Summer Olympics in Paris, where volleyball was played as part of an American sports demonstration event. After the foundation of FIVB and some continental confederations, it began to be considered for official inclusion. In 1957, a special tournament was held at the 53rd IOC session in Sofia, Bulgaria to support such request. The competition was a success, and the sport was officially included in the programme for the 1964 Summer Olympics.

The Olympic volleyball tournament was originally a simple competition, whose format paralleled the one still employed in the World Cup: all teams played against each other team and then were ranked by wins, set average, and point average. One disadvantage of this round-robin system is that medal winners could be determined before the end of the games, making the audience lose interest in the outcome of the remaining matches. To cope with this situation, the competition was split into two phases with the addition of a "final round" elimination tournament consisting of quarterfinals, semifinals, and finals matches in 1972. The number of teams involved in the Olympic tournament has grown steadily since 1964. Since 1996, both men's and women's events count twelve participant nations. Each of the five continental volleyball confederations has at least one affiliated national federation involved in the Olympic Games.

The U.S.S.R. won men's gold in both 1964 and 1968. After taking bronze in 1964 and silver in 1968, Japan finally won the gold for men's volleyball in 1972. Women's gold went to Japan in 1964 and again in 1976. That year, the introduction of a new offensive skill, the backrow attack, allowed Poland to win the men's competition over the Soviets in a very tight five-set match. Since the strongest teams in men's volleyball at the time belonged to the Eastern Bloc, the American-led boycott of the 1980 Summer Olympics did not have as great an effect on these events as it had on the women's. The U.S.S.R. collected their third Olympic Gold Medal in men's volleyball with a 3-1 victory over Bulgaria (the Soviet women won that year as well, their third gold as well). With the U.S.S.R. boycotting the 1984 Olympic Games in Los Angeles, the U.S. was able to sweep Brazil in the finals to win the men's gold medal. Italy won its first medal (bronze in the men's competition) in 1984, foreshadowing a rise in prominence for their volleyball teams.

At the 1988 Games, Karch Kiraly and Steve Timmons led the U.S. men's team to a second straight gold medal. In 1992, underrated Brazil upset favourites C.I.S., Netherlands, and Italy in the men's competition for the country's first Olympic gold medal. Runner-up Netherlands, men's silver medalist in 1992, came back under team leaders Ron Zwerver and Olof van der Meulen in the 1996 Games for a five-set win over Italy. A men's bronze medalist in 1996, Serbia and Montenegro (playing in 1996 and 2000 as the Federal Republic of Yugoslavia) beat Russia in the gold medal match in 2000, winning their first gold medal ever. In 2004, Brazil won its second men's volleyball gold medal beating Italy in the finals. In the 2008 Games, the USA beat Brazil in the men's volleyball final.

Rules of the Game

Volleyball Court

The Court: The game is played on a volleyball court 18 meters (59 feet) long and 9 meters (29.5 feet) wide, divided into two 9 m × 9 m halves by a one-meter (40-inch) wide net placed so that the top of the net is 2.43 meters (7 feet 11 5/8 inches) above the center of the court for men's competition, and 2.24 meters (7 feet 4 1/8 inches) for women's competition (these heights are varied for veterans and junior competitions).

There is a lino 3 meters from and parallel to the net in each team court which is considered the "attack line". This "3 moter" (or 10 foot) line divides the court into "back row" and "front row" areas (also back court and front court). These are in turn divided into 3 areas each: these are numbered as follows, starting from area "1", which is the position of the serving player:

After a team gains the serve (also known as siding out), its members must rotate in a clockwise direction, with the player previously in area "2" moving to area "1" and so on, with the player from area "1" moving to area "6".

The team courts are surrounded by an area called the free zone which is a minimum of 3 meters wide and which the players may enter and play within after the service of the ball. All lines denoting the boundaries of the team court and the attack zone are drawn or painted within the dimensions of the area and are therefore a part of the court or zone. If a ball comes in contact with the line, the ball is considered to be "in". An antenna is placed on each side of the net perpendicular to the sideline and is a vertical extension of the side boundary of the court. A ball passing over the net must pass completely between the antennae (or their theoretical extensions to the ceiling) without contacting them.

The Ball

FIVB regulations state that the ball must be spherical, made of leather or synthetic leather, have a circumference of 65–67 cm, a weight of 260–280 g and an inside pressure of 0.30–0.325 kg/cm2. Other governing bodies have similar regulations.

Game Play

Each team consists of six players. To get play started, a team is chosen to serve by coin toss. A player from the serving team throws the ball into the air and attempts to hit the ball so it passes over the net on a course such that it will land in the opposing team's court (the serve). The opposing team must use a combination of no more than three contacts with the volleyball to return the ball to the opponent's side of the net. These contacts usually consist first of the bump or pass so that the ball's trajectory is aimed towards the player designated as the setter; second of the set (usually an over-hand pass using wrists to push finger-tips at the ball) by the setter so that the ball's trajectory is aimed towards a spot where one of the players designated as an attacker can hit it, and third by the attacker who spikes (jumping, raising one arm above the head and hitting the ball so it will move quickly down to the ground on the opponent's court) to return the ball over the net. The team with possession of the ball that is trying to attack the ball as described is said to be on offense.

The team on defense attempts to prevent the attacker from directing the ball into their court: players at the net jump and reach above the top (and if possible, across the plane) of the net in order to block the attacked ball. If the ball is hit around, above, or through the block, the defensive players arranged in the rest of the court attempt to control the ball with a dig (usually a fore-arm pass of a hard-driven ball). After a successful dig, the team transitions to offense.

The game continues in this manner, rallying back and forth, until the ball touches the court within the boundaries or until an error is made. The most frequent errors that are made are either to fail to return the ball over the net within the allowed three touches, or to cause the ball to land outside the court. A ball is "in" if any part of it touches a sideline or end-line, and a strong spike may compress the ball enough when it lands that a ball which at first appears to be going out may actually be in. Players may travel well outside the court to play a ball that has gone over a sideline or end-line in the air.

Other common errors include a player touching the ball twice in succession, a player "catching" the ball, a player touching the net while attempting to play the ball, or a player penetrating under the net into the opponent's court. There are a large number of other errors specified in the rules, although most of them are infrequent occurrences. These errors include back-row or libero players spiking the ball or blocking (back-row players may spike the ball if they jump from behind the attack line), players not being in the correct position when the ball is served, attacking the serve in the front court and above the height of the net, using another player as a source of support to reach the ball, stepping over the back boundary line when serving, taking more than 8 seconds to serve, or playing the ball when it is above the opponent's court.

Scoring

When the ball contacts the floor within the court boundaries or an error is made, the team that did not make the error is awarded a point, whether they served the ball or not. The team that won the point serves for the next point. If the team that won the point served in the previous point, the same player serves again. If the team that won the point did not serve the previous point, the players of the team rotate their position on the court in a clockwise manner. The game continues, with the first team to score 25 points (and be two points ahead) awarded the set. Matches are best-of-five sets and the fifth set (if necessary) is usually played to 15 points. (Scoring differs between leagues, tournaments, and levels; high schools sometimes play best-of-three to 25; in the NCAA games are played best-of-five to 25 as of the 2008 season.)

Before 1999, points could be scored only when a team had the serve (side-out scoring) and all sets went up to only 15 points. The FIVB changed the rules in 1999 (with the changes being compulsory in 2000) to use the current scoring system (formerly known as rally point system), primarily to make the length of the match more predictable and to make the game more spectator-and television-friendly.

Libero

In 1998 the libero player was introduced internationally, the term meaning free in Italian is pronounced LEE-beh-ro (although many players and coaches pronounce it lih-BEAR-oh). The NCAA introduced the libero in 2002. The libero is a player specialized in defensive skills: the libero must wear a contrasting jersey colour from his or her teammates and cannot block or attack the ball when it is entirely above net height. When the ball is not in play, the libero can replace any back-row player, without prior notice to the officials. This replacement does not count against the substitution limit each team is allowed per set, although the libero may be replaced only by the player whom they replaced. The libero may function as a setter only under certain restrictions. If she/he makes an overhand set, she/he must be standing behind (and not stepping on) the 3-meter line; otherwise, the ball cannot be attacked above the net in front of the 3-meter line. An underhand pass is allowed from any part of the court.

The libero is, generally, the most skilled defensive player on the team. There is also a libero tracking sheet, where the referees or officiating team must keep track of who the libero subs in and out for. There may only be one libero per set (game), although there may be a different libero in the beginning of any new set (game). Furthermore, a libero is not allowed to serve, according to international rules, with the exception of the NCAA women's volleyball games, where a 2004 rule change allows the libero to serve, but only in a specific rotation. That is, the libero can only serve for one person, not for all of the people for whom she goes in. That rule change was also applied to high school and junior high play soon after.

Recent Rule Changes

Other rule changes enacted in 2000 include allowing serves in which the ball touches the net, as long as it goes over the net into the opponents' court. Also, the service area was expanded to allow players to serve from anywhere behind the end line but still within the theoretical extension of the sidelines. Other changes were made to lighten up calls on faults for carries and double-touches, such as allowing multiple contacts by a single player ("double-hits") on a team's first contact provided that they are a part of a single play on the ball.

In 2008, the NCAA changed the minimum number of points needed to win any of the first four sets from 30 to 25 for women's volleyball (men's volleyball remained at 30.) If a fifth (deciding) set is reached, the minimum required score remains at 15. In addition, the word "game" is now referred to as "set".

Skills

Competitive teams master six basic skills: serve, pass, set, attack, block and dig. Each of these skills comprises a number of specific techniques that have been introduced over the years and are now considered standard practice in high-level volleyball.

Serve

Setting up for an overhand serve.

A man making a jump serve.

A player stands behind the inline and serves the ball, in an attempt to drive it into the opponent's court. His or her main objective is to make it land inside the court; it is also desirable to set the ball's direction, speed and acceleration so that it becomes difficult for the receiver to handle it properly. A serve is called an "ace" when the ball lands directly onto the court or travels outside the court after being touched by an opponent.

In contemporary volleyball, many types of serves are employed:

- *Underhand and Overhand Serve:* refers to whether the player strikes the ball from below, at waist level, or first tosses the ball in the air and then hits it above shoulder level. Underhand serve is considered very easy to receive and is rarely employed in high-level competitions.
- *Sky Ball Serve:* a specific type of underhand serve occasionally used in beach volleyball, where the ball is hit so high it comes down almost in a straight line. This serve was invented and employed almost exclusively by the Brazilian team in the early 1980s and is now considered outdated. In Brazil, this serve is called Jornada nas Estrelas (Star Trek).
- *Line and Cross-Court Serve:* refers to whether the ball flies in a straight trajectory parallel to the side lines, or crosses through the court in an angle.
- *Top Spin:* an overhand serve where the ball gains topspin through wrist snapping. This spin causes the ball to drop faster than it appears to a passer receiving it.
- *Floater:* an overhand serve where the ball is hit with no spin so that its path becomes unpredictable. This type of serve can be administered while jumping or standing. This is akin to a knuckleball in baseball.
- *Jump Serve:* an overhand serve where the ball is first tossed high in the air, then the player makes a timed approach and jumps to make contact with the ball. There is usually much topspin imparted on the ball. This is the most popular serve amongst college and professional teams.
- *Jump Float:* This is a serve like the jump serve and the floater. The ball is tossed lower than a topspin jump

serve, but contact is still made while in the air. This serve is becoming more popular amongst college and professional players because it has a certain unpredictability in its flight pattern.

- *Round-House Serve:* the player stands with one shoulder facing the net, tosses the ball high and hits it with a fast circular movement of the arm. The ball is hit with the palm of the hand, creating a lot of topspin.
- *Hybrid Serve:* An overhand serve delivered similarly to a top spin serve; however, it has more pace than a floater, but has a similar unpredictable path.

Pass

A woman making a forearm pass or bump.

Also called reception, the pass is the attempt by a team to properly handle the opponent's serve, or any form of attack. Proper handling includes not only preventing the ball from touching the court, but also making it reach the position where the setter is standing quickly and precisely.

The skill of passing involves fundamentally two specific techniques: underarm pass, or bump, where the ball touches the inside part of the joined forearms or platform, at waist line; and overhand pass, where it is handled with the fingertips, like a set, above the head. Either form (joined forearm or overhand pass) are acceptable in professional and beach volleyball, however there are much tighter regulations on the overhand pass in beach volleyball.

Set

The set is usually the second contact that a team makes with the ball. The main goal of setting is to put the ball in the air in such a way that it can be driven by an attack into the opponent's court. The setter coordinates the offensive movements of a team, and is the player who ultimately decides which player will actually attack the ball.

As with passing, one may distinguish between an overhand and a bump set. Since the former allows for more control over the speed and direction of the ball, the bump is used only when the ball is so low it cannot be properly handled with fingertips, or in beach volleyball where rules regulating overhand setting are more stringent.

In the case of a set, one also speaks of a front or back set, meaning whether the ball is passed in the direction the setter is facing or behind the setter. There is also a jump set that is used when the ball is too close to the net. In this case the setter usually jumps off his or her right foot straight up to avoid going into the net. The setter usually stands about 2/3 of the way from the left to the right of the net and faces the left (the larger portion of net that he or she can see).

Sometimes a setter refrains from raising the ball for a teammate to perform an attack and tries to play it directly onto the opponent's court. This movement is called a "dump". The most common dumps are to 'throw' the ball behind the setter or in front of the setter to zones 2 and 4. More experienced setters toss the ball into the deep corners or spike the ball on the second hit.

Attack

An Attack in Progress: The attack (or spike, the slang term) is usually the third contact a team makes with the ball. The object of attacking is to handle the ball so that it lands on the opponent's court and cannot be defended. A player makes a series of steps (the "approach"), jumps, and swings at the ball.

Ideally the contact with the ball is made at the apex of the hitter's jump. At the moment of contact, the hitter's arm is fully extended above his or her head and slightly forward, making the highest possible contact while maintaining the ability to deliver a powerful hit.

The hitter uses arm swing, wrist snap, and a rapid forward contraction of the entire body to drive the ball. A 'bounce' is a slang term for a very hard/loud spike that follows an almost straight trajectory steeply downward into the opponent's court and bounces very high into the air. A "kill" is the slang term for an attack that is not returned by the other team thus resulting in a point.

Contemporary volleyball comprises a number of attacking techniques:

- *Backcourt (or backrow) / Pipe Attack:* an attack performed by a back row player. The player must jump from behind the 3-meter line before making contact with the ball, but may land in front of the 3-meter line.
- *Line and Cross-court Shot:* refers to whether the ball flies in a straight trajectory parallel to the side lines, or crosses through the court in an angle. A cross-court shot with a very pronounced angle, resulting in the ball landing near the 3-meter line, is called a cut shot.
- *Dip / Dink / Tip / Cheat:* the player does not try to make a hit, but touches the ball lightly, so that it lands on an area of the opponent's court that is not being covered by the defense.
- *Tool / Wipe / Block-abuse:* the player does not try to make a hard spike, but hits the ball so that it touches the opponent's block and then bounces off-court.
- *Off-speed Hit:* the player does not hit the ball hard, reducing its speed and thus confusing the opponent's defense.
- *Quick hit / "One":* an attack (usually by the middle blocker) where the approach and jump begin before the setter contacts the ball. The set (called a "quick set") is placed only slightly above the net and the ball is struck by the hitter almost immediately after leaving the setter's hands. Quick attacks are often effective because they isolate the middle blocker to be the only blocker on the hit.
- *Slide:* a variation of the quick hit that uses a low back set. The middle hitter steps around the setter and hits from behind him or her.
- *Double quick hit / "Stack" / "Tandem":* a variation of quick hit where two hitters, one in front and one behind the setter or both in front of the setter, jump to perform a quick hit at the same time. It can be used to deceive opposite blockers and free a fourth hitter attacking from backcourt, maybe without block at all.

Block

A block that is aimed at completely stopping an attack, thus making the ball remain in the opponent's court, is called offensive. A well-executed offensive block is performed by jumping and reaching to penetrate with one's arms and hands over the net and into the opponent's area. It requires anticipating the direction the ball will go once the attack takes place. It may also require calculating the best foot work to executing the "perfect" block. The jump should be timed so as to intercept the ball's trajectory prior to it crossing over the net. Palms are held deflected downward about 45-60 degrees toward the interior of the opponents court. A "roof" is a spectacular offensive block that redirects the power and speed of the attack straight down to the attacker's floor, as if the attacker hit the ball into the underside of a peaked house roof.

By contrast, it is called a defensive, or "soft" block if the goal is to control and deflect the hard-driven ball up so that it slows down and becomes more easy to be defended. A well-executed soft-block is performed by jumping and placing one's hands above the net with no penetration into the opponent's court and with the palms up and fingers pointing backward.

Blocking is also classified according to the number of players involved. Thus, one may speak of single (or solo), double, or triple block. Successful blocking does not always result in a "roof" and many times does not even touch the ball. While it's obvious that a block was a success when the attacker is roofed, a block that consistently forces the attacker away from his or her 'power' or preferred attack into a more easily controlled shot by the defense is also a highly successful block.

At the same time, the block position influences the positions where other defenders place themselves while opponent hitters are spiking.

Dig

Woman going for a dig.

Digging is the ability to prevent the ball from touching one's court after a spike or attack, particularly a ball that is nearly touching the ground. In many aspects, this skill is similar to passing, or bumping: overhand dig and bump are also used to distinguish between defensive actions taken with fingertips or with joined arms.

Some specific techniques are more common in digging than in passing. A player may sometimes perform a "dive", i.e., throw his or her body in the air with a forward movement in an attempt to save the ball, and land on his or her chest. When the player also slides his or her hand under a ball that is almost touching the court, this is called a "pancake". The pancake is frequently used in indoor volleyball.

Sometimes a player may also be forced to drop his or her body quickly to the floor in order to save the ball. In this situation, the player makes use of a specific rolling technique to minimize the chances of injuries.

Coaching

Basic: Coaching for volleyball can be classified under two main categories: match coaching and developmental coaching. The objective of match coaching is to win a match by managing a team's strategy. Developmental coaching emphasizes player development through the reinforcement of basic skills during exercises known as "drills." Drills promote repetition and refinement of volleyball movements, particularly in footwork patterns, body positioning relative to others, and ball contact. A coach will construct drills that simulate match situations thereby encouraging speed of movement, anticipation, timing, communication, and team-work. At the various stages of a player's career, a coach will tailor drills to meet the strategic requirements of the team. The American Volleyball Coaches Association is the largest organization in the world dedicated exclusively to volleyball coaching.

Strategy: An image from an international match between Italy and Russia in 2005. A Russian player on the left has just served, with three men of his team next to the net moving to their assigned block positions from the starting ones. Two others, in the back-row positions, are preparing for defense. Italy, on the right, has three men in a line, each preparing to pass if the ball reaches him. The setter is waiting for their pass while the middle hitter with no. 10 will jump for a quick hit if the pass is good enough. Alessandro Fei (no. 14) has no passing duties and is preparing for a back-row hit on the right side of the field. Note the two liberos with different colour dress. Middle hitters/blockers are commonly substituted by liberos in their back-row positions.

Player Specialization

There are 5 positions filled on every volleyball team at the elite level. Setter, Outside Hitter/Left Side Hitter, Middle Hitter, Opposite Hitter/Right Side Hitter and Libero/Defensive Specialist. Each of these positions plays a specific, key role in winning a volleyball match.

- Setters have the task for orchestrating the offense of the team. They aim for second touch and their main responsibility is to place the ball in the air where the attackers can place the ball into the opponents' court for a point. They have to be able to operate with the hitters, manage the tempo of their side of the court and choose the right attackers to set. Setters need to have swift and skillful appraisal and tactical accuracy, and must be quick at moving around the court.
- Liberos are defensive players who are responsible for receiving the attack or serve. They are usually the players on the court with the quickest reaction time and best passing skills. Libero means 'free' as they have the ability to substitute for any other player on the court during each play. They do not necessarily need to be tall, as they never play at the net, which allows shorter players with strong passing and defensive skills to excel in the position and play an important role in the team's success. A player designated as a libero for a match may not play other roles during that match. Liberos wear a different colour jersey than their teammates.
- Middle blockers or Middle hitters are players that can perform very fast attacks that usually take place near

the setter. They are specialized in blocking, since they must attempt to stop equally fast plays from their opponents and then quickly set up a double block at the sides of the court. In non-beginners play, every team will have two middle hitters.

- Outside hitters or Left side hitters attack from near the left antenna. The outside hitter is usually the most consistent hitter on the team and gets the most sets. In accurate first passes usually result in a set to the outside hitter rather than middle or opposite. Since most sets to the outside are high, the outside hitter may take a longer approach, always starting from outside the court sideline. In non-beginners play, there are again two outside hitters on every team in every match.
- Opposite hitters or Right side hitters carry the defensive workload for a volleyball team in the front row. Their primary responsibilities are to put up a well formed block against the opponents Outside Hitters and serve as a backup settor. Sets to the opposite usually go to the right side of the antennae.

Formations

The three standard volleyball formations are known as "4-2", "6-2" and "5-1", which refers to the number of hitters and setters respectively. 4-2 is a basic formation used only in beginners' play, while 5-1 is by far the most common formation in high-level play.

4-2

The 4-2 formation has four hitters and two setters. The setters usually set from the middle front or right front position. The team will therefore have two front-row attackers at all times. In the international 4-2, the setters set from the right front position. The international 4-2 translates more easily into other forms of offense.

The setters line up opposite each other in the rotation. The typical lineup has two outside hitters. By aligning like positions opposite themselves in the rotation, there will always be one of each position in the front and back rows. After service, the players in the front row move into their assigned positions, so that the setter is always in middle front. Alternatively, the setter moves into the right front and has both a middle and an outside attacker; the disadvantage here lies in the lack of an offside hitter, allowing one of the other team's blockers to "cheat in" on a middle block.

The clear disadvantage to this offensive formation is that there are only two attackers, leaving a team with fewer offensive weapons.

Another aspect is to see the setter as an attacking force, albeit a weakened force, because when the setter is in the front court they are able to 'tip' or 'dump', so when the ball is close to the net on the second touch, the setter may opt to hit the ball over with one hand. This means that the blocker who would otherwise not have to block the setter is engaged and may allow one of the hitters to have an easier attack.

6-2

In the 6-2 formation, a player always comes forward from the back row to set. The three front row players are all in attacking positions. Thus, all six players act as hitters at one time or another, while two can act as setters. So the 6-2 formation is actually a 4-2 system, but the back-row setter penetrates to set.

The 6-2 lineup thus requires two setters, who line up opposite to each other in the rotation. In addition to the setters, a typical lineup will have two middle hitters and two outside hitters. By aligning like positions opposite themselves in the rotation, there will always be one of each position in the front and back rows. After service, the players in the front row move into their assigned positions.

The advantage of the 6-2 is that there are always three front-row hitters available, maximizing the offensive possibilities. However, not only does the 6-2 require a team to possess two people capable of performing the highly specialized role of setter, it also requires both of those players to be effective offensive hitters when not in the setter position. At the international level, only the Cuban National Women's Team employs this kind of formation. It is also used in Women's NCAA play, partially due to the variant rules used which allow 12 substitutions per set (as opposed to the 6 allowed in the standard rules).

5-1

The 5-1 formation has only one player who assumes setting responsibilities regardless of his or her position in the rotation. The team will therefore have three front-row attackers when the setter is in the back row, and only two when the setter is in the front row, for a total of five possible attackers.

The player opposite the setter in a 5-1 rotation is called the opposite hitter. In general, opposite hitters do not pass; they stand behind their teammates when the opponent is serving.

The opposite hitter may be used as a third attack option (back-row attack) when the setter is in the front row: this is the normal option used to increase the attack capabilities of modern volleyball teams. Normally the opposite hitter is the most technical skilled hitter of the team. Back-row attacks generally come from the back-right position (position 1), but are increasingly performed from back-center in high-level play.

The big advantage of this system is that the setter always has 3 hitters to vary sets with. If the setter does this well, the opponent's middle blocker may not have enough time to block with the outside hitter, increasing the chance for the attacking team to make a point.

There is another advantage: when the setter is a front-row player, he or she is allowed to jump and "dump" the ball onto the opponent's side. This too can confuse the opponent's blocking players: the setter can jump and dump or can set to one of the hitters. A good setter knows this and thus won't only jump to dump or to set for a quick hit, but as well to confuse the opponent.

The 5-1 offense is actually a mix of 6-2 and 4-2: when the setter is in the front row, the offense looks like a 4-2; when the setter is in the back row, the offense looks like a 6-2.

Variations and Related Games

There are many variations on the basic rules of volleyball. By far the most popular of these is beach volleyball, which is played on sand with two people per team, and rivals the main sport in popularity.

Some games related to volleyball include:

- Newcomb ball (or sometimes spelled "Nuke 'Em")-where the ball is caught and thrown instead of hit, and which rivalled volleyball in popularity until the 1920s
- Prisoner Ball-also played with volleyball court and a volleyball. People can be called out, back in.
- Footvolley-a sport from Brazil in which the hands and arms are not used but most else is like beach volleyball.

Basic Skills of Volleyball

The worst situation that a volleyball team could be in is to show up at a game without knowing what skills they needed to win the game. Hitting the ball, being in the right place, and playing competitively can help to win the game as well as gain confidence in the sport. Focusing on the basics for volleyball can help you to gain the skills you need for every game.

1. *Serving:* This is what always starts the game and helps to keep the game. There are two basic types of serves. One is overhand; where the player will throw the ball in the air first, then hit it. The second is underhand, where the server will hold the ball and swing their other arm underneath the ball to hit it. There are a variety of other serves beyond these basics, all which help to get the ball over the net, and get the game going.
2. *Pass or Reception:* This is usually set up by the setter of the game. It is used in order to take the ball and give it to the other players on your own team. They will then have the ability to put the ball to the other side like they want to. You can either pass by the forearm or by hitting the ball overhead.
3. *Tip:* A tip is used as a way to trick the other team into thinking that the ball is going further than it will. The

player will hit the ball lightly, making it go over the net but not too far into the other player's area so that they can't hit it back.

4. *Dig:* This is the ability for a player to save the ball from hitting the court after it has been spiked. It usually requires a player to slide underneath the ball on the court or to dive underneath the ball.
5. *Rebound:* This occurs when the ball stays on one side, making the players rebound, or take the ball back.

With all of these different hits for a ball, you will want to make sure that the players have the ability to move freely and effectively with every move. With all of these different hits, the players will need to connect where they want to hit the ball with the way that their feet move. For example, a dig will require the feet to move under the body in order to save the ball. A serve will require more balance on both feet in order to hit the ball more effectively. This will be important to keep in mind as you are training players.

The basics of volleyball hits can lead a long way when you are working towards playing the game. If you are finding ways to teach techniques to players, this is the place to start. It will allow everyone to have a good chance at controlling and hitting the ball, no matter what the set up is.

Volleyball Basic Rules

The Serve:

(A) Server must serve from behind the restraining line (end line) until after contact.

(B) Ball may be served underhand or overhand.

(C) Ball must be clearly visible to opponents before serve.

(D) Served ball may graze the net and drop to the other side for point.

(E) First game serve is determined by a volley, each subsequent game shall be served by the previous game loser.

(F) Serve must be returned by a bump only. no setting or attacking a serve.

Scoring:

1. Rally scoring will be used.
2. There will be a point scored on every score of the ball.
3. Offense will score on a defense miss or out of bounds hit.
4. Defense will score on an offensive miss, out of bounds hit, or serve into the net.
5. Game will be played to 25 pts.
6. Must win by 2 points.

Rotation:

(A) Team will rotate each time they win the serve.

(B) Players shall rotate in a clockwise manner.

(C) There shall be 4-6 players on each side.

Playing The Game (Volley):

(A) Maximum of three hits per side.

(B) Player may not hit the ball twice in succession (A block is not considered a hit).

(C) Ball may be played off the net during a volley and on serve.

(D) A ball touching a boundary line is good.

(E) A legal hit is contact with the ball by a player body above and including the waist which does not allow the ball to visibly come to a rest.

(F) If two or more players contact the ball simultaneously, it is considered one play and the players involved may not participate in the next play.

(G) A player must not block or attack a serve.

(H) Switching positions will be allowed only between front line players. (After the serve only).

Basic Violations:

(A) Stepping on or over the line on a serve.

(B) Failure to serve the ball over the net successfully.

(C) Hitting the ball illegally (Carrying, Palming, Throwing, etc.).

(D) Touches of the net with any part of the body while the ball is in play. If the ball is driven into the net with such force that it causes the net to contact an opposing player, no foul will be called, and the ball shall continue to be in play.

(E) Reaching over the net, except under these conditions:
1. When executing a follow-through.
2. When blocking a ball which is in the opponents court but is being returned (the blocker must not contact the ball until after the opponent who is attempting to return the ball makes contact). Except to block the third play.

(F) Reaches under the net (if it interferes with the ball or opposing player).

(G) Failure to serve in the correct order.

(H) Blocks or spikes from a position which is clearly not behind the 10-foot line while in a back row position.

The Court

Playing Area

Both indoor and outdoor courts are 18 m x 9mi (29'6" x 59').

Indoor courts also include an attack area designated by a line 3 m (9'10") back from the center line.

Lines on the court are 5cm (2" wide).

Net Height

Net height for men, co-ed mixed 6, & outdoor is 2.43 meters or 7'11-5/8".

Net height for women, 7'4-1/8".

The height of the net shall be 8'.

Ball

The ball weighs between 9 and 10 ounces. Ball pressure is between 4.5 and 6.0 pounds

Volleyball Lingo	Translation
"Ace"	When the ball is served to the other

	team, and no one touches it.
"Sideout"	When the team that served the ball makes a mistake, causing the ball to go to the other team.
"Roof"	When a player jumps above the height of the net, and blocks the ball.
"Stuff"	When a player jumps about the height of the net, blocks the ball, and the ball goes back at the person who attacked(spiked) the ball.
"Dig"	When a player makes a save from a very difficult spike.
"Kill"	When a team spikes the ball and it either ends in a point or a sideout.

Throwball

Throwball is a non-contact ball sport played across a net between two teams of seven players on a rectangular court. Throwball is popular in Asia, moreover on the Indian subcontinent and was played as a women's sport in Chennai (formerly Madras) during the 1940s. The game's roots are closely linked with the YMCA (Young Men's Christian Association) as are those of volleyball which, while older, shares many similarities with throwball. Rules were drafted in 1955 and India's first national level throwball championship was played in 1980.

History

According to the Throwball Federation of India, throwball is thought to have been taken from a recreational sport popular among women in England and Australia during the 1930s. The YMCA is believed to have brought throwball to Chennai, India where it was played as a women's sport in the 1940s. Harry Crowe Buck of the YMCA College of Physical Education in Chennai (which had become co-educational in 1940) drafted guidelines for throwball rules and regulations in 1955. The game reached Bangalore in the 1950s.

T. Ramanna, a sports enthusiast from Bangalore, organized a national level throwball championship in 1980. In 1985 the Throwball Federation of India (TFI) was formed along with the Indian National Throwball Championship and by 1990 throwball in India had become a sport for both men and women.

Rules and Play

The playing court is somewhat larger than a volleyball court at 12.20 by 18.30 metres (40.03 ft × 60.04 ft) with a neutral box 1.5 metres (4 ft 11.06 in) on either side of the centre. The height of the net is 2.2 metres (7.22 ft). The ball is similar to a volleyball but may be slightly larger. While in volleyball the ball is hit or volleyed throughout play, in throwball the ball is thrown over the net, where a member of the other team tries to catch the ball and quickly throw it back across the net.

An official game is played between two teams of seven players. A maximum of five substitute players is allowed for each team, which can make a maximum of five substitutions during a set. A team can take two time-outs of 30 seconds each during a set. The first team to score 25 points wins a set. A match is three sets.

Service is within five seconds after the referee whistles and is done from the service zone, without crossing the end line. A player can jump while serving the ball. The service ball must not touch the net. Double touch is not allowed for receiving the service ball and players stay in 2-3-2 position during the serve.

During a rally, the ball must be caught at once with both hands, without any sound or movement of the ball within the hands (dubs) and the player should have contact with the ground. Two players are not allowed to catch the ball simultaneously. The ball is thrown within three seconds after being caught, only from above the shoulder-line and only with one hand. A player can jump when throwing the ball, which can touch the net (but not the antenna). The player should have contact with the ground when catching the ball. However, the ball is not touched with any part of the body other than the palm when catching or throwing (body touch). The ball can neither be shifted (passed) to the left or right, nor deliberately pushed. In official play, teams wear a shorts and jersey uniform with numbers only in the range of 1-12 printed front and back.

Major Competitions

Domestic Competitions

India: In India, National Throwball Championship is organized by All India Throwball Federation. In 2009, the 31st National Championship is scheduled to be held in Vijayawada.

Basic Skills

The Thunder-swipe, Thunder-Smash, White Disc Thunder, Thunder-Crush, Thunder-Check, Thunder-Punch, Thunder-Push, Thunder-Fist etc.... Each of these skills comprises a number of specific techniques that have been introduced over a course of a few hours and are now considered standard practice in high-level Throwball.

Thunder-Swipe

The arm of Derek Sigmeth displaying the grip for the Thunder Fist (Derek invented this move).

A player stands behind the endline and serves the ball, in an attempt to drive it into the opponent's court. His or her main objective is to make it land inside the court; it is also desirable to set the ball's direction, speed and acceleration so that it becomes difficult for the receiver to handle it properly. A serve is called an "ace" when the ball lands directly onto the court or travels outside the court after being touched by an opponent.

In contemporary Throwball (Thunderball), many types of serves are employed:

* *Thunder Swipe:* refers to the standard serve of the Thunderball. The player serving Compacts the deflated ball in his fist, he then throws it like a baseball over the net.
* *Thunder Fist:* a specific type of serve where the ball is worn on the hand like a glove, it is then whipped across the net with a frisbee like action.

- *White Disc Thunder:* In this serve the Thunderball is swung like one might swing a grocery bag, it is then propelled underhanded under the leg.

Thunder-Pass

Also called Thunder-reception, the pass is the attempt by a team to properly handle the opponent's serve, or any form of attack. Proper handling includes not only preventing the ball from touching the court, but also making it reach the position where the Thunder-pirate is standing quickly and precisely.

The skill of passing involves fundamentally two specific techniques: 1) Grab the ball 2) pass the ball.

Thunder-Smash

- The basic smash the ball is drilled by a offensive player towards the oppenents area over the net
- Rainbow thunder smash-A backhanded smash where an offensive player jumps rotating his hand backwards and smashing over the net.

Thunder-Hits

- Thunder-Punch-when a defensive player punches an offensive player with two fists (this motion must begin with the fists near the players chest and arms up, the fists then swing out from the defensive players chest)
- Thunder-check-Like a check similar to one you might see in hockey. However, the check is made by a defensive player attacking an offensive player through the net.
- Thunder-push-A defensive push through the net on an offensive player.

Kho-Kho

Kho-Kho ranks as one of the most popular traditional sports in India. The origin of Kho-Kho is difficult to trace, but many historians believe, that it is a modified form of 'Run Chase', which in its simplest form involves chasing and touching a person. With its origins in Maharashtra, Kho-Kho in ancient times, was played on 'raths' or chariots, and was known as Rathera.

Like all Indian games, it is simple, inexpensive and enjoyable. It does, however, demand physical fitness, strength, speed and stamina, and a certain amount of ability. Dodging, feinting and bursts of controlled speed make this game quite thrilling. To catch by pursuit-to chase, rather than just run-is the capstone of Kho-Kho.The game develops qualities such as obedience, discipline, sportsmanship, and loyalty between team members.

The rules of the game were framed in the beginning of the 20th century. At Gymkhana Poona, a Committee was formed in 1914, to frame its rules. The first ever rules on Kho-Kho were published from Gymkhana Baroda, in 1924. In 1959-60, the first national Kho-Kho championship was organised in Vijayawada (Andhra Pradesh). The Government has initiated the following awards for the game: Arjuna Award, Eklavya Award for men, Rani Laxmi Bai award for women, Veer Abhimanyu award for boys under 18, and Janaki award for girls under 16.

How the Game is Played

Each team consists of twelve players, but only nine players take the field for a contest. A match consists of two innings. An innings consists of chasing and running turns of 7 minutes each. Eight members of the chasing team sit in their eight squares on the central lane, alternately facing the opposite direction, while the ninth member is an active chaser, and stands at either of the posts, ready to begin the pursuit. Members of the chasing team have to put their opponent out, touching them with their palms, but without committing a foul. All the action in Kho-Kho is provided by the defenders, who try to play out the 7 minutes time, and the chasers who try to dismiss them. A defender can be dismissed in three ways: 1) if he is touched by an active chaser with his palm without committing a foul, 2) if he goes out of the limits on his own, 3) if he enters the limit late.

Defenders enter the limit, in batches of three. After the third and last defender of batch is out, the next batch must enter the limits, before a 'kho' is given by the successful active chaser. Defenders have full freedom of movement on both sides of the central lane, but the active chaser cannot change the direction to which he is committed. He cannot cross the central lane. An active chaser can change position with a seated chaser, by touching him from behind by palm, and uttering the word 'kho' loudly, and simultaneously, chase or attack is build up through a series of 'khos' as the chase continues with a relay of chasers.

At the end of the innings there is an interval of 5 minutes and an interval of 2 minutes, in between the turns. Each side alternates between chasing and defence. Kho-Kho can be played by men, women, and children of all ages. The game requires a very small piece of evenly surfaced ground, rectangular in shape, and 27m by 15m. The only equipment required are the two poles. The game lasts no more than 37 minutes.

Domestic Seasons and Tournaments

The following championships are organised for this game:

National Championships, Junior National, Sub Junior National Championship, School Championship, Mini School Championship, Primary Mini School Championship, National Women Championship, All India Inter University Championship and Federation Cup.

Organisations Involved with the Sport in India

The primary sports body for this game is called the Kho-Kho Federation of India (K.K.F.I.). It has its branches in all the states and it has been conducting Mini, Junior and Open National Championships for both sexes, in many parts of India.

Rules

* The back kho rules will only depend on the wrong motion of the body.
* The back kho will be cleared if the chaser goes to either pole or gives kho to another player.
* The bunch of 3 players should enter the playing area within 10 seconds after the last player of the previous bunch gets out.

* In the free area the chaser can go in any direction.
* The runner will be out if he/she crosses the field boundaries.
* The referee's decision is final. Teams will be disqualified if they misbehave with the referee.
* The format of the tournament (knockout or league) and other such details will be decided once registration is over and we know how many teams are participating.

Key Players

A number of players have bagged the Arjuna Award. Some of these players are:

Shri Shekhar Dharwadkar, Shri Shrirang Inamdar, Usha Nagarkar, Nilima Sarolkar, Achala Devare.

UNIT-III

Methods, Organization and Administration

Methods of Teaching Physical Activities

Participation in regular physical activity at a level sufficient to promote health-related physical fitness is an essential behavior for professionals in all fields of physical activity at all levels (this includes coaches, K-12 teachers, physical education and kinesiology faculty in higher education, fitness professionals, athletes, all advocates of physically active lifestyles). From the beginning of the twentieth century to present times, authorities in our field have stressed the importance of modeling an active lifestyle and physical fitness for professionals in all fields related to physical activity. (Cadinal, 2001; Corbin, 1984; McCloy, 1940; Melville, 1999; Sargeant, 1900; Staffo & Stier, 2000; Wilmore, 1982). A recent survey of physical activity-related professionals and pre-professionals shows that there is continued strong support for this view (Cardinal & Cardinal, 2001).Respondents agreed (4.56 on a 5-point Likert scale) that "role modeling is a powerful teaching tool for HPERD professionals." Several key aspects related to modeling in general, and modeling physical activity and fitness in particular, are presented here.

- The behaviors of models can influence the learning of others.
- Participation in regular physical activity is an essential behavior of physical educators and professionals in physical activity as role models as well as for personal health-related wellness.

- Achievement and maintenance of health-related physical fitness (based on accepted criterion-referenced standards) is an appropriate expectation for all professionals in the field of physical activity.

Together these points provide support for the position statement. The behaviors of models can influence the learning of others. There is considerable research in diverse domains to support the tenets of social cognitive theory, pointing to the effectiveness of modeling as an important factor in altering human behaviors (Bandura, 1997). Modeling has been shown to be an effective method in working with negative eating behaviors, substance abuse (e.g., alcohol, smoking), and influencing seat belt use (Baranowsky, Perry, & Parcel, 1997). In the psychomotor domain, extensive research has found that modeling can play a major role in the acquisition of motor skills (Ferrari, 1996; Maddalozzo, Stuart, Rose, & Cardinal, 1999; McCullagh, 1993). The use of models can promote competence and feelings of self-confidence and self-efficacy.

Research on modeling related to a physically active lifestyle indicates that children of physically active parents (parent models) are more likely to be active than children of sedentary parents (Freedson & Evenson, 1991; Moore, Lombardi, White, Campbell, Oliveria & Ellison, 1991). Furthermore, the evidence suggests that children who are active with their parents are likely to be more active than children who do not exercise with their parents (Sallis, 1988a; Sallis, 1988b). Physical education teachers may be less powerful role models than parents, however, teachers are among the more important models for children and youth (Cardinal, 2001). In a study of sixth through eighth grade school children, Gilmer, Speck, Bradley, Harrell, and Belyea (1996) found teachers and coaches to be the most frequently cited non-family member adult role models. Modeling a physically active lifestyle by physical education teachers could have effects on youth similar to those of parents (Melville & Maddalozzo, 1988).

Implication: Models can influence attitudes and behaviors in many ways, including health practices, motor skill acquisition, and the adoption of physical activity patterns. Physical educators, coaches, and all professionals in fitness and physical activity have strong modeling status for many children and youth.Participation in regular physical activity is an essential behavior of physical educators and other physical activity-related professionals as role models as well as for personal health-related wellness. Since a primary goal of the profession is to promote an active healthy lifestyle (AAHPERD, AAHPERD vision statement, 1998) for everyone, those involved in professions related to physical activity and fitness should teach and model the most current "established" behaviors and processes for improving health and physical fitness. Presently, those behaviors include participating in a variety of physical activities as noted in the Physical Activity Pyramid (Corbin & Lindsey, 1997; Heyward, 1998).

The foundation of this model calls for an accumulation of at least 30 minutes of moderate "lifestyle physical activities" on all or most days of the week. To further guide the selection of physical activities, the model recommends moderate to vigorous aerobic activities 3 to 6 times per week, muscle fitness exercises 2 to 3 times per week, and flexibility or range of motion exercises 3 to 7 times per week. Physical activity professionals should demonstrate a personal understanding and appreciation of the basic physiological training principles such as warm-up, cool-down, gradual overload, progression, and the application of the principles of frequency, intensity, and time as they relate to improving and maintaining fitness (Howley & Franks, 1997; AAHPERD, 1999). Modeling these principles in their own fitness endeavors will have a positive influence on those who expect fitness and exercise leaders to be leaders in their profession and to set a positive example for young people and the community.

Studies by Cardinal and Sachs (1995, 1996) have found that most people are more likely to adopt moderate intensity "lifestyle physical activities" as opposed to traditional, more structured forms of exercise. This finding suggests that encouragement and modeling of "lifestyle physical activities" by fitness and exercise professionals and physical educators may be especially important to young people and a community that is already inclined to adopt moderate physical activity to improve the quality of life.In addition to the importance of a physical activity professional's potential influence on others as a model, engaging in a physically active lifestyle is very important for personal reasons. There are studies that show that participation in organized fitness programmes (e.g., corporate fitness programmes) results in greater productivity, reduced absenteeism, lower health care costs, and greater job satisfaction among employees (Opatz, 1994).

It is reasonable to assume that physical educators and other physical activity professionals who exhibit active lifestyles, similar to those of corporate employees involved in physical activity programmes, can expect to experience similar benefits. This was confirmed in one study conducted among 117 schoolteachers (Blair et al., 1984). Those involved in the school district's experimental wellness programme demonstrated significantly greater improvements compared to those not involved in the wellness programme on a number of physiological variables, as well as general well-being, level of job satisfaction, and self-concept. Moreover, both self-and principal-ratings of the teachers' stress management and performance were higher among those in the wellness programme compared to those not in the programme.

Implications: When children and youth see physical activity professionals participating in accordance with established activity guidelines, applying sound physiological training principles, and actively modeling a physically active lifestyle, it reinforces student learning and will likely lead some to adopt similar activity patterns. The active lifestyle of professionals promotes credibility among parents and colleagues and exemplifies evidence of the value of a physically active lifestyle.

Furthermore, the physical activity professionals who exercise regularly provide examples of the positive physiological, health-related effects of an active lifestyle.Achievement and maintenance of health-related physical fitness (based on accepted criterion referenced standards) is an appropriate expectation for all professionals in the field of physical activity.

Throughout the years, leaders in our discipline have claimed that physical educators need to maintain acceptable physical fitness levels to be totally effective teachers (Cadinal, 2001; Corbin, 1984; McCloy, 1940; Melville, 1999; Sargeant, 1900; Staffo & Stier, 2000; Wilmore, 1982). Physical educators also need to maintain and exhibit acceptable physical fitness levels to be totally effective fitness role models. Professionals and pre-service professionals are adamant that fitness is important and that the components of health-related fitness, cardio-vascular endurance, muscular endurance,muscular strength, flexibility, and body composition (Howley & Franks, 1997) should be a measure of that fitness level. Cardinal & Cardinal (2001) found that physical education professionals strongly believe, "it is important for health, physical education, recreation, and dance professionals to maintain a healthy body fat percentage." Those same people strongly concurred (4.4 on a 5-point scale) with the statement "involvement in regular physical activity at a level sufficient to promote health-related physical fitness is a desirable and recommended behavior for physical education teachers." Such models are worthy of commendation if they are careful to keep long-term health considerations ahead of shorter-term performance ones.

Administrators have also expressed that they value teacher fitness. School administrators have identified lack of teacher fitness as a barrier to implementing quality elementary physical education programmes (Sallis, McKenzie, Kolody, & Curtis, 1996). Surveys of individual's responsible for hiring physical educators have shown that applicants perceived to be unfit have a much-reduced chance of employment (Melville & Cardinal, 1997). Although these studies present a topic that requires further study, it should be noted that there has been little research undertaken to determine whether or not a teacher's fitness level actually affects student learning and behavior or teacher effectiveness.

Implications: Although the physical activity professional's physical fitness level is only one of many characteristics which contribute to the learning process, modeling an appropriate fitness level and an active lifestyle needs to be considered a significant factor in encouraging young people, colleagues, and communities to do the same. The level of physical fitness we model may have a powerful influence on youth and our success in the advocacy for our profession to the public.

Lesson Plan—Parts and Preparation of General Lesson Plan

A lesson plan is a teacher's detailed description of the course of instruction for an individual lesson.

Developing an instructional unit

While there are many formats for a lesson plan, most lesson plans contain some or all of these elements, typically in this order:

* The title of the lesson
* The amount of time required to complete the lesson
* A list of required materials
* *A List of Objectives:* These may be stated as behavioral objectives (what the student is expected to be able to do upon completion of the lesson) or as knowledge objectives (what the student is expected to know upon completion of the lesson).
* *The Set or Lead-in to the Lesson:* This is designed to focus students on the skill or concept about to be instructed. Common sets include showing pictures or models, asking leading questions, or reviewing previously taught lessons.
* *The Instructional Component:* This describes the sequence of events which will take place as the lesson is delivered. It includes the instructional input—what the teacher plans to do and say, and guided practice—an opportunity for students to try new skills or express new ideas with the modeling and guidance of the teacher.
* *Independent Practice:* This component allows students to practice the skill or extend the knowledge on their own.

* *The Summary:* This is an opportunity for the teacher to wrap up the discussion and for the students to pose unanswered questions.
* *Evaluation:* Some, but not all, lessons have an evaluative component where the teacher can check for mastery of the instructed skills or concepts. This may take the form of a set of questions to be answered or a set of instructions to be followed. The evaluation may be formative; that is to say, used to guide subsequent learning, or summative; that is to say, used to determine a grade or other achievement criterion.
* *Analysis:* Often not part of a lesson plan, this component allows the teacher to reflect on the lesson and answer questions such as what went well, what needs improving, and how students reacted to the lesson.
* *Continuity* : The content/ideas/theme/rules etc. from previous day are reflected upon or reviewed.

A Well Developed Unit

A well developed lesson plan will be established dependent on the interests and needs of your students. It will incorporate the best practices for the educational field. The lesson plan will also correlate with the teacher's philosophy of education, which is what the teacher feels is the purpose of educating his or her students.

There are usually four topics that lesson plans, in a secondary English programme, are centered around. They are literary theme, elements of language and composition, literary history, and literary genre. A broad, thematic lesson plan is preferred because it allows a teacher to create various research, writing, speaking, and reading assignments. It allows an instructor to teach various genres of literature and incorporate the use of videotapes, films, and television programmes in classroom activities. It also allows for literature and English to be taught together.

The exact format chosen for a lesson plan will be driven by school requirements and personal tastes of the teacher, in that order. Unit plans follow much the same format, but are intended to cover an entire unit of work, which may be delivered over several days or weeks.

In today's constructivist teaching style, the individual lesson plan may not be required. Specific objectives and timelines may be included in the unit plan, but lesson plans are more fluid as they cater to student needs and learning styles.

Setting an Objective

The first thing a teacher must do is decide what the lesson plan will focus on. Based on this answer, the teacher should create one idea or question that he or she wants to be explored or answered. Next, the teacher should create classroom activities that will correlate with the established idea or question. This should include individual and group activities. Once these activities are established, the teacher must identify what language arts skills will be covered in the lesson plan.

After the teacher has completed these activities, he or she must guarantee that the lesson plan is equivalent to the best practices used in language arts; this includes conducting research on what teaching methods will result in a high success rate for students in language arts. The teacher must ensure that the goals in the lesson plan are compatible to the developmental level of the students. The teacher must also ensure that his or her expectations for student achievement are reasonable.

Selecting Lesson Plan Material

The lesson plan you create must correlate to the text book you will be using for the class. These text books are usually books selected by the school and are limited. Because of this dilemma, the teacher must take great care in selecting the most appropriate book for his or her students.

Unit Structure

The instructor must decide whether class assignments are going to be whole-class, small groups, workshops, independent work, peer learning, or contractual. Whole-class is when the teacher lectures to the class as a whole and has the class collectively participate in classroom discussions. Small groups are when students are placed in groups of three or four to work on assignments together. Although the teacher has control of this process, it may pose a problem if the students do not know how to work well together. Workshops are when students are performing various tasks simultaneously. The activities executed in the workshop must be tailored to the lesson plan. Independent work is when a student is given assignments that must be completed individually. Peer learning allows students to work together, face to face, so they can learn from one another. Contractual work establishes an agreement between the teacher and the student in which the student agrees to perform a certain amount of work by a set deadline.

Testing

The teacher must decide how she is going to evaluate each student's performance.

Summative Assessment Summative assessment evaluates learning needs. It usually consists of tests, semester exams, end of unit or end of chapter tests which evaluate a student's progress, performance, and knowledge. The final grade of a student is calculated based upon the student's performance in these exams. These assessments may assist teachers in adjusting future curriculum based upon how well the students retain information.

Formative Assessment Formative assessment evaluates the process of learning in its process, and is a part of the teaching process. Teachers use formative assessment to discover holes and modify their teaching and the learning of their students. As opposed to the adjustments in a summative assessment programme, the student needs are recognized immediately during the course of learning. Such an approach enables educators to raise the learning standards right. By knowing the current needs of each student, including those with lower abilities, a teacher can address them immediately. The information provided by formative assessment is to be used for modifying the teaching and learning activities in the classroom in order to get the best possible learning results.

Reliability of Classroom Assessment

Reliability of classroom assessment is an controversial issue. Teachers have different grading and evaluating standards, so some put more emphasis on the amount of work performed, while others value quality. Formative and summative assessment procedures should be equally applied in the classroom. However, it seems that more stress in the modern education system (see NCLB) is put upon summative assessment, and student's performance is evaluated mainly by means of exams. Summative assessments are easy and they provide an objective picture of the students' skills and knowledge. However, formative assessments should be applied in the classroom more often in order for a teacher to always have adequate current information about students' learning needs.

Evaluate the Lesson Plan

As mentioned above, a teacher must ensure he or she is using the best practices to make certain that his or her students have a high success rate.

Organisation of Intramural and Extramural Competitions

Intramural activities consist of all the sport and fitness activities carried on inside the campus of routine. The morning fitness programme for the masses, which start at 6.00 a.m. in summer & 6.30 p.m. in winter includes Yogasans, Marshal Arts, Conditioning & Fitness exercise & Aerobics. All these Activities are carried out simultaneously at different station at Vidula Maidan. Students join various activities according to their interest & choice.

The evening programme at Viduala Maidan starts at 4.30 pm. which includes match practice for various games like Basketball ,Volleyball, Athletics, Hockey, Football, Tennis, Marshal Arts, Kho-Kho, Kabaddi, Handball, Netball, Softball, Archery, Cricket & Swimming (Seasonal). Match Practice session are for the preparation of the teams for extramural competitions.

Games and Sports

Inter-faculty/ Inter house completions are one of the important events in the intramural programme. The intramural programme is formally opened every year with a festive look. It represented by all the faculties of the university houses of the Higher Secondary and Primary schools. All the teams assemble at Vidula Maidan representing their faculty/ houses projecting some contemporary political, cultural & social issues in a colorful procession.

With the opening ceremony of intramurals, the year long inter-faculty/ house competition take off. The intramural competitions are organized in approximately 15-20 games according to the time and facilities available. These competitions are organized through out the session. A formal valedictory function is organized to declare the winner faculty/ house of year and to conclude the year long intramural programme.

Mass Demonstrations : Mass Demonstrations of indigenous skills such as Sword Fighting, Yogasanas, Javelin, Lezium, Lathi etc. are also taught and performed on various occasions.

Horse Riding: *Horse riding* is a regular activity for the Students in the campus. Interested students avail this facility.

Swimming: Swimming is a seasonal activity, this facility is also available to all the students of Banasthali. More than 50 % of the students learn swimming in the campus every year.

Banasthali Seva Dal: *Banasthali Seva Dal* was introduced in the University to train the students in *March past, Ceremonial Parade* and *Rifle Shooting*. Banasthali Seva Dal also runs the programme of girl guide, which was registered with "Bharat Scouts and Guides" in the year 1988-89. It organizes the camps for girl guides and the eligible guides are selected to take part in state and national level camps. Number of students from the University has been honoured with "Rashtrapati Award". Two of our guides were selected to attend the international events of the World Association of Girl Guides and Girl Scouts at Pune (WAGGGS).

Shooting: Banasthali University has a Rifle Club named, Banasthali University Rifle Club. It is the member of National Rifle Association of India. We have a shooting range where training is imparted to the students for the shooting skills in accordance with the various competitions/programmes of Rifle Association of India.

Flying: Banasthali University has its own licensed airfield (09/26); and has a Pushpak Aircraft VTDNB. The University provides training to the eligible selected students for SPL (Students Pilot License), for which they have to undergo an entrance test.

Extramural Programmes

Various Teams of Banasthali University participated in various Inetr Iniversity, Open and Women festival competition every year.

Inter University Competitions: The University teams participate in various Inter University competition e.g. Basketball, Hockey, Badminton, Table tennis, Kho-Kho, Handball and Shooting, Archery, Swimming, Chess, Cricket, Tennis, Judo, Volleyball.

Open Tournaments: The participation in open Tournament of the University at District, State and National level is in following games and sports : Basketball, Hockey, Kho-kho and Kabbadi, Archery, Cricket, Volleyball, Marshal Arts, Tennis.

Women Festival Competitions: Participation of the University in the women festival competition is also very regular. The games in which the university takes part are Basketball, Hockey, tennis, Kho-Kho and Kabbadi.

Organization of Tournaments: Banasthali University has been organizing various inter-university tournaments since it's inception. The University has organized All India Inter University and Southwest Zone Inter University Championships in various games e.g. Hockey, Basketball, Shooting and Tennis. In the year 2001-2002 AIU sponsored Inter University South-West-Zone (Women) Basketball Championship was organized. Recently in February 2006, Banasthali University organized the National Inter University Women Hockey Tournament. Apart from Inter-university tournaments, Rajasthan State Senior and Junior Women Hockey Championship, District level Competitions are also organized at regular intervals.

Infrastructure: The University has developed infrastructure for physical education over the past seven decades. At present, there are adequate and varied resources available to sustain the various activities on campus. Significant among them are :

Play Fields (Outdoors)

I. *Vidula Maidan:* Basket Ball courts (two) one court with flood lights, Tennis courts (two) one court with flood lights, Hockey field (one), Four Hundred meters cinder track with Eight lanes, Kho-Kho courts (two), Kabbadi courts (two) Volley Ball Courts (one) Throw Ball court (one) Hand Ball Court (one) Facility for field events (shot) discus, Javlin, High Jump, Long Jump etc.), Archery Range, Netball, Softball, Cricket Pitch, Floodlit, Basketball Stadium and Tennis Stadium

II. *Lakshmi Bai Maidan:* Field for mass demonstrations, Field for march-past and ceremonial parade.

III. Swimming Pool

IV. Horseriding field

V. Air Strip

VI. Shooting Range

Play Field (Indoors) Table Tennis Hall (Gyan Mandir), Partially enclosed Badminton Court (Gyan Mandir), Multigym (16 Stations) installed at Apaji Arogya Mandir.

Tournament : Preparation of Fixtures

A tournament is a competition involving a relatively large number of competitors, all participating in a sport or game. More specifically, the term may be used in either of two overlapping senses:

1. One or more competitions held at a single venue and concentrated into a relatively short time interval.

2. A competition involving multiple matches, each involving a subset of the competitors, with the overall tournament winner determined based on the combined results of these individual matches. These are common in those sports and games where each match must involve a small number of competitors: often precisely two, as in most team sports, racket sports and combat sports, many card games and board games, and many forms of competitive debating. Such tournaments allow large numbers to compete against each other in spite of the restriction on numbers in a single match.

These two senses are distinct. All golf tournaments meet the first definition, but while match play tournaments meet the second, stroke play tournaments do not, since there are no distinct matches within the tournament. In contrast, football (soccer) leagues like the Premier League are tournaments in the second sense, but not the first, having matches spread across many stadia over a period of up to a year. Many tournaments meet both definitions; for example, the Wimbledon tennis championship.

A tournament-match (or tie or fixture or heat) may involve multiple game-matches (or rubbers or legs) between the competitors. For example, in the Davis Cup tennis tournament, a tie between two nations involves five rubbers between the nations' players. The team that wins the most rubbers wins the tie. In the later rounds of UEFA Champions League of football (soccer), each fixture is played over two legs. The scores of each leg are added, and the team with the higher aggregate score wins the fixture, with away goals used as a tiebreaker and a penalty shootout if away goals cannot determine a winner.

History

The word and general meaning derive from the mediaeval tournament or tourney. The word is still occasionally used for a military event such as the Royal Tournament. It was also based on the Renaissance Jousting tournament.

Knockout Tournaments

A knockout tournament is divided into successive rounds; each competitor plays in at most one fixture per round. The top-ranked competitors in each fixture progress to the next round. As rounds progress, the number of competitors and fixtures decreases, and the final round consists of just one fixture, the winner of which is the overall champion.

In a single-elimination tournament, only the top-ranked competitors in a fixture progress; in 2-competitor games, only the winner progresses. All other competitors are eliminated. This ensures a winner is decided with the minimum number of fixtures. However, most competitors will be eliminated after relatively few matches; a single bad or unlucky performance can nullify many preceding excellent ones. Some single-elimination tournaments such as NBA use a multiple-game format, in which teams would play each other more than one game (e.g. best-of-seven series in NBA) in order to determine who is the winner of this round. Other knockout formats provide a "second chance" for some or all losers.

A double-elimination tournament may be used in 2-competitor games to allow each competitor a single loss without being eliminated from the tournament. All losers from the main bracket enter a losers' bracket, the winner of which plays off against the main bracket's winner.

Some formats allow losers to play extra rounds before re-entering the main competition in a later round. Rowing regattas often have repechage rounds for the "fastest losers" from the heats. The winners of these progress, but are at a disadvantage in later rounds owing to the extra effort expended during the repechage.

In the playoffs of the Australian Football League, the teams with the best record before the playoffs are allowed to lose a game without being eliminated, whereas the lesser qualifiers are not. In athletics meetings, fastest losers may progress in a running event held over several rounds; e.g. the qualifiers for a later round might be the first 4 from each of 6 heats, plus the 8 fastest losers from among the remaining runners.

An extreme form of the knockout tournament is the step-ladder format where the strongest team is assured of a berth at the final round while the next strongest teams are given byes according to their strength/seeds; for example, in a four team tournament, the fourth and third seed figure in the first round, then the winner goes to the semifinals against the second seed, while the survivor faces the first seed at the final.

Group Tournaments

A group tournament, league, division or conference involves all competitors playing a number of fixtures. Points are awarded for each fixture, with competitors ranked based either on total number of points or average points per fixture. Usually each competitor plays an equal number of fixtures, in which case rankings by total points and by average points are equivalent.

In a round-robin tournament, each competitor plays all the others an equal number of times, once in a single round-robin tournament and twice in a double round-robin tournament. This is often seen as producing the most reliable rankings. However, for large numbers of competitors it may require an unfeasibly large number of rounds. A Swiss system tournament attempts to determine a winner reliably, based on a smaller number of fixtures. Fixtures are scheduled one round at a time; a competitor will play another who has a similar record in previous rounds of the tournament. This allows the top (and bottom) competitors to be determined with fewer rounds than a round-robin, though the middle rankings are unreliable.

There may be other considerations besides reliability of rankings. In some professional team sports, weaker teams are given an easier slate of fixtures as a form of handicapping. This occurs in the National Football League in the USA. Sometimes schedules are weighted in favour of local derbies or other traditional rivalries. For example, NFL teams play two games against each of the other three teams in their division, one game against half of the other twelve teams in their conference, and one game against a quarter of the sixteen teams in the other conference.

American sports are also unusual in providing fixtures between competitors who are, for ranking purposes, in different groups. Another, systematic, example of this was the 2006 Women's Rugby World Cup: each of the teams in Group A played each of the teams in Group B, with the groups ranked separately based on the results. (Groups C and D intertwined similarly.) An elaboration of this system is the Mitchell movement in duplicate bridge, discussed below, where North-South pairs play East-West pairs.

In 2-competitor games where ties are rare or impossible, competitors are typically ranked by number of wins, with ties counting half; each competitors' listings are usually ordered Wins-Losses(-Ties). Where draws are more common, this may be 2 points for a win and 1 for a draw, which is mathematically equivalent but avoids having too many half-points in the listings. These are usually ordered Wins-Draws-Losses. If there are more than 2 competitors per fixture, points may be ordinal (for example, 3 for first, 2 for second, 1 for third).

Multi-stage Tournaments

Many tournaments are held in multiple stages, with the top teams in one stage progressing to the next. American professional team sports have a "regular season" (group tournament) acting as qualification for the "post season" or "playoffs" (single-elimination tournament). In the FIFA World Cup, each continent has one or more qualifying tournaments, some of which are themselves multi-stage. The top teams in each qualify for the finals tournament. There, the 32 teams are divided into eight round-robin groups of four, with the top two in each progressing to the knockout phase, which involves four single-elimination rounds including the final.

Sometimes, results from an earlier phase are carried over into a later phase. In the Cricket World Cup, the second stage, known as the Super Eight since 2007 and before that the Super Six, features two teams from each of four preliminary groups (previously three teams from two preliminary groups), who do not replay the teams they have already played, but instead reuse the original results in the new league table. Formerly in the Swiss Football League, teams played a double round-robin, at which point they were split into a top "championship" group and a bottom "relegation" group; each played a separate double round-robin, with results of all 32 matches counting for ranking each group. A similar system is also used in the Scottish Premier League since 2000. After 33 games, when every club has played every other club three times, the division is split into two halves. Clubs play a further 5 matches, against the teams in their half of the division. This can (and often does) result in the team placed 7th having a higher points total than the team placed 6th, because their final 5 games are considerably easier.

The top Slovenian basketball league has a unique system. In its first phase, 12 of the league's 13 clubs compete in a full home-and-away season, with the country's representative in the Euroleague (an elite pan-European club competition) exempt. The league then splits. The top seven teams are joined by the Euroleague representative for a second home-and-away season, with no results carrying over from the first phase. These eight teams compete for four spots in a final playoff. The bottom five teams play their own home-and-away league, but their previous results do carry over. These teams are competing to avoid relegation, with the bottom team automatically relegated and the second-from-bottom team forced to play a mini-league with the second-and third-place teams from the second level for a place in the top league.

Promotion and Relegation

Where the number of competitors is larger than a tournament format permits, there may be multiple tournaments held in parallel, with competitors assigned to a particular tournament based on their ranking. In chess, scrabble, and many other individual games, many tournaments over one or more years contribute to a player's ranking. However, many team sports involve teams in only one major tournament per year. In European sport, including football, this constitutes the sole ranking for the following season; the top teams from each division of the league are promoted to a higher division, while the bottom teams from a higher division are relegated to a lower one. This promotion and relegation occurs mainly in league tournaments, but also features in Davis Cup tennis, where each group is a single-elimination tournament: while the team which wins each round is the champion, the one which loses each round will be relegated. The hierarchy of divisions may be linear, or tree-like, as with the English football league pyramid.

Bridge Tournaments

In contract bridge a "tournament" is a tournament in the first sense above, composed of multiple "events", which are tournaments in the second sense. Some events may be single-elimination, double-elimination, or Swiss style. However, "Pair events" are the most widespread. In these events, an identical deal (or board) is played in multiple rubbers. The North-South (NS) pair in one such rubber is measured not against the East-West (EW) pair in that same rubber, but rather against all the other NS pairs playing the same board in other rubbers. Thus pairs are rewarded for playing the same cards better than others have played them. Several systems provide a predetermined schedule of fixtures based on the number of pairs and boards to be played, to ensure a good mix of opponents, and that no pair plays the same board twice.

Poker Tournaments

In poker tournaments, as players are eliminated, the number of tables is gradually reduced, with the remaining players redistributed among the remaining tables. Play continues until one player has won all of the chips in play. Finishing order is determined by the order in which players are eliminated: last player remaining gets 1st place, last player eliminated gets 2nd, previous player eliminated gets 3rd, etc.

In a "shootout" tournament, players do not change tables until every table has been reduced to one player.

Rummy Tournaments

In rummy tournaments, multiple players join a single tournament. There can be tournaments between multiple players in multiples of 2. Eg: 4, 16, 32, 64, 128 players so on and so forth. As part of overall tournament, all players join one-on-one individual matches. Winners in each match move to the next round. Tournament continues until one player has won the final match. Finishing order of winners is determined by the order in which players are eliminated: last player remaining gets 1st place, last player eliminated gets 2nd, previous player eliminated gets 3rd, etc.

Single-elimination Tournament (Knock out) and Single League

A single-elimination tournament, also called a knockout, cup or sudden death tournament, is a type of elimination tournament where the loser of each match is immediately eliminated from winning the championship or first prize in the event. (However, it does not always mean that the defeated competitor will not participate further in the tournament: in some such tournaments, consolation or "classification" contests are subsequently held among those already defeated to determine the awarding of lesser places, for example, a Third place playoff.)

Format

This article may require cleanup to meet Wikipedia's quality standards. Please improve this article if you can. (February 2007)

Often, the number of participants in a single-elimination tournament is fixed as a power of two; for example, the tennis Grand Slam singles championships are tournaments of 128 players. This ensures all competitors will face opponents who have previously played the same number of matches. The full schedule of pairings across all rounds (the bracket) may be allocated before the start of the tournament; or each round may be allocated at the end of the preceding round. Each successive round halves the number of competitors remaining (assuming there are no byes — see below). The round in which only sixteen remain is sometimes called the "Round of Sixteen" or "Last Sixteen", when eight remain at the start it is generally called the quarter-final round; this is followed by the semi-final round in which only four are left, the two winners of which then meet in the final or championship round.

In cases where the number of competitive entities at the start of the tournament is not a power of two, some competitors may receive a bye in the first round, which entitles these competitors to advance to the second round automatically without playing. Often, these byes will be awarded to the highest-rated competitors in the event as a reward for some previous accomplishment; indeed, in some American team sports-most notably football-the number of teams qualifying for the postseason tournament will be intentionally set at a number which is not a power of two, in order to provide such an advantage to a high-achieving team in the just-completed regular season.

Multiple rounds of byes are also possible: in the FA Cup, the teams in the top two league divisions enter in the third round "proper" (of eight); the two next-highest divisions' teams will have entered in the first round; lower-division teams in one of 6 preliminary rounds.

When matches are held to determine places or prizes lower than first and second (the loser of the final-round match gaining the latter position), these typically include a match between the losers of the semifinal matches, the winner therein placing third and the loser fourth; sometimes contests are also held among the losers of the quarterfinal matches to determine fifth through eighth places (this is most commonly encountered in the Olympic Games, with the exception of boxing, where both fighters are deemed to be third place). In one scenario, two "consolation semifinal" matches may be conducted, with the winners of these then facing off to determine fifth and sixth places and the losers playing for seventh and eighth; those are used often in qualifying tournaments where only the top five teams advance to the next round; or some method of ranking the four quarterfinal losers might be employed, in which case only one round of additional matches would be held among them, the two highest-ranked therein then playing for fifth and sixth places and the two lowest for seventh and eighth.

In a tournament where more than two opponents or teams can play together at once, such as in a shootout poker tournament, players are removed when they can no longer play until one player remains from the group. This player moves on to the next round.

SOP for tournament brackets.

N = the number of teams in the tournament

Start with x = 1; Repeat x = 2x (i.e. keep doubling x) until x exceeds N.

The number of teams with a bye for the play-in bracket, B = x – N;

The number of teams in the play-in bracket, N – B (which also equals 2N-x) will be an even number. It is possible for B to equal N, in which case there will be no play-in games.

For the play-in bracket, the team in position B+1 plays team N with the winner taking position B+1, team B+2 plays team N-1 with the winner taking position B+2, etc.

After the play-in games are complete, the number of teams left, F = x/2 (N-(2N-x)/2), will be a number for a normal bracket (2, 4, 8, 16, etc)

In the next round, team 1 plays team F with the winner taking position 1, team 2 play team F-1 with the winner taking position 2, etc.

Subsequent rounds proceed likewise.

Seeding

Opponents may be allocated randomly (such as in the FA Cup); however, since the "luck of the draw" may result in the highest-rated competitors being scheduled to face each other early in the competition, seeding is often used to prevent this. Brackets are set up so that the top two seeds could not possibly meet until the final round (should both advance that far), none of the top four can meet prior to the semifinals, and so on.

One version of seeding is where brackets are set up so that the quarterfinal pairings (barring any upsets) would be the 1 seed vs. the 8 seed, 2 vs. 7, 3 vs. 6 and 4 vs. 5; however, this is not the procedure that is followed in most tennis tournaments, where the 1 and 2 seeds are placed in separate brackets, but then the 3 and 4 seeds are assigned to their brackets randomly, and so too are seeds 5 through 8, and so on. This may result in some brackets consisting of stronger players than other brackets, and since only the top 32 players are seeded at all in Tennis Grand Slam tournaments, it is conceivable that the 33rd-best player in a 128-player field could end up playing the top seed in the first round. While this may seem unfair to a casual observer, it should be pointed out that rankings of tennis players are generated by computers, and players tend to change ranking positions very gradually, so that a more equitable method of determining the pairings might result in many of the same head-to-head matchups being repeated over and over again in successive tournaments.

Sometimes the remaining competitors in a single-elimination tournament will be "re-seeded" so that the highest surviving seed is made to play the lowest surviving seed in the next round, the second-highest plays the second-lowest, etc. This may be done after each round, or only at selected intervals. In American team sports, for example, both the NFL and NHL employ this tactic, but the NBA does not (and neither does the NCAA college basketball tournament). MLB does not have enough teams in its playoff tournament where re-seeding would make a difference in the matchups, (The NFL is at the minimum, which is 6 from each league (or conference in the NFL, NBA or NHL) for a total of 12).

The NBA's format calls for the winner of the first-round series between the first and eighth seeds (within each of the two conferences the league has) to face the winner of the first-round series between the fourth and fifth seeds in the next round, even if one or more of the top three seeds had been upset in their first-round series; critics have claimed that this gives a team fighting for the fifth and sixth seeding positions near the end of the regular season an incentive to tank (deliberately lose) games, so as to finish sixth and thus avoid a possible matchup with the top seed until one round later. In some situations, a seeding restriction will be implemented; from 1978 until 1989, the NFL and since 1995, MLB have a rule where at the conference or league semifinal, should the top seed and last seed (wild card) be from the same division, they may not play each other; in that case, the top seed plays the worst division champion; the second-best division champion plays the wild card team.

Evaluation

The single-elimination format enables a relatively large number of competitors to participate. There are no "dead" matches (perhaps excluding "classification" matches), and no matches where one competitor has more to play for than the other.

The format is less suited to games where draws are frequent. In chess, each fixture in a single-elimination tournament must be played over multiple matches, because draws are common, and because white has an advantage over black. In soccer, games ending in a draw may be settled in extra time and eventually by a penalty shootout, viewed by many fans as an unsatisfactory conclusion to a fixture, or by replaying the fixture. In various forms of one-day cricket, a bowl-out has been used in recent years to settle tied matches.

Another perceived disadvantage is that most competitors are eliminated after relatively few games. Variations such as the double-elimination tournament allow competitors a single loss while remaining eligible for overall victory.

Other Tournament Systems

Variations of the single-elimination tournament include:

* Elimination tournament
* Double-elimination tournament
* Triple-elimination tournament

Other common tournament types are:

* Round-robin tournament
* Swiss system tournament
* Playoffs-a variation of the single-elimination tournament where instead of one win, a team needs to win a specific number of games in a series in order to advance.

Single Knockout Tournament Format

Single Knockout Tournament Format, also known as Single Elimination, is a format for pairing players to play games in tournaments.

In the first round, players are paired to play. Those players that lose are eliminated, knocked out of, the tournament. Those players that win, are promoted to the second round. This procedure is repeated till only a single player remains, that player is the tournament winner.

The number of rounds required is the ceiling of the log base 2 of the number of players in the tournament. (Example: 30 players necessitates 5 rounds of play because 2^5 == 32.) As a result, unless the number of players is equal to a power of 2, some players will play one more round than the others. Often the strongest players are not paired in the first round.

Mark Glickman, creator of the Glicko Rating system adopted by the FIDE, has a paper entitled: [ext] Bayesian Optimal Design of Knockout Tournaments. The paper presents two approaches:

1. maximize the probability that the best player will advance to the next round (goal focused on a single player)
    - maximize the expected log-probability of game outcomes over all possible sets of pairings (goal focused on all players)

UNIT-IV

Concepts of Health Education

Meaning, Definition, Aims and Objectives of Health Education

When defining health ethics, it is the decisions that people make that relate to the health issues of people all around the world. Health ethics came about for the dignity and human rights that need to be given to everyone. When asking the question, "what is the meaning of health ethics?", you have to think of terms such as privacy, decency, rights, and equity. Health Ethics has evolved in the health care industry to not being just an individual aspect but to a much larger spectrum of taking care of the well-being of the general public as a whole.

When becoming a doctor or medical specialist, you will get asked the question, "what is the meaning of health ethics?". Having a career in the medical industry not only requires you to know the technical issues of your job but also the ethical issues as well. Doctors or medical staff who have a lack of health ethics often find themselves in the middle of a lawsuit brought on by the patient that they serviced. Their lack of health ethics may have caused them discriminate or treat their patient with no respect. They may have even compromised their patient's private information by joking with a co-worker.

There are rules and regulations that are put in to place in order to make sure that all people get the respect and treatment that they deserve. When asking "what is the meaning of health ethics?", you should be able to answer the specific ways that your health ethics are administered. A person should be able to go into any medical facility and get serviced no matter their race, political belief, religion, or what social and economic condition they are in. The health ethics of the medical community is based on making sure that every person gets the same treatment that any other person would get.

Doctors today and long since have had the requirement of taking a Hippocratic oath that states they have to perform ethically in their medical career. They have to know what is the meaning of health ethics so that they can give their patients the kind of treatment that they deserve along with the respect that they deserve as well. Ways of doing this is treating each person as you would want someone to treat you. Also by keeping information pertaining to your patients confidential. And by treating their illness to the best of your ability.

Definition of Health Education

Health Education comprises consciously constructed opportunities for learning involving some form of communication designed to improve health literacy, including improving knowledge, and developing life skills which are conducive to individual and community health.

Health education is not only concerned with the communication of information, but also with fostering the motivation, skills and confidence (self-efficacy) necessary to take action to improve health. Health education includes the communication of information concerning the underlying social, economic and environmental conditions impacting on health, as well as individual risk factors and risk behaviors, and use of the health care system. Thus, health education may involve the communication of information, and development of skills which demonstrates the political feasibility and organizational possibilities of various forms of action to address social, economic and environmental determinants of health.

In the past, health education was used as a term to encompass a wider range of actions including social mobilization and advocacy. These methods are now encompassed in the term health promotion, and a more narrow definition of health education is proposed here to emphasize the distinction.

Physical Education Aims and Objectives

Aim of Physical Education-The ultimate goal or direction is referred to as an aim, it point out way. It is final end. Aim is achieved some certain objectives.

Aim of physical education, like general education, is to develop human personality in its totality well planned activity programmes. In some words, physical education aim at the all round development of the personality of an individual or wholesome development of human personality and it includes physical, mental, social, emotional and moral aspects to make an individual a good citizen who is able to make contribution in process of nation in one's own way. Thus physical education means at making an individual physical fit, mentally alert, emotionally balanced, socially well adjusted, morally true and spiritually uplifted.

Objectives of Physical Education-Objectives are steps considered towards the attainment of the aim. They are the particular and precise means employed to realize an aim. The moment an aim is achieved it becomes an objective in the action that goal on continuing.

The three Objectives of physical education are:

1. *The Objective of Physical Fitness :* It refers to that state where an individual has developed great endurance, speed, strength etc. Physical fitness is essential to leading a happy, vigorous and abundant life.
2. *The Objective of Social Efficiency :* It concerned with one's proper adaptation to group living. Physical education activities provides ample opportunities to develop traits such as cooperation, respect to others, loyalty, sportsmanship, self confidence etc. All these qualities help a person to make him a good citizen.
3. *The Objective of Culture :* It aims at developing an understanding and appreciation of one's own local environment as well as the environment which is world-wide in scope. By participation in various physical education activities such as dance, sports and games, a person fully understand the history, culture, tradition,

religious practices etc and the aesthetic values associated with these activities

Effectiveness of Different Methods of Health Education: A Comparative Assessment in a Scientific Conference

Every individual mode of health education has its own merits, drawbacks as well as their own sphere of effectiveness. A specific mode of communication is more useful in a specific setting on a specific group than others. To search for optimum mode of communication for a specific audience is a major area of research in health education. The issue of imparting health education to a gathering of educated people, representing different fields of knowledge has remained a relatively less lighted aspect of health education research. In this backdrop this study was initiated for making a comparative assessment of different methods of dissemination of health education among educated people.

Methods

A cross-sectional interviewer administered questionnaire survey was conducted involving 142 randomly selected subjects during the last session of a five-day conference having health as main theme when the opinion of the delegates regarding different communication methods was asked for. Collected data was analyzed not only to find out the optimum mode of education dissemination in such a setting but also to find the contribution of different factors in the preferences of the study subjects.

Results

The participants opted more (60%) for focused programmes of smaller audience (sectional programme). In both broad area (main programme) and focused area programmes (sectional), the participants preferred lectures (62% and 65.7% respectively). Specific topics were preferred both in lectures (67.6%) and symposia (57.7%). In the exhibition, exhibits seemed to be more attractive (62%) than the posters. Qualification has emerged to be a contributing factor in peoples' choice towards sectional programme and also in their affinity to symposia. Increased age was a significant contributor in participants' preference towards specific topics. Physical barriers of communication appeared to be a problem in the main programme as well as in the exhibition. Lack of coherence among the speakers was reported (69%) to be a major reason for which symposia was not preferred.

Conclusion

This study concluded that while planning for health education dissemination in an educated group a focused programme should be formulated in small groups preferably in the form of lectures on specific topics, more so while dealing with participants of higher age group having higher educational qualification.

Methods of Imparting Health Education in Schools—Health Instruction, Health Services, Health Suvervision

Children's health and learning are unquestionably linked. Healthy children are more able to learn and achieve academic success.

According to one study comparing students at low and high risk for food insufficiency, students who were undernourished scored lower on math tests, were more likely to have been suspended from school, and had more problems getting along with others (Alaimo, Olson, & Frongillo, 2001). Conversely, schools that offer physical education and health education produce students with higher scores on tests of reading, writing, and mathematics; higher grade point averages; and better attendance than comparable schools without an emphasis on health (Improving Academic Performance, 2000).

Schools are often described as being ideal environments for teaching children about health because they provide access to large numbers of children, are staffed by professionally trained educators and nurses, and frequently offer services that promote health, such as nutrition programmes and health centers. This digest examines the preparation of classroom teachers in health and what teachers should know to effectively provide school health education.

Who Teaches Health?

About 90% of the states and school districts in the United States require some health education for students (Marx, 2001, in press). Fewer than 20% of states and districts require health to be taught as a separate subject at the elementary level; 28-44% require a separate subject at the middle school level; and more than half require a separate subject in high school.

In U.S. elementary schools (grades kindergarten through 5 or 6), health education is most commonly taught by regular classroom teachers rather than trained health education specialists. In middle schools (grades 6-8), health is often taught by regular classroom teachers who have obtained certification in health, science, home economics, or physical education. At the high school level (grades 9-12), health education is most often taught by teachers with a health credential. According to the results of the School Health Policies and Programmes Study (2000), health education specialists are the only teachers who teach required health education in 25.8% of the senior high schools in the United States (Kann, Brener, & Allensworth, 2001).

However, the 50 states vary widely in the requirements for obtaining that credential. The evidence is clear: regular classroom teachers have a significant influence on the quantity and the quality of health education. In addition, at all levels of education, trusted teachers of any subject may be seen as health resources by students who need information.

How Well are Teachers Prepared in Health?

Teacher licensure or certification (academic and other requirements teachers must meet to get a teaching certificate) is governed by the states, and each state may have different regulations for what teachers need to know to become licensed or certified. A 1999 survey found that only eight states require coursework in health for prospective elementary teachers, and four states require health or physical education coursework; 16 states require elementary teachers to demonstrate competency or knowledge of health. Half of the states require coursework in health for middle school teachers (Marx, 2002, in press).

About half of the teacher training programmes in the United States are approved by the National Council for Accreditation of Teacher Education (NCATE). The NCATE recently released new Programme Standards for Elementary Teacher Preparation, which state (in standard 2g) that teacher education candidates "must know, understand, and use the major concepts in the subject matter of health education to create opportunities for student development and practice of skills that contribute to good health" (NCATE, 2000). This standard can be met in a different way by each teacher education institution. Some institutions require one or more health courses for teacher education students, while others justify using first aid or psychology courses to meet health requirements. It's no surprise that first year elementary school teachers report considerable discomfort when teaching health education (Hausman & Ruzek, 1995).

Lack of teacher preparation has been called "a major obstacle to implementing high-quality school health instruction" (Peterson, Cooper, & Laird, 2001). Inservice training cannot make up for this. For example, a CDC study examining HIV/AIDS education found that in states mandating HIV prevention education, only one-third of teachers attended inservice training on the topic in the past two years (School-based HIV prevention education, 1994).

What Hinders Teacher Preparation in Health?

Several factors may account for poor teacher preparation in health:

* *Lack of Time in the Teacher Education Curriculum:* The increased demands placed on teacher education programmes to produce teachers who are competent in numerous subject areas, as well as proficient in classroom management, technology, and multicultural education, results in fewer hours to devote to subjects seen as less important, such as health.
* *Emphasis on Standardized Testing:* Teacher education programmes must produce teachers who are able to prepare students to take state-mandated standardized

tests in math, reading, science, social studies, and several other areas. Subjects like health, for which standardized testing is rare, may be de-emphasized in favour of devoting more time to subjects that are tested.

* *Lack of Comfort:* Health education includes many sensitive and controversial topics. Teacher education faculty may find it difficult to overcome their own discomfort with these topics and fail to prepare student teachers adequately to address such topics.

What Should Teachers Know About Health and Health Instruction?

Teachers who will be providing health education need to have teacher health literacy. This is defined as, "the capacity to obtain, interpret, and understand basic health information and services, with the competence to use such information and services in ways that enhance the learning of health concepts and skills by school students" (Peterson et al., 2001).

There is no nationally recognized standard for teacher preparation in health education to achieve health literacy. However, several groups have developed what they believe such a standard should be.

* The Institute of Medicine issued a report in 1997 that recommended substantive preservice preparation in health education content and methodology for all elementary teachers. "This preparation should give elementary generalist teachers strategies for infusing health instruction into the curriculum and prepare upper elementary teachers to lay the groundwork for the intensive middle or junior high health education programme" (Allensworth, 1997).
* The American Cancer Society convened a conference in 1992 that made two recommendations for PreK-12 teacher preparation: that all teacher preparation programmes include content and process courses in health instruction, and that K-6 student teachers in regular and special education be supervised by a health educator or health coordinator when teaching health

lessons. The full report is printed in the Journal of School Health, January 1993, vol. 63, No. 1.

* The American Association for Health Education (AAHE) has developed Health Instruction Responsibilities for Elementary (K-6) Classroom Teachers, and Responsibilities of Teachers of Young Adolescents in Coordinated School Health Programmes for Middle School-Level (Grades 5-9) Classroom Teachers. AAHE suggests there are five responsibilities and 17 competencies at the elementary level and eight responsibilities and 27 competencies at the middle school level. To access these, visit their web site www.aahperd.org/aahe/aahe-main.html.

The competencies in health education that are generally recommended for elementary, middle school, and special education teachers include (Peterson et al., 2001):

* Use the National Health Education Standards. Forty of the 50 states use the National Health Education Standards in curriculum planning (Bennett, Perko, & Herstine, 2000).
* Demonstrate knowledge of community health, consumer health, environmental health, family life, mental and emotional health, injury prevention and safety, nutrition, personal health, disease prevention and control, and alcohol, tobacco, and other drugs.
* Incorporate health concepts into other curricular areas.
* Develop age-appropriate and culturally relevant health lessons.
* Help children develop not only health knowledge but health skills.
* Select and use valid and reliable sources of health information.

These competencies may be met by requiring a separate health course for preservice teachers or by integrating health education into other curricular areas in the teacher education programme (Pateman, 2002; in press). For example, a children's literature course might include readings from books dealing with specific diseases, death, and customs. A math methods course might teach math concepts using health data from federal health databases.

Health Services in the Schools: Building Interdisciplinary Partnerships

There are two essential social systems with which virtually all children and families have routine, significant contact: school and health care settings. The school is an environment wherein children not only engage in academic learning and growth, but where they also experience social and emotional interactions with adults and peers so as to build self-esteem and social competence. These essential experiences can serve to increase later prospects for success in relationships, the work place, and personal pursuits. It is vital that schools support the broad developmental needs of children and families.

Schools are being asked to address the needs of children and youth at a time when fundamental transformations of schooling structures and outcome expectations are also being demanded (Children's Defense Fund, 1992). Restructured schools alone cannot satisfactorily address the multidimensional needs of children and youth. Schools and other child-and family-service organizations must collaborate to enhance the likelihood of educational and personal success for all children. Recent legislative and policy initiatives, such as Healthy People 2000 (1990), a blueprint for disease prevention and health promotion, highlight the important role that schools must play in assuring the well-being of our nation's children and youth.

In order to address the developmental needs of children and families in a comprehensive and preventive manner, schools and communities must coordinate services. Therefore, a service integration perspective that recognizes the central role that schools play in the lives of children should guide efforts to establish an empowering, healthy climate for them and their families within the community at large (Institute for Educational Leadership, 1992; Oomes & Herendeen, 1989). Such a view acknowledges the complex, reciprocal interaction among social systems, including families, when problems are conceptualized and service systems are designed. It assumes that children and families are most likely to benefit from collaborative, focused efforts among the various systems responsible for addressing their needs, both formal and informal.

Interdisciplinary Partnerships in Health Care

There is an emerging consensus among professionals and consumers that the current health care service delivery system is not meeting the needs of children and families (Knitzer, 1982; National Commission on Child Welfare and Family Preservation, 1990). Solutions must move beyond adding resources (e.g., more funding, more programmes) and toward fundamental changes in how the system operates. Social and political institutions have not considered the needs of children and families as funding priorities (Melaville & Blank, 1991, 1993). Individual service delivery systems for children (e.g., health care, education, social service, mental health) are funded and designed to address isolated and crisis-oriented needs, rather than to promote healthy development for all children and families in a comprehensive fashion. In addition, some parents either have no knowledge of how to access available services, or they may not value them. Thus, services provided to children and families frequently are not comprehensive, responsive, or integrated.

Key sources of difficulty in the current service delivery system are the lack of clarity, coordination, and comprehensiveness, resulting in inflexible patterns of funding, training, and service provision. Since the cognitive, social, emotional, educational, and physical needs of children are complex, an integrated services model provides for a more coherent, needs-based response to these complex problems (Chaudry, Maurer, Oshinsky & Mackie, 1993; Dunst, Trivette, Gordon, & Pletcher, 1989).

Health Care in Schools Through Service Integration

The efficacy of services to children and families can be viewed from the perspective of the families themselves. When examined in this manner, emphasis is placed upon the nature of service delivery events or episodes that occur, and the impact these events have on children and families. Within a well-integrated programme, typically:

1. services are available in close proximity and are accessible without reference to physical, psychological, social, linguistic, sexual orientation, or other barriers;
2. services are comprehensive and appropriate, in that they possess features that address priority needs the family has identified, at a level of service sufficient to their need;
3. services are formulated and delivered at a high level of quality such that the family perceives them as an organized whole and can participate in a consistent and effective manner;
4. services promote psychological competence and self sufficiency rather than focusing exclusively on dysfunction and pathology;
5. services are oriented toward full participation, partnership, and empowerment of family members;
6. services are sensitive to cultural, gender, racial, linguistic, class, disability, and sexual orientation issues; and,
7. interventions are driven by concern for the needs and desires of the consumers (i.e., children and families) and emphasize explicit outcomes stated in a positive manner. (Paavola et al., 1995).

Features of an Integrated Service System

Relative to the definition offered previously, there is a continuum of integrated services that varies as a function of need, service availability, problem severity, and related dimensions. From the perspective of children and families, many opportunities and services can best be accessed through a single provider and implemented in an integrative manner. An integrated services model also assumes that the greater the number of providers involved (e.g., psychologists, nurses, teachers, social workers, physicians, day care workers), the greater the need for effective collaboration. Timely and responsive interventions on behalf of children and families therefore rely on effective communication, coordination, and collaboration among service providers, agencies and organizations, and the consumers of services (children and families).

Thus, "coordinated and collaborative services" should be the essential standard by which effective services are delivered. The service system must respond to the multiplicity of needs exhibited by children and families through carefully orchestrated teamwork. At a minimum, this collaboration takes the form of different providers (from independent agencies) communicating regularly by phone regarding a child or family. Or, it may involve regular face-to-face meetings and case conferences among providers. Ideally, providers and family members would work as an integrated team to provide needed services. The net result of the integrated team concept could be service delivery models such as "one-stop shopping" or more staff sharing and programme development activity.

The service delivery system should also allow for both "ease of entry and flexibility of movement." For example, if the point of initial contact in a community is a school setting, there should be a clear connection between the school and the array of community services that the family needs, regardless of categorical restrictions. This requires that individual providers and agencies see themselves as part of a much larger ecology that is community-wide and geared to aiding the overall climate within which children grow and develop. The point of initial entry into such a system should be less critical than the fact that child and family needs are considered paramount in responding to the concerns presented. The flexibility of movement concept allows for a child or family to enter such a system at any point and move flexibly between services as their needs dictate without having to confront barriers.

The service delivery system must be organized for both "maximum development of the child and for accountability," first to the family, and also to the community within which the child lives. This means that providers need to be re-trained within a consumer-oriented model, with children and families seen as customers with whom one must collaborate, rather than as patients or adversaries. Community accountability refers to concern for improving the quality of life in communities through community resource development, advocacy, and related activities.

"Funding for coordinated and collaborative service needs to be both flexible and shared" (where possible) among agencies, such that different agencies can be encouraged to develop together programmes that serve children and families holistically. Funding and programme decisions need to be made from the "bottom up" and those providers who have on-going contact and communication with the family should be the major decision makers about how pooled and/or flexible funds can be utilized most effectively, with direct input from the consumers of services. "Interdisciplinary interaction and training" for providers needs to be a top priority in an integrated service model. It will be necessary for providers from different disciplines to know what other disciplines can contribute to solutions for issues confronting families. Collaborative effort outside of traditional disciplinary lines creates opportunities for true communication and integration among providers.

Relevance to Psychology

"Role of Psychologists"

Psychologists develop systems that ensure the healthy development of children and the strengthening and empowerment of families. In both primary health care and school settings, psychology can play an integral role in "prevention, assessment, treatment, consultation, and advocacy" for children and families. Psychologists employed in other social service, mental health, and related organizational settings can also have considerable impact on the welfare of children and families through early intervention and treatment activities. In all settings, psychological services must be integrated with other necessary services and then provided in a manner that does not artificially separate the physical, emotional, and social needs of children and families.

There are a number of integrated service efforts underway,

many of which involve or are led by psychologists. For example, the School of the Future project (Holtzman, 1992) in Austin, Dallas, Houston, and San Antonio, Texas (partially funded by the Hogg Foundation) focuses on the coordination and delivery of an extensive array of health and human services through neighborhood schools. In the Memphis City Schools, educational, mental health, and social services have been integrated within a "one-stop shopping" paradigm (Paavola, Hannah, & Nichol, 1989). The National Institute of Mental Health promotes the Child and Adolescent Service System Programme (CASSP) initiative, designed to improve mental health services for children with severe emotional disabilities by encouraging states to provide more comprehensive and coordinated services through interagency collaboration and service coordination (Day & Roberts, 1991).

The Robert Wood Johnson Foundation is extensively involved in health promotion and in improving systems of care for children with emotional and behavioral problems. Other prominent foundations sponsor large-scale family support and integrated services demonstration projects in a number of states (e.g., Annie B. Casey Foundation, Pew Charitable Trust). Scattered across the country are numerous other projects and activities in this same vein (e.g., within Head Start and related early education programmes). Emerging from these projects is evidence that integrated services can be effective, responsive, and cost-efficient (Illback, 1992, 1993). Furthermore, there is a recognition of the need to extend these findings to the health-service system as a whole.

Implications for School Health Psychology

The concept of service integration has several implications for psychology as a profession and psychologists as health-service providers in schools. Implications for psychological training, practice, research, and leadership, are discussed below.

Training: Service integration has major implications for both graduate and in-service training of psychologists since this integration will require greater breadth and flexibility among practitioners. A school health psychologist with expertise in behavioral health who serves an elementary school, for example, will need to be competent in a broad number of skills and approaches, ranging from typical developmental concerns and issues, to guidelines for monitoring commonly used child psychotropic medications, family interventions, and community consultation. Professionals who are "generalists" in human services will have greater possibilities for employment in an integrated service system than those whose background is limited specifically to traditional psychological practice specialties. There will, of course, always be some need for specialization, particularly with respect to low-incidence or highly technical problems. Psychologists will need more systematic training in collaborative and consultation-based approaches to practice.

Practice: Psychological services within an integrated services framework will look and feel substantially different. Practitioners will be able to exercise greater flexibility in the range of activities in which they engage, and will not be as constrained in regard to funding source and eligibility considerations. They will spend more time working as part of a team, in concert with a variety of providers, caregivers, and community members. In addition to the school-based services they provide, school-health psychologists are likely to spend more time in homes and other community settings. These psychologists will routinely work across interdisciplinary boundaries among various social systems that impinge on children and families to coordinate activities, manage conflict, and insure focus and quality of services.

Leadership: Psychologists should be trained and encouraged to assume leadership roles within integrated service programmes. In addition to the more traditional aspects of programme administration and supervision, leadership activities should focus on establishing an integrative strategic vision for child-serving organizations, building collaborative teams, and facilitating planned organizational change in the direction of more integrated services.

Research: Psychological research on the efficacy of integrated service delivery approaches for children and families represents a unique contribution for psychology. Such research is distinct from traditional controlled experimentation, in that the array of target problems is vast, treatment programmes are diverse and multifaceted, and outcome measurements complicated. Practicing psychologists need to become proficient in a broader range of methods and procedures (e.g., quasi-experimental design, multivariate analysis, programme evaluation techniques, qualitative research) in order to conduct such social policy and programme-related investigations. Psychologists would also be in a unique position to help service systems develop and validate information systems to allow for on-going programme monitoring and management.

Pediatric Health Supervision Guidelines Part-1: Introduction

You child will be making frequent visits to your pediatrician, especially in his first few years. In addition to giving immunizations, these well child visits are an important way to monitor your child's growth and development. Specific health supervision topics for each visit vary depending on the age and developmental stage of your child. In general, you can expect the following topics to be covered at each visit:

- Examination of your child's growth and development.
- Review of feeding and sleep schedules.
- Screening height, weight, head circumference and/or blood pressure.
- Counseling for proper discipline, injury prevention, dental health, and a healthy diet.

AAP Preventative Health Care Guidelines		
Infants	**Children**	**Adolescents**
Newborn	Fifteen Months	Eleven Years
Two Weeks	Eighteen Months	Twelve Years
Two Months	Two Years	Thirteen Years
Four Months	Three Years	Fourteen Years
Six Months	Four Years	Fifteen Years
Nine Months	Five Years	Sixteen Years
Twelve Months	Six Years	Seventeen Years
Fifteen Months	Eight Years	Eighteen Years
Eighteen Months	Ten Years	Nineteen Years
		Twenty Years
		Twenty One Years

Remember to write down any questions you may have for your doctor before you child's checkups.

Part-2: Infants

You will be making frequent visits to your Pediatrician now. For newborns discharged in less than 48 hours, the first visit should be within two to four days of life, especially for mothers breastfeeding for the first time.

Age specific topics that should be discussed at well child visits include toilet training (eighteen months) and dealing with temper tantrums (toddlers).

In general, you can expect the following topics to be covered at each visit:

- Examination of your infant's growth and development.
- Review of feeding and sleep schedules.
- Screening height, weight, and head circumference.
- Counseling for effective discipline, injury prevention, dental health (first visit to the dentist by age three unless high risk), and diet.
- Immunizations: by eighteen months your child will have completed the Hepatitis B, Prevnar, and Hib immunizations. He will also have received the primary series of Polio, DTaP, and MMR vaccines and the Chickenpox vaccine.
- Screening test: newborn screen according to state law, subjective tests of vision and hearing, blood level to check for anemia (by nine months), screening questionnaire for lead poisoning risk (routinely at nine months and two years), tuberculosis test if high risk.

Remember to write down any questions you may have for your doctor before you child's checkups.

Part-3: Children

You will be making less frequent visits to your Pediatrician now. Age specific topics that should be discussed at well child visits include toilet training (eighteen months to three years), school readiness in preschool age children, and school performance in school age children. Remember that by the middle childhood years, it is important to talk about avoiding drugs and alcohol and to begin sexuality education.

In general, you can expect the following topics to be covered at each visit:

- Examination of your child's growth and development.
- Review of feeding and sleep schedules.
- Screening height, weight, head circumference (up to age three) and/or blood pressure (usually routine after age three years).
- Counseling for effective discipline, injury prevention, dental health (first visit to the dentist by age three unless high risk), and diet.
- Immunizations: MMR, DTaP and IPV boosters at the four to six year checkup.
- Screening test: vision (formal test by three years), hearing (formal test by four years), blood level to check for anemia (at two years), screening questionnaire for lead poisoning risk (routinely at nine months and two years), tuberculosis test if high risk.

Remember to write down any questions you may have for your doctor before you child's checkups.

Part-4: Adolescents

The American Academy of Pediatrics recommends yearly visits for children over the age of eleven, at which your Pediatrician will provide an:

- Examination of your teen's growth, development, and pubertal stage.
- Screening height, weight and blood pressure.
- Review of school performance.
- Counseling for effective discipline, injury prevention, substance abuse, sexual behavior, dental health, diet and exercise.
- Immunizations: Tetanus (Td) booster, Hepatitis B series if not already given

- Screening tests: scoliosis, anemia (for menstruating teens), urinalysis, vision and hearing test (if not already passed), tuberculosis test if high risk.
- Sexually active teenagers should have yearly checks for sexually transmitted diseases and a pelvic exam (females).

Remember to write down any questions you may have for your doctor before you teenager's checkups.

The Nature of Children's Play

In play, children expand their understanding of themselves and others, their knowledge of the physical world, and their ability to communicate with peers and adults. This digest discusses children's play and its relationship to developmental growth from infancy to middle childhood. The digest also suggests ways in which educators and other adults can support children's play.

Sensorimotor Play

In what Piagot (1962) aptly described as sensorimotor practice play, infants and toddlers experiment with bodily sensation and motor movements, and with objects and people. By 6 months of age, infants have developed simple but consistent action schemes through trial and error and much practice. Infants use action schemes, such as pushing and grasping, to make interesting things happen. An infant will push a ball and make it roll in order to experience the sensation and pleasure of movement.

As children master new motor abilities, simple schemes are coordinated to create more complex play sequences. Older infants will push a ball, crawl after it, and retrieve it. When infants of 9 months are given an array of objects, they apply the same limited actions to all objects and see how they react. By pushing various objects, an infant learns that a ball rolls away, a bile spins, and a rattle makes noise. At about 12 months, objects bring forth more specific and differentiated actions. At this age, children will throw or kick a ball, but will shake rattles.

In a toddler's second year, there is growing awareness of the functions of objects in the social world. The toddler puts a cup on a saucer and a spoon in her mouth. During the last half of this year, toddlers begin to represent their world symbolically as they transform and invent objects and roles. They may stir an imaginary drink and offer it to someone (Bergen, 1988). Adults initiate and support such play. They may push a baby on a swing or cheer its first awkward steps. Children's responses regulate the adult's actions. If the swing is pushed too high, a child's cries will guide the adult toward a gentler approach. In interactions with adults such as peekaboo, children learn to take turns, act with others, and engage others in play.

Pretend Play

As children develop the ability to represent experience symbolically, pretend play becomes a prominent activity. In this complex type of play, children carry out action plans, take on roles, and transform objects as they express their ideas and feelings about the social world (Garvey, 1984).

Action plans are blueprints for the ways in which actions and events are related and sequenced. Family-related themes in action plans are popular with young children, as are action plans for treating and healing and for averting threats.

Roles are identities children assume in play. Some roles are functional: necessary for a certain theme. For example, taking a trip requires passengers and a driver. Family roles such as mother, father and baby are popular, and are integrated into elaborate play with themes related to familiar home activities. Children also assume stereotyped character roles drawn from the larger culture, such as nurse, and fictional character roles drawn from books and television, such as He-Man. Play related to these roles tends to be more predictable and restricted than play related to direct experiences such as family life (Garvey, 1984).

As sociodramatic play emerges, objects begin to influence the roles children assume. For example, household implements trigger family-related roles and action plans, but capes stimulate superhero play. Perceptually bound younger children may be aided by the provision of realistic objects (Fein, 1981). Even three-year-olds can invent and transform objects to conform to plans.

By the age of four or five, children's ideas about the social world initiate most pretend play. While some pretend play is solitary or shared with adults, preschoolers' pretend or sociodramatic play is often shared with peers in the school or neighborhood. To implement and maintain pretend play episodes, a great deal of shared meaning must be negotiated among children. Play procedures may be talked about explicitly, or signaled subtly in role-appropriate action or dialogue. Players often make rule-like statements to guide behavior ("You have to finish your dinner, baby"). Potential conflicts are negotiated. Though meanings in play often reflect real world behavior, they also incorporate children's interpretations and wishes. The child in a role who orders a steak and piece of candy from a pretend menu is not directly copying anything he has seen before. Construction play with symbolic themes is also popular with preschoolers, who use blocks and miniature cars and people to create model situations related to their experience. A kind of play with motion, rough and tumble play, is popular in preschool years. In this play, groups of children run, jump, and wrestle. Action patterns call for these behaviors to be performed at a high pitch. Adults may worry that such play will become aggressive, and they should probably monitor it. Children who participate in this play become skilled in their movements, distinguish between real and feigned aggression, and learn to regulate each other's activity (Garvey, 1984).

Games with Rules

Children become interested in formal games with peers by age five or younger. Older children's more logical and socialized ways of thinking make it possible for them to play games together. Games with rules are the most prominent form of play during middle childhood (Piaget, 1962).

The main organizing element in game play consists of explicit rules which guide children's group behavior. Game play is very organized in comparison to sociodramatic play. Games usually involve two or more sides, competition, and agreed-upon criteria for determining a winner. Children use games flexibly to meet social and intellectual needs. For example, choosing sides may affirm friendship and a pecking order. Games provide children with shared activities and goals. Children often negotiate rules in order to create the game they wish to play (King, 1986).

They can learn reasoning strategies and skills from strategy games like checkers. In these games, children must consider at the same time both offensive alternatives and the need for defense. Many card games encourage awareness of mathematics and of the psychology of opponents. Such games can be intellectually motivating parts of pre-and primary school curriculum (Kamii & DeVries, 1980, Kamii, 1985).

Safety Education—Play Field, Road, Home, School

These general guidelines may be helpful:

* Value children's play and talk to children about their play. Adults often say "I like the way you're working," but rarely, "I like the way you're playing."
* Play with children when it is appropriate, especially during the early years. If adults pay attention to and engage in children's play, children get the message that play is valuable.
* Create a playful atmosphere. It is important for adults to provide materials which children can explore and adapt in play.
* When play appears to be stuck or unproductive, offer a new prop, suggest new roles, or provide new experiences, such as a field trip.
* Intervene to ensure safe play. Even in older children's play, social conflicts often occur when children try to negotiate. Adults can help when children cannot solve these conflicts by themselves (Caldwell, 1977). Adults should identify play which has led to problems for particular children. They should check materials and

equipment for safety. Finally, adults should make children aware of any hidden risks in physical challenges they set for themselves.

Road Safety Education

No one is born knowing how to use the road system. Children and young people have a high involvement in road crashes, so they must learn to use the road safely. As they grow and develop they need to learn to be safe in different environments – as passengers, pedestrians, bicycle riders, public transport users and learner drivers.

Parents/carers play a pivotal role in teaching their children to be safe at all times, with the support of Maternal and Child Health Nurses, child carers, family day carers, preschools, primary and secondary schools.

VicRoads and its partners provide a range of road safety resources and programmes that deliver developmentally appropriate education to prepare children and young people to become safe and independent road users.

Home Safety Education and Providing Safety Equipment for Injury Prevention

Injuries are the leading cause of childhood death in industrialised countries. People living in disadvantaged circumstances are at greater risk of injury than those more advantaged. This review examined whether home safety education and providing safety equipment increased safety behaviours and safety equipment use and reduced injuries. It also looked at whether home safety education was more or less effective in families which are disadvantaged. The review authors found 80 studies, which reported many different safety behaviours, but few studies included information on injuries.

The results often varied between studies, but overall families who received home safety education were more likely to have a safe hot tap water temperature, a working smoke alarm, to store medicines, cleaning products and sharp objects out-of-reach, to have fitted stair gates and socket covers on unused sockets and to have syrup of ipecac and poison control centre numbers accessible. The reviewers did not find that home safety education reduced injury rates, but this may have been due to the small number of studies which measured injuries, and more research is needed to answer this question. The reviewers did not find that home safety education was less effective in families whose children were at greater risk of injury.

Safety: Home Safety, Child Safety and More

There are a lot of potential dangers and hazards which we take for granted. Much more than that, there are prospective pitfalls that we are often not even aware of. You'll be able to find a large database of tips and information here regarding an extensive variety of situations and environments to help you and your entire family stay safe. Thousands of accidents occur every year that could potentially have been avoided had the right safety information been known to those victims. You can look forward to helpful pointers, guides and checklists that will help you ensure optimal safety in your daily life.

And because the most comprehensive safety comes with a little extra help, we've also dedicated a great deal of effort in researching and organizing information regarding today's best safety products. From office safety products to first-aid kits, there are countless safety products to choose from in today's market. Variety is usually a positive element, but it can make sifting through these countless choices quite a challenge. We understand that you want the very best for your family and trying to decide on the best safety products can create immense pressure. From childproofing your home to avoiding accidents in your backyard, we'll help you decide what's best for your specific needs. We make sure to provide our information in well-organized and enlightening safety articles so you can make well-informed decisions.

One of the specific areas you'll be able to find information about is home safety. Granted, the home is often thought of as a safe haven, but there are countless potential perils that exist within the home. We'll not only provide you with clear and simple steps for maintaining an accident-free home environment, but we'll inform you as to which products will assist you in doing so. And most important of all, you'll also be able to find articles regarding child safety. From newborns to toddlers and teens, we've done our homework to find what will keep your loved ones safe at all times.

We also hope that this safety education site will be able to do much more than teach you about daily potential hazards, but will be able to help you then teach others. We encourage you to share the resources you find most interesting and helpful on this site so that we can help as many people as possible. Comprehensive safety is a collaborative effort and the onus is on all of us.

Getting to School Safely

From fall to spring, millions of children are on the streets every day making their way to and from school. They walk, bike, ride the school bus, or are driven by parents. When hundreds converge on one building—or sometimes a complex of buildings—the traffic can be a nightmare and the risks to kids can be numerous.

Ideally, every school would have one loading zone for buses and another for cars. Bike racks would be located in an area that allows safe and easy access. The parking lot would be designed to allow cars to enter without crossing paths with students who walk or bike. In reality, many schools are cramped for space and are located in high-traffic areas. Separating all these vehicles and children can be a real challenge.

We've already discussed in Teaching Kids to Navigate Streets, Buying the Right Bike for Your Child, and Bike Helmets: Buying Them, Using Them what you can do at home to make your kids street smart. But what about your school? What can it do?

Form a Committee

Safety measures can take a variety of forms, everything from stepped-up traffic enforcement to in-class education on such topics as school bus safety rules. Your school already may be using some of these effectively. Many schools have adult crossing guards and school safety patrols, for example. Still, there probably are traffic situations that could use improvement. To get a comprehensive look at the issues, your school could do a safety audit with the help of a school safety committee that includes staff, parents, police, and someone from your community's traffic engineering department.

The engineer can look at signs, traffic lights, street markings, and other features of the streets around your school and make recommendations on additional traffic control measures that might be needed, for example.

Safety Savvy

The American Automobile Association has materials for parents and school staff on working together to make the school trip safer. To get information for your school, check your phone book for the number of the chapter near you.

Safest Route Maps

One project of the school safety committee should be preparing maps that show the safest routes to school. The maps would indicate, for example, which intersections have crossing guards and therefore are the best places for children to cross. The maps should be big enough to incorporate the entire enrollment area. That way parents can plan the entire route for their children to follow, either to school or to the bus stop.

Once you pick a route, walk it with your child and point out any hazards he should watch for. You also may notice places where you might need to modify the route, because of large bushes that obstruct the view of an intersection, for example.

Watch Out!

The safest route for your walker to take may not be the same one your child should use to bike to school. The walker could be safer on a route with intersections where there are traffic lights, but the biker might be better off on streets with less traffic.

The Problem with Parents

Many of the traffic problems around schools are caused by parents. Some ignore the pick-up zones, double park, or block the buses. One dangerous, and all too common, practice is dropping children off on the wrong side of the street and jaywalking with them mid-block. Traffic troubles usually are worse in bad weather, as more parents drive their kids and everyone tries to take shortcuts to hurry into the building without getting wet.

Schools can alleviate congestion by taking such steps as staggering the dismissal of walkers and riders, having them exit on different sides of the building, and creating more pick-up-lane space if possible.

Traffic rule violations put kids in danger. If this is a problem at your school, talk to the parent-teacher association or the school staff—both about ways to ease congestion and to enforce the rules.

UNIT-V

Common Communicable Diseases and Athletic Injuries

Common Communicable Diseases

A communicable disease is one that can be passed from one person or animal to another.Most communicable diseases are caused by small life-forms. Chances are you've had some experiences with communicable diseases like the common flu or cold.

But there are more serious cases like the measles and rabies. Luckily these aren't as common and have vaccines, or cures for these unwanted illnesses. But if you think you are coming down with something it is a good idea to take your temperature and if you suspect something, visit your local pharmacy and see a doctor.

The invasion of the body!

As you may know communicable diseases can come in many forms like a virus, or a fungus. Here is a list of communicable diseases that kids catch regularly all around the U.S.

Strep Throat: Symptoms-Sore or scratchy throat, fever, swollen glands, headache, abominable pain. Nausea and vomiting in severe cases. It is most contagious during the infection and until 24 hours after effective treatment begins. See your doctor for medication.

Athlete's Foot: Common mainly if your in sporting events and is caused by a fungi. Can be spread by the sweat of other athletes, ten days after exposure itch between toes develop. Skin between toes begin to crack, thin peel and then puss. This is caused by a fungus. See doctor for information and medication.

Chicken Pox: Caused by a virus is usually mild with children but get more severe as you get older. There is a vaccine for it to prevent it witch you may want to get if you haven't had it yet. Anyway chicken pox is caused by a virus that invades the skin and throat cells. Slight fever and rash in mouth and throat are common symptoms. But the one that chicken pox is known for is the itching. It usually goes away after a week the virus first struck and just bout everyone gets it some point in their life.

Measles: Not as common with the vaccines taken regularly but it can be pretty severe. Caused by another virus that again invades the throat, covering of the eye, or skin. Frequently begins with fever, runny nose, and a cough. Spots then appear(much like the chicken pox) all over body, including mouth and throat. By the time the infection reaches the feet your feeling better but it's not over yet. It can also prey to the lungs and even your brain.

Influenza: Influenza or the flu is caused by you getting the spray of mucus from someone else who already has the flu inside of you. Or by getting germs in your mouth by not washing your hands. So please cover your mouth when you sneeze and try to wash your hands regularly. It will run its course in a matter of days so don't worry, it won't last long.

Bacteria: These tiny one-celled organisms are neither animals or plants. They belong to a third family of life forms known as Monera. Bacteria are all around us-in the air, soil, water, and everything we touch. Even inside of us. Some bacteria can cause disease, but most are not capable of making us sick. Many bacteria in our bodies are kept from multiplying and causing disease by our body's natural resistance. We can become resistant to a disease after we have been exposed to the bacterium that causes it. But when a disease causing bacterium to which our body has not been exposed to, chances are much greater it will make us sick. Here is a picture of bacteria.

Virus: Virus are not alive. Living organisms digest food, use oxygen, grow, and reproduce themselves. Viruses can do none of these things on their own. Thy are particle, shaped like balls or rods, many times smaller than bacteria. A single virus particle consists of an inner core of chemicals called nucleic acids surrounded by one or two protective shells made up of protein (see 1-800-Health). Here is picture of a virus

Viruses can take one important quality of life, that of reproduction-when they invade cells.So basically if you stop the virus from getting inside you, you'll stop it from reproducing more viruses and eventually making you sick.

Whooping Cough: Is an infection of the windpipe, or trachea, and the main passegways to the lungs, called bronchi. The infection starts with the symtoms of cold-cough, sneezing, runny nose ,fever, sore eyes. Then a more severe cough develops. As the person struggles to inhale inbetween coughs, he or he mkes a wooping sound. Violent coughing sometimes causes vomitting. A vaccination givin to babies has made whooping cough a rare disease.

Maleria: Is a transmitted disease then travels from victim to victim by small insects such as mosquitoes who deliver the disease right into the bloodstream. Symtoms include perspiration, shivering, sick to the stomach, hurt all over, high temperature, pain in head and back, and exhaustion. Symptoms can last somewhere around three months without proper treatment. Go to your local doctor for more info and treatment.

Lyme Disease: Lyme disease is transmitted by the bite of a bacteria infected tick(a small blood sucking animal) that normally infects deer(that's how it became a deer tick. Lyme disease starts with a red dot that appears on the body where the infected tick bite occurred. This develops into an inch-wide blotch with a red ring around it. Then fever develops along with headache, muscle pains, and tiredness. As if the person had the flue. Redness and swelling of joints is next followed by numbness and tingling in different parts of the body, and double vision. Sense of taste may also be lost.

Antibiotics will cure the disease but there is no shot to immunize against it.

All this caused by a little tick.

Meningitis: Is a rare but rather serious illness. Symptoms include, feverish, severe headache, and stiff neck. Not to mention highly sensitive to light. Soon vomiting begins, then the person become drowsy and then unconscious. Red rash may develop. Meningitis is usually the result of the spirea of an infection from the throat, and ear. This disease can also cause brain damage. But that depends on where brain is infected.

This can also be caused by a virus.

Pneumonia: This is an infection of the lungs. Usually follows less serious infection like a cold. When the organism invades the lungs, fluid fills part of the lungs, the person develops a fever and difficulty breathing. Pneumonia is often caused by a virus but can sometimes be caused by a bacteria. There is a vaccine for the bacteria but none for the virus.

Diptheria: Is an infection that begins in the persons throat, where the outer layer of cells in the throat are destroyed. The throat reacts by oozing a fluid, making it difficult for the person to breathe. Diptheria can cause damage to the heart and other parts of the body. Because this one dangerous disease can be prevented by vaccination it is now uncommon.

Typhoid Fever: Is an intestinal infection. Symtoms include: fever, appetite loss, fatigue, stomach pain, and constipation, followed by diarrhea and the development of tiny red dots on the skin of the stomach and chest. Unless treated with antibiotic, the oranisms will cause internal bleeding and spread the infection to other parts of the body,which can be lead to death. Prevent by only drinking purified water.

Typhus: Is caused by a bacteria-like organism that lives inside the cells of other organisms. The organism is transmitted from rats to humans by the bite of a small bloodsucking insect called a louse. The infected person develops a hedache, backache, high fever, and rash. The organism invades the blood vessels of most of the major organs of the body. The person dies when the heart, lungs. or kidneys fail. Typhus can be treated with antibiotics, and killing the lice controls the disease.

Malaria

Malaria is a vector-borne infectious disease caused by protozoan parasites. It is widespread in tropical and subtropical regions, including parts of the Americas, Asia, and Africa. Each year, there are approximately 350–500 million cases of malaria, killing between one and three million people, the majority of whom are young children in Sub-Saharan Africa. Ninety percent of malaria-related deaths occur in Sub-Saharan Africa. Malaria is commonly associated with poverty, but is also a cause of poverty and a major hindrance to economic development.

Malaria is one of the most common infectious diseases and an enormous public health problem. The disease is caused by protozoan parasites of the genus *Plasmodium*. Five species of the plasmodium parasite can infect humans; the most serious forms of the disease are caused by *Plasmodium falciparum*. Malaria caused by *Plasmodium vivax*, *Plasmodium ovale* and *Plasmodium malariae* causes milder disease in humans that is not generally fatal. A fifth species, *Plasmodium knowlesi*, causes malaria in macaques but can also infect humans. This group of human-pathogenic *Plasmodium* species is usually referred to as *malaria parasites*.

Usually, people get malaria by being bitten by an infective female *Anopheles* mosquito. Only Anopheles mosquitoes can transmit malaria, and they must have been infected through a previous blood meal taken on an infected person. When a mosquito bites an infected person, a small amount of blood is taken, which contains microscopic malaria parasites. About one week later, when the mosquito takes its next blood meal, these parasites mix with the mosquito's saliva and are injected into the person being bitten. The parasites multiply within red blood cells, causing symptoms that include symptoms of anemia (light-headedness, shortness of breath, tachycardia, etc.), as well as other general symptoms such as fever, chills, nausea, flu-like illness, and, in severe cases, coma, and death. Malaria transmission can be reduced by preventing mosquito bites with mosquito nets and insect repellents, or by mosquito control measures such as spraying insecticides inside houses and draining standing water where mosquitoes lay their eggs. Work has been done on malaria vaccines with limited success and more exotic controls, such as genetic manipulation of mosquitoes to make them resistant to the parasite have also been considered.

Although some are under development (such as RTS,S), no vaccine is currently available for malaria that provides a high level of protection; preventive drugs must be taken continuously to reduce the risk of infection. These prophylactic drug treatments are often too expensive for most people living in endemic areas. Most adults from endemic areas have a degree of long-term infection, which tends to recur, and also possess partial immunity (resistance); the resistance reduces with time, and such adults may become susceptible to severe malaria if they have spent a significant amount of time in non-endemic areas. They are strongly recommended to take full precautions if they return to an endemic area. Malaria infections are treated through the use of antimalarial drugs, such as quinine or artemisinin derivatives. However, parasites have evolved to be resistant to many of these drugs. Therefore, in some areas of the world, only a few drugs remain as effective treatments for malaria.

History

Malaria has infected humans for over 50,000 years, and may have been a human pathogen for the entire history of the species. Close relatives of the human malaria parasites remain common in chimpanzees. References to the unique periodic fevers of malaria are found throughout recorded history, beginning in 2700 BC in China. The term malaria originates from Medieval Italian: *mala aria*—"bad air"; and the disease was formerly called ague or marsh fever due to its association with swamps and marshland. Malaria was once common in most of Europe and North America, where it is now for all purposes non-existent.

Scientific studies on malaria made their first significant advance in 1880, when a French army doctor working in the military hospital of Constantine in Algeria named Charles Louis Alphonse Laveran observed parasites for the first time, inside the red blood cells of people suffering from malaria. He, therefore, proposed that malaria is caused by this protozoan, the first time protozoa were identified as causing disease. For this and later discoveries, he was awarded the 1907 Nobel Prize for Physiology or Medicine. The protozoan was called *Plasmodium* by the Italian scientists Ettore Marchiafava and Angelo Celli. A year later, Carlos Finlay, a Cuban doctor treating patients with yellow fever in Havana, provided strong evidence that mosquitoes were transmitting disease to and from humans. This work followed earlier suggestions by Josiah C. Nott, and work by Patrick Manson on the transmission of filariasis.

However, it was Britain's Sir Ronald Ross working in the Presidency General Hospital in Calcutta who finally proved in 1898 that malaria is transmitted by mosquitoes. He did this by showing that certain mosquito species transmit malaria to birds and isolating malaria parasites from the salivary glands of mosquitoes that had fed on infected birds. For this work Ross received the 1902 Nobel Prize in Medicine. After resigning from the Indian Medical Service, Ross worked at the newly-established Liverpool School of Tropical Medicine and directed malaria-control efforts in Egypt, Panama, Greece and Mauritius. The findings of Finlay and Ross were later confirmed by a medical board headed by Walter Reed in 1900, and its recommendations implemented by William C. Gorgas in the health measures undertaken during construction of the Panama Canal. This public-health work saved the lives of thousands of workers and helped develop the methods used in future public-health campaigns against this disease.

The first effective treatment for malaria came from the bark of cinchona tree, which contains quinine. This tree grows on the slopes of the Andes, mainly in Peru. A tincture made of this natural product was used by the inhabitants of Peru to control malaria, and the Jesuits introduced this practice to Europe during the 1640s, where it was rapidly accepted. However, it was not until 1820 that the active ingredient, quinine, was extracted from the bark, isolated and named by the French chemists Pierre Joseph Pelletier and Joseph Bienaime Caventou.

In the early twentieth century, before antibiotics, patients with syphilis were intentionally infected with malaria to create a fever, following the work of Julius Wagner-Jauregg. By accurately controlling the fever with quinine, the effects of both syphilis and malaria could be minimized. Although some patients died from malaria, this was preferable to the almost-certain death from syphilis.

Although the blood stage and mosquito stages of the malaria life cycle were identified in the 19th and early 20th centuries, it was not until the 1980s that the latent liver form of the parasite was observed. The discovery of this latent form of the parasite finally explained why people could appear to be cured of malaria but still relapse years after the parasite had disappeared from their bloodstreams.

Distribution and Impact

Malaria causes about 250 million cases of fever and approximately one million deaths annually. The vast majority of cases occur in children under 5 years old; pregnant women are also especially vulnerable. Despite efforts to reduce transmission and increase treatment, there has been little change in which areas are at risk of this disease since 1992. Indeed, if the prevalence of malaria stays on its present upwards course, the death rate could double in the next twenty years. Precise statistics are unknown because many cases occur in rural areas where people do not have access to hospitals or the means to afford health care. As a consequence, the majority of cases are undocumented.

Although co-infection with HIV and malaria does cause increased mortality, this is less of a problem than with HIV/tuberculosis co-infection, due to the two diseases usually attacking different age-ranges, with malaria being most common in the young and active tuberculosis most common in the old. Although HIV/malaria co-infection produces less severe symptoms than the interaction between HIV and TB, HIV and malaria do contribute to each other's spread. This effect comes from malaria increasing viral load and HIV infection increasing a person's susceptibility to malaria infection.

Malaria is presently endemic in a broad band around the equator, in areas of the Americas, many parts of Asia, and much of Africa; however, it is in sub-Saharan Africa where 85–90% of malaria fatalities occur. The geographic distribution of malaria within large regions is complex, and malaria-afflicted and malaria-free areas are often found close to each other. In drier areas, outbreaks of malaria can be predicted with reasonable accuracy by mapping rainfall. Malaria is more common in rural areas than in cities; this is in contrast to dengue fever where urban areas present the greater risk. For example, the cities of Vietnam, Laos and Cambodia are essentially malaria-free, but the disease is present in many rural regions. By contrast, in Africa malaria is present in both rural and urban areas, though the risk is lower in the larger cities.

The global endemic levels of malaria have not been mapped since the 1960s. However, the Wellcome Trust, UK, has funded the Malaria Atlas Project to rectify this, providing a more contemporary and robust means with which to assess current and future malaria disease burden.

Socio-economic Effects

Malaria is not just a disease commonly associated with poverty but also a cause of poverty and a major hindrance to economic development. Tropical regions are affected most, however malaria's furthest extent reaches into some temperate zones with extreme seasonal changes. The disease has been associated with major negative economic effects on regions where it is widespread. During the late 19th and early 20th centuries, it was a major factor in the slow economic development of the American southern states.. A comparison of average per capita GDP in 1995, adjusted for parity of purchasing power, between countries with malaria and countries without malaria gives a fivefold difference ($1,526 USD versus $8,268 USD). In countries where malaria is common, average per capita GDP has risen (between 1965 and 1990) only 0.4% per year, compared to 2.4% per year in other countries. Poverty is both cause and effect, however, since the poor do not have the financial capacities to prevent or treat the disease. The lowest income group in Malawi carries the burden of having 32% of their annual income used on this disease compared with the 4% of household incomes from low-to-high groups. In its entirety, the economic impact of malaria has been estimated to cost Africa $12 billion USD every year. The economic impact includes costs of health care, working days lost due to sickness, days lost in education, decreased productivity due to brain damage from cerebral malaria, and loss of investment and tourism. In some countries with a heavy malaria burden, the disease may account for as much as 40% of public health expenditure, 30-50% of inpatient admissions, and up to 50% of outpatient visits.

Symptoms

Symptoms of malaria include fever, shivering, arthralgia (joint pain), vomiting, anemia (caused by hemolysis), hemoglobinuria, retinal damage, and convulsions. The classic symptom of malaria is cyclical occurrence of sudden coldness followed by rigor and then fever and sweating lasting four to six hours, occurring every two days in *P. vivax* and *P. ovale* infections, while every three for *P. malariae*. *P. falciparum* can have recurrent fever every 36–48 hours or a less pronounced and almost continuous fever. For reasons that are poorly understood, but that may be related to high intracranial pressure, children with malaria frequently exhibit abnormal posturing, a sign indicating severe brain damage. Malaria has been found to cause cognitive impairments, especially in children. It causes widespread anemia during a period of rapid brain development and also direct brain damage. This neurologic damage results from cerebral malaria to which children are more vulnerable.

Typhoid

Typhoid fever, also known as enteric fever,Salmonella Typhi or commonly just typhoid, is an illness caused by the bacterium *Salmonella enterica* serovar Typhi. Common worldwide, it is transmitted by the ingestion of food or water contaminated with feces from an infected person. The bacteria then perforate through the intestinal wall and are phagocytosed by macrophages. Salmonella Typhi then alters its structure to resist destruction and allow them to exist within the macrophage. This renders them resistant to damage by PMN's, complement and the immune response. The organism is then spread via the lymphatics while inside the macrophages. This gives them access to the reticuloendothelial system and then to the different organs throughout the body. The organism is a Gram-negative short bacillus that is motile due to its peritrichous flagella. The bacteria grows best at 37 °C/99 °F – human body temperature.

Symptoms

Typhoid fever is characterized by a sustained fever as high as 40 °C (104 °F), profuse sweating, gastroenteritis, and nonbloody diarrhea. Less commonly a rash of flat, rose-colored spots may appear.

Classically, the course of untreated typhoid fever is divided into four individual stages, each lasting approximately one week. In the first week, there is a slowly rising temperature with relative bradycardia, malaise, headache and cough. A bloody nose (epistaxis) is seen in a quarter of cases and abdominal pain is also possible. There is leukopenia, a decrease in the number of circulating white blood cells, with eosinopenia and relative lymphocytosis, a positive diazo reaction and blood cultures are positive for Salmonella Typhi or Paratyphi. The classic Widal test is negative in the first week.

In the second week of the infection, the patient lies prostrated with high fever in plateau around 40 °C (104 °F) and bradycardia (Sphygmo-thermic dissociation), classically with a dicrotic pulse wave. Delirium is frequent, frequently calm, but sometimes agitated. This delirium gives to typhoid the nickname of "nervous fever". Rose spots appear on the lower chest and abdomen in around 1/3 patients. There are rhonchi in lung bases. The abdomen is distended and painful in the right lower quadrant where borborygmi can be heard. Diarrhea can occur in this stage: six to eight stools in a day, green with a characteristic smell, comparable to pea-soup. However, constipation is also frequent. The spleen and liver are enlarged (hepatosplenomegaly) and tender and there is elevation of liver transaminases. The Widal reaction is strongly positive with antiO and antiH antibodies. Blood cultures are sometimes still positive at this stage.

In the third week of typhoid fever a number of complications can occur:

- Intestinal hemorrhage due to bleeding in congested Peyer's patches; this can be very serious but is usually non-fatal.
- Intestinal perforation in distal ileum: this is a very serious complication and is frequently fatal. It may occur without alarming symptoms until septicaemia or diffuse peritonitis sets in.
- Encephalitis
- Metastatic abscesses, cholecystitis, endocarditis and osteitis

The fever is still very high and oscillates very little over 24 hours. Dehydration ensues and the patient is delirious (typhoid state). By the end of third week the fever has started reducing (defervescence). This carries on into the fourth and final week.

Diagnosis

Diagnosis is made by any blood, bone marrow or stool cultures and with the Widal test (domonstration of salmonella antibodies against antigens O-somatic and H-flagellar). In epidemics and less wealthy countries, after excluding malaria, dysentery or pneumonia, a therapeutic trial time with chloramphenicol is generally undertaken while awaiting the results of Widal test and blood cultures.

Treatment

Typhoid fever in most cases is not fatal. Antibiotics, such as ampicillin, chloramphenicol, trimethoprim-sulfamethoxazole, Amoxicillin and ciprofloxacin, have been commonly used to treat typhoid fever in developed countries. Prompt treatment of the disease with antibiotics reduces the case-fatality rate to approximately 1%. When untreated, typhoid fever persists for three weeks to a month. Death occurs in between 10% and 30% of untreated cases.

Resistance

Resistance to ampicillin, chloramphenicol, trimethoprim-sulfamethoxazole and streptomycin is now common, and these agents have not been used as first line treatment now for almost 20 years. Typhoid that is resistant to these agents is known as multidrug-resistant typhoid (MDR typhoid).

Ciprofloxacin resistance is an increasing problem, especially in the Indian subcontinent and Southeast Asia. Many centres are therefore moving away from using ciprofloxacin as first line for treating suspected typhoid originating in South America, India, Pakistan, Bangladesh, Thailand or Vietnam. For these patients, the recommended first line treatment is ceftriaxone. It has also been suggested Azithromycin is better at treating typhoid in resistant populations than both fluoroquinolone drugs and ceftriaxone. Azithromycin significantly reduces relapse rates compared with ceftriaxone.

There is a separate problem with laboratory testing for reduced susceptibility to ciprofloxacin: current recommendations are that isolates should be tested simultaneously against ciprofloxacin (CIP) and against nalidixic acid (NAL), and that isolates that are sensitive to both CIP and NAL should be reported as "sensitive to ciprofloxacin", but that isolates testing sensitive to CIP but not to NAL should be reported as "reduced sensitivity to ciprofloxacin". However, an analysis of 271 isolates showed that around 18% of isolates with a reduced susceptibility to ciprofloxacin (MIC 0.125–1.0 mg/l) would not be picked up by this method. It is not certain how this problem can be solved, because most laboratories around the world (including the West) are dependent disc testing and cannot test for MICs.

Prevention

Sanitation and hygiene are the critical measures that can be taken to prevent typhoid. Typhoid does not affect animals and therefore transmission is only from human to human. Typhoid can only spread in environments where human feces or urine are able to come into contact with food or drinking water. Careful food preparation and washing of hands are therefore crucial to preventing typhoid.

There are two vaccines currently recommended by the World Health Organization for the prevention of typhoid: these are the live, oral Ty21a vaccine (sold as *Vivotif Berna*) and the injectable Typhoid polysaccharide vaccine (sold as *Typhim Vi* by Sanofi Pasteur and *Typherix* by GlaxoSmithKline). Both are between 50 to 80% protective and are recommended for travelers to areas where typhoid is endemic. There exists an older killed whole-cell vaccine that is still used in countries where the newer preparations are not available, but this vaccine is no longer recommended for use, because it has a higher rate of side effects (mainly pain and inflammation at the site of the injection).

Transmission

Flying insects feeding on feces may occasionally transfor the bacteria through poor hygiene habits and public sanitation conditions. Public education campaigns encouraging people to wash their hands after defecating and before handling food are an important component in controlling spread of the disease. According to statistics from the United States Center for Disease Control, the chlorination of drinking water has led to dramatic decreases in the transmission of typhoid fever in the U.S.

A person may become an asymptomatic carrior of typhoid fever, suffering no symptoms, but capable of infecting others. According to the Centers for Disease Control approximately 5% of people who contract typhoid continue to carry the disease after they recover. The most famous asymptomatic carrier was Typhoid Mary. She was a young cook who was responsible for infecting about 47 people during her lifetime, killing three of the infected. This was the first time a perfectly healthy person was known to be responsible for an "epidemic".

Many carriers of typhoid were locked into an isolation ward never to be released in order to prevent further typhoid cases.

These people often deteriorated mentally, driven mad by the conditions they lived in.

Epidemiology

With an estimated 16-33 million cases of annually resulting in 500,000 to 600,000 deaths in endemic areas, the World Health Organization identifies typhoid as a serious public health problem. Its incidence is highest in children and young adults between 5 and 19 years old.

Cholera

Cholera, sometimes known as Asiatic or epidemic cholera, is an infectious gastroenteritis caused by enterotoxin-producing strains of the bacterium *Vibrio cholerae*. Transmission to humans occurs through eating food or drinking water contaminated with *cholera vibrios* from other cholera patients. The major reservoir for cholera was long assumed to be humans themselves, but considerable evidence exists that aquatic environments can serve as reservoirs of the bacteria.

Vibrio cholerae is a Gram-negative bacterium that produces cholera toxin, an enterotoxin, whose action on the mucosal epithelium lining of the small intestine is responsible for the disease's infamous characteristic, exhaustive diarrhea. In its most severe forms, cholera is one of the most rapidly fatal illnesses known, and a healthy person's blood pressure may drop to hypotensive levels within an hour of the onset of symptoms; infected patients may die within three hours if medical treatment is not provided. In a common scenario, the disease progresses from the first liquid stool to shock in 4 to 12 hours, with death following in 18 hours to several days, unless oral rehydration therapy is provided.

Symptoms

The incubation period is the period from infection until symptoms occur. In cholera this is usually 18–72 hours. The severity of symptoms depends on the dose, i.e. the number of bacteria ingested. Some otherwise healthy individuals may not develop any symptoms at all. Of those who do, only a small proportion develop severe disease.

The principal symptom of infection is diarrhea, which is watery and brown at first, but quickly changes to large volumes of pale fluid stools ('rice-water stools'). In the most severe cases dramatic fluid loss from the continuous diarrhea can lead to hypovolemic shock and collapse within 1 to 4 hours. Depending upon the treatment provided, unconsciousness and death can occur anytime from 12 to 18 hours afterwards, although some individual cases may persist for several days.

Fever is not a prominent feature of cholera.

Other symptoms include nosebleed, rapid pulse, dry skin, tiredness, abdominal cramps, nausea, leg cramps, and vomiting.

Treatment

In most cases cholera can be successfully treated with oral rehydration therapy. Prompt replacement of water and electrolytes is the principal treatment for cholera, as dehydration and electrolyte depletion occur rapidly. Oral rehydration therapy or ORT is highly effective, safe, and simple to administer. In situations where commercially produced ORT sachets are too expensive or difficult to obtain, alternative homemade solutions using various formulas of water, sugar, table salt, baking soda, and fruit offer less expensive methods of electrolyte repletion. In severe cholera cases with significant dehydration, the administration of intravenous rehydration solutions may be necessary.

Antibiotics shorten the course of the disease, and reduce the severity of the symptoms. However Oral rehydration therapy remains the principal treatment. Tetracycline is typically used as the primary antibiotic, although some strains of *V. cholerae* exist that have shown resistance.

Other antibiotics that have been proven effective against *V. cholerae* include cotrimoxazole, erythromycin, doxycycline, chloramphenicol, and furazolidone. Fluoroquinolones such as norfloxacin also may be used, but resistance has been reported. Recently Hemendra Yadav reported findings at the All India Institute of Medical Sciences, New Delhi, noting that ampicillin resistance has again decreased in the *V. Cholerae* strains of Delhi.

Rapid diagnostic assay methods are available for the identification of multidrug resistant *V. cholerae*. New generation antimicrobials have been discovered which are effective against *V. cholerae* in *in vitro* studies.

The success of treatment is significantly affected by the speed and method of treatment. If cholera patients are treated quickly and properly, the mortality rate is less than 1%; however, with untreated cholera the mortality rate rises to 50–60%.

Epidemiology

Prevention: Although cholera can be and is, if left untreated, life-threatening, prevention of the disease is normally straightforward if proper sanitation practices are followed. In the first world, due to nearly universal advanced water treatment and sanitation practices, cholera is no longer a major health threat. The last major outbreak of cholera in the United States occurred in 1910-1911. Travelers should be aware of how the disease is transmitted and what can be done to prevent it. Effective sanitation practices, if instituted and adhered to in time, are usually sufficient to stop an epidemic. The main procedure involves exposing as many microbes as possible to treatments or processes that kill or remove them. Heat, chlorine, ozone, ultra-violet light, and microbal filters are all some of the methods used to kill or remove the germs. There are several points along the cholera transmission path at which its spread may be (and should be) halted:

- *Sterilization:* Proper disposal and treatment of the germ infected fecal waste water produced by cholera victims (and all clothing, bedding, people, etc. that come in contact with it) is of primary importance. All materials that come in contact with cholera patients should be sterilized by washing in hot water using chlorine bleach if possible. Hands that touch cholera patients or their clothing, bedding etc. should be thoroughly cleaned and sterilized with chlorinated water or other effective anti-microbal.
- *Sewage:* anti-bacterial treatment of general sewage by chlorine, ozone, ultra-violet light or other effective

treatment before it enters the waterways or underground water supplies helps prevent undiagnosed patients from inadvertently spreading the disease.

- *Sources:* Warnings about possible cholera contamination should be posted around contaminated water sources with directions on how to decontaminate the water (boiling, chlorination etc.) for possible use.
- *Water Purification:* All water used for drinking, washing, or cooking should be sterilized by boiling,chlorination, ozone water treatment, ultra-violet light sterilization, or anti-microbal filtration in any area where cholera may be present. Chlorination, and boiling are nearly always the cheapest and most effective means of halting transmission. Cloth filters, though very basic, have significantly reduced the occurrence of cholera when used in poor villages in Bangladesh that rely on untreated surface water. Better anti-microbal filters like those present in up-scale individual water treatment hiking kits are required to remove all microbes. Public health education and adherence to appropriate sanitation practices are of primary importance to help prevent and control transmission of cholera and other diseases.

A vaccine is available in some countries (not the U.S.), but this prophylactic is not currently recommended for routine use by the U.S. Centers for Disease Control and Prevention (CDC). During recent years, substantial progress has been made in developing new oral vaccines against cholera. Two oral cholera vaccines, which have been evaluated with volunteers from industrialized countries and in regions with endemic cholera, are commercially available in several countries: a killed whole-cell *V. cholerae* O1 in combination with purified recombinant B subunit of cholera toxin and a live-attenuated live oral cholera vaccine, containing the genetically manipulated *V. cholerae* O1 strain CVD 103-HgR. The appearance of *V. cholerae* O139 has influenced efforts in order to develop an effective and practical cholera vaccine since none of the currently available vaccines is effective against this strain. The newer vaccine (brand name:

Dukoral), an orally administered inactivated whole cell vaccine, appears to provide somewhat better immunity and have fewer adverse effects than the previously available vaccine. This safe and effective vaccine is available for use by individuals and health personnel. Work is under way to investigate the role of mass vaccination.

Sensitive surveillance and prompt reporting allow for containing cholera epidemics rapidly. Cholera exists as a seasonal disease in many endemic countries, occurring annually mostly during rainy seasons. Surveillance systems can provide early alerts to outbreaks, therefore leading to coordinated response and assist in preparation of preparedness plans. Efficient surveillance systems can also improve the risk assessment for potential cholera outbreaks. Understanding the seasonality and location of outbreaks provide guidance for improving cholera control activities for the most vulnerable. This will also aid in the developing indicators for appropriate use of oral cholera vaccine.

Susceptibility

Recent epidemiologic research suggests that an individual's susceptibility to cholera (and other diarrheal infections) is affected by their blood type: those with type O blood are the most susceptible, while those with type AB are the most resistant. Between these two extremes are the A and B blood types, with type A being more resistant than type B.

About one million *V. cholerae* bacteria must typically be ingested to cause cholera in normally healthy adults, although increased susceptibility may be observed in those with a weakened immune system, individuals with decreased gastric acidity (as from the use of antacids), or those who are malnourished.

It has also been hypothesized that the cystic fibrosis genetic mutation has been maintained in humans due to a selective advantage: heterozygous carriers of the mutation (who are thus not affected by cystic fibrosis) are more resistant to *V. cholerae* infections. In this model, the genetic deficiency in the cystic fibrosis transmembrane conductance regulator channel proteins interferes with bacteria binding to the gastrointestinal epithelium, thus reducing the effects of an infection.

Transmission

People infected with cholera suffer acute diarrhea. This highly liquid diarrhea, colloquially referred to as "rice-water stool," is loaded with bacteria that can infect water used by other people. Cholera is transmitted from person to person through ingestion of water contaminated with the cholera bacterium, usually from faeces or other effluent. The source of the contamination is typically other cholera patients when their untreated diarrhea discharge is allowed to get into waterways or into groundwater or drinking water supplies. Any infected water and any foods washed in the water, as well as shellfish living in the affected waterway, can cause an infection. Cholera is rarely spread directly from person to person. *V. cholerae* harbors naturally in the zooplankton of fresh, brackish, and salt water, attached primarily to their chitinous exoskeleton. Both toxic and non-toxic strains exist. Non-toxic strains can acquire toxicity through a lysogenic bacteriophage. Coastal cholera outbreaks typically follow zooplankton blooms, thus making cholera a zoonotic disease.

Potential Human Contribution to Transmissibility

Cholera bacteria grown *in vitro* encounter difficulty subsequently growing in humans without additional stomach acid buffering. In a 2002 study at Tufts University School of Medicine, it was found that stomach acidity is a principal factor that contributes to epidemic spread. In their findings, the researchers found that human colonization creates a hyperinfectious bacterial state that is maintained after dissemination and that may contribute to epidemic spread of the disease. When these hyperinfectious bacteria underwent transcription profiles, they were found to possess a unique physiological and behavioral state, characterized by high expression levels of genes required for nutrient acquisition and motility, and low expression levels of genes required for bacterial chemotaxis. Thus, the spread of cholera can be expedited by host physiology.

Diagnosis

In epidemic situations a clinical diagnosis is made by taking a history of symptoms from the patient and by a brief examination only. Treatment is usually started without or before confirmation by laboratory analysis of specimens. Stool and swab samples collected in the acute stage of the disease, before antibiotics have been administered, are the most useful specimens for laboratory diagnosis. If an epidemic of cholera is suspected, the most common causative agent is *Vibrio cholerae* O1. If *V. cholerae* serogroup O1 is not isolated, the laboratory should test for *V. cholerae* O139. However, if neither of these organisms is isolated, it is necessary to send stool specimens to a reference laboratory. Infection with *V. cholerae* O139 should be reported and handled in the same manner as that caused by *V. cholerae* O1. The associated diarrheal illness should be referred to as cholera and must be reported as a case of cholera to the appropriate public health authorities.

A number of special media have been employed for the cultivation for cholera vibrios. They are classified as follows:

Holding or Transport Media

1. *Venkataraman-Ramakrishnan (VR) medium:* This medium has 20g Sea Salt Powder and 5g Peptone dissolved in 1L of distilled water.
2. *Cary-Blair Medium:* This the most widely-used carrying media. This is a buffered solution of sodium chloride, sodium thioglycollate, disodium phosphate and calcium chloride at pH 8.4.
3. Autoclaved sea water

Enrichment Media

1. Alkaline peptone water at pH 8.6
2. Monsur's taurocholate tellurite peptone water at pH 9.2

Plating Media

1. *Alkaline Bile Salt Agar (BSA)*: The colonies are very similar to those on nutrient agar.

2. *Monsur's Gelatin Tauro Cholate Trypticase Tellurite Agar (GTTA) Medium*: Cholera vibrios produce small translucent colonies with a greyish black centre.
3. *TCBS Medium*: This the mostly widely used medium. This medium contains thiosulphate, citrate, bile salts and sucrose. Cholera vibrios produce flat 2-3 mm in diameter, yellow nucleated colonies.

Direct microscopy of stool is not recommended as it is unreliable. Microscopy is preferred only after enrichment, as this process reveals the characteristic motility of *Vibrios* and its inhibition by appropriate antiserum. Diagnosis can be confirmed as well as serotyping done by agglutination with specific sera.

Biochemistry

Most of the *V. cholerae* bacteria in the contaminated water consumed by the host do not survive the highly acidic conditions of the human stomach. The few bacteria that do survive conserve their energy and stored nutrients during the passage through the stomach by shutting down much protein production. When the surviving bacteria exit the stomach and reach the small intestine, they need to propel themselves through the thick mucus that lines the small intestine to get to the intestinal wall where they can thrive. *V. Cholerae* bacteria start up production of the hollow cylindrical protein flagellin to make flagella, the curly whip-like tails that they rotate to propel themselves through the mucus that lines the small intestine.

Once the cholera bacteria reach the intestinal wall, they do not need the flagella propellers to move themselves any longer. The bacteria stop producing the protein flagellin, thus again conserving energy and nutrients by changing the mix of proteins that they manufacture in response to the changed chemical surroundings. On reaching the intestinal wall, *V. Cholerae* start producing the toxic proteins that give the infected person a watery diarrhea. This carries the multiplying new generations of *V. cholerae* bacteria out into the drinking water of the next host—if proper sanitation measures are not in place.

Microbiologists have studied the genetic mechanisms by which the *V. cholerae* bacteria turn off the production of some proteins and turn on the production of other proteins as they respond to the series of chemical environments they encounter, passing through the stomach, through the mucous layer of the small intestine, and on to the intestinal wall. Of particular interest have been the genetic mechanisms by which cholera bacteria turn on the protein production of the toxins that interact with host cell mechanisms to pump chloride ions into the small intestine, creating an ionic pressure which prevents sodium ions from entering the cell.

The chloride and sodium ions create a salt water environment in the small intestines which through osmosis can pull up to six liters of water per day through the intestinal cells creating the massive amounts of diarrhea. The host can become rapidly dehydrated if an appropriate mixture of dilute salt water and sugar is not taken to replace the blood's water and salts lost in the diarrhea.

By inserting separate, successive sections of *V. cholerae* DNA into the DNA of other bacteria such as *E. coli* that would not naturally produce the protein toxins, researchers have investigated the mechanisms by which *V. cholerae* responds to the changing chemical environments of the stomach, mucous layers, and intestinal wall.

Researchers have discovered that there is a complex cascade of regulatory proteins that control expression of *V. cholerae* virulence determinants. In responding to the chemical environment at the intestinal wall, the *V. cholerae* bacteria produce the TcpP/TcpH proteins, which, together with the ToxR/ToxS proteins, activate the expression of the ToxT regulatory protein.

ToxT then directly activates expression of virulence genes that produce the toxins that cause diarrhea in the infected person and that permit the bacteria to colonize the intestine. Current research aims at discovering "the signal that makes the cholera bacteria stop swimming and start to colonize (that is, adhere to the cells of) the small intestine."

Diarrhea

In medicine, diarrhea (from the Greek, "diarrhoia" meaning "a flowing through"), also spelled diarrhoea (see spelling differences), is characterized by frequent loose or liquid bowel movements. Acute diarrhea is a common cause of death in developing countries and the second most common cause of infant deaths worldwide. The loss of fluids through diarrhea can cause severe dehydration which is one cause of death in diarrhea sufferers. Along with water, sufferers also lose dangerous amounts of important salts, electrolytes, and other nutrients.

Causes

Diarrhea commonly results from gastroenteritis caused by viral infections, parasites or bacterial toxins. In sanitary living conditions where there is ample food and a supply of clean water, an otherwise healthy patient usually recovers from viral infections in a few days. However, for ill or malnourished individuals diarrhea can lead to severe dehydration and can become life-threatening without treatment.

Diarrhea can also be a symptom of more serious diseases, such as dysentery, cholera, or botulism, and can also be indicative of a chronic syndrome such as Crohn's disease or severe mushroom poisoning syndromes. Though appendicitis patients do not generally have violent diarrhea, it is a common symptom of a ruptured appendix. It is also an effect of severe radiation sickness.

Diarrhea can also be caused by dairy intake in those who are lactose intolerant.

Symptomatic treatment for diarrhea involves the patient consuming adequate amounts of water to replace that loss, preferably mixed with electrolytes to provide essential salts and some amount of nutrients. For many people, further treatment is unnecessary. The following types of diarrhea indicate medical supervision is required:

- Diarrhea in infants
- Moderate or severe diarrhea in young children;

- Diarrhea associated with blood
- Diarrhea that continues for more than two days;
- Diarrhea that is associated with more general illness such as non-cramping abdominal pain, fever, weight loss, etc;
- Diarrhea in travelers, since they are more likely to have exotic infections such as parasites;
- Diarrhea in food handlers, because of the potential to infect others;
- Diarrhea in institutions such as hospitals, child care centers, or geriatric and convalescent homes.

A severity score is used to aid diagnosis in children.

Types of Diarrhea

There are at least four types of diarrhea: secretory diarrhea, osmotic diarrhea, motility-related diarrhea, and inflammatory diarrhea.

Secretory Diarrhea

Secretory diarrhea means that there is an increase in the active secretion, or there is an inhibition of absorption. There is little to no structural damage. The most common cause of this type of diarrhea is a cholera toxin that stimulates the secretion of anions, especially chloride ions. Therefore, to maintain a charge balance in the lumen, sodium is carried with it, along with water.

Osmotic Diarrhea

Osmotic diarrhea occurs when too much water is drawn into the bowels. This can be the result of maldigestion (e.g., pancreatic disease or Coeliac disease), in which the nutrients are left in the lumen to pull in water. Osmotic diarrhea can also be caused by osmotic laxatives (which work to alleviate constipation by drawing water into the bowels). In healthy individuals, too much magnesium or vitamin C or undigested lactose can produce osmotic diarrhea and distention of the bowel. A person who does not have lactose intolerance can have difficulty absorbing lactose after an extraordinarily high intake of dairy products. In persons who do not have fructose malabsorption, excess fructose intake can still cause diarrhea. High-fructose foods that also have a high glucose content are more absorbable and less likely to cause diarrhea. Sugar alcohols such as sorbitol (often found in sugar-free foods) are difficult for the body to absorb and, in large amounts, may lead to osmotic diarrhea.

Motility-related Diarrhea

Motility-related diarrhea is caused by the rapid movement of food through the intestines (hypermotility). If the food moves too quickly through the GI tract, there is not enough time for sufficient nutrients and water to be absorbed. This can be due to a vagotomy or diabetic neuropathy, or a complication of menstruation. Hyperthyroidism can produce hypermotility and lead to pseudodiarrhea and occasionally real diarrhea. Diarrhea can be treated with antimotility agents (such as loperamide).

Inflammatory Diarrhea

Inflammatory diarrhea occurs when there is damage to the mucosal lining or brush border, which leads to a passive loss of protein-rich fluids, and a decreased ability to absorb these lost fluids. Features of all three of the other types of diarrhea can be found in this type of diarrhea. It can be caused by bacterial infections, viral infections, parasitic infections, or autoimmune problems such as inflammatory bowel diseases. It can also be caused by tuberculosis, colon cancer, and enteritis.

Dysentery

Generally, if there is blood visible in the stools, it is not diarrhea, but dysentery. The blood is trace of an invasion of bowel tissue. Dysentery is caused by an excess of water by a release of antidiuretic hormone from the posterior pituitary gland. Dysentery is a symptom of, among others, *Shigella*, *Entamoeba histolytica*, and *Salmonella*.

Infectious Diarrhea

Infectious diarrhea is diarrhea caused by a microbe such as a bacterium, parasite, or virus.

Malabsorption

Malabsorption is the inability to absorb food, mostly in the small bowel but also due to the pancreas.

Causes include celiac disease (intolerance to wheat, rye, and barley gluten, the protein of the grain), lactose intolerance (intolerance to milk sugar, common in non-Europeans), fructose malabsorption, pernicious anemia (impaired bowel function due to the inability to absorb vitamin B12), loss of pancreatic secretions (may be due to cystic fibrosis or pancreatitis), short bowel syndrome (surgically removed bowel), radiation fibrosis (usually following cancer treatment), and other drugs, including agents used in chemotherapy.

Inflammatory Bowel Disease

The two overlapping types here are of unknown origin:

- Ulcerative colitis is marked by chronic bloody diarrhea and inflammation mostly affects the distal colon near the rectum.
- Crohn's disease typically affects fairly well demarcated segments of bowel in the colon and often affects the end of the small bowel.

Irritable Bowel Syndrome

Another possible cause of diarrhea is Irritable Bowel Syndrome (IBS). Symptoms defining IBS: abdominal discomfort or pain relieved by defecation and unusual stool (diarrhea or constipation or both) or stool frequency, for at least 3 days a week over the previous 3 months.

IBS symptoms can be present in patients with a variety of conditions including food allergies, infective diarrhea, celiac, and inflammatory bowel diseases. Treating the underlying condition (celiac disease, food allergy, bacterial dysbiosis, etc.) usually resolves the diarrhea. IBS can cause visceral hypersensitivity. While there is no direct treatment for undifferentiated IBS, symptoms, including diarrhea, can sometimes be managed through a combination of dietary changes, soluble fiber supplements, and/or medications.

It is important to note that IBS can often be confused with Giardiasis since false negative tests for giardia can result in a misdiagnoses of the actual cause, a parasitic infection.

Other Important Causes

- Ischemic bowel disease. This usually affects older people and can be due to blocked arteries.
- Bowel cancer: Some (but not all) bowel cancers may have associated diarrhea. Cancer of the large intestine is most common.
- Hormone-secreting tumors: some hormones (e.g. serotonin) can cause diarrhea if excreted in excess (usually from a tumor).
- Bile salt diarrhea: excess bile salt entering the colon rather than being absorbed at the end of the small intestine can cause diarrhea, typically shortly after eating. Bile salt diarrhea is a bad side-effect of gallbladder removal. It is usually treated with cholestyramine, a bile acid sequestrant.
- Celiac Disease
- Intestinal protozoa such as Giardiasis

Alcohol

Chronic diarrhea can be caused by chronic ethanol ingestion. Consumption of alcohol affects the body's capability to absorb water-this is often a symptom that accompanies a hangover after a binge drinking session. The alcohol itself is absorbed in the intestines and as the intestinal cells absorb it, the toxicity causes these cells to lose their ability to absorb water. This leads to an outpouring of fluid from the intestinal lining, which is in turn poorly absorbed. The diarrhea usually lasts for several hours until the alcohol is detoxified and removed from the digestive system. Symptoms range from person to person and are influenced by both the amount consumed as well as physiological differences.

Treatment

In many cases of diarrhea, replacing lost fluid and salts is the only treatment needed. This is usually by mouth–oral rehydration therapy–or, in very severe cases, intravenously. Diet restriction such as limiting milk has no effect on the duration of diarrhea. Medicines such loperamide (Imodium), bismuth subsalicylate (as found in Pepto Bismol and Kaopectate) may be beneficial, however they may be contraindicated in certain situations. Prescribed medications sometimes contain pain-killers, such as morphine or codeine, to counter the cramps that can accompany diarrhea.

Evolutionary Medicine

According to two researchers into evolutionary medicine, Nesse and Williams, diarrhea functions as an evolved expulsion defense mechanism. As a result, if it is stopped, there might be a delay in illness recovery. They cite in support of this argument research carried out by DuPont and Hornick that was published in the Journal of the American Medical Association (JAMA) showed that treating *Shigella* with the anti-diarrhea drug (Lomotil) caused people to stay feverish twice as long as those not so treated. The researchers indeed themselves observed that: “Lomotil may be contraindicated in shigellosis. Diarrhea may represent a defense mechanism”.

Smallpox

Smallpox is an infectious disease unique to humans, caused by either of two virus variants, *Variola major* and *Variola minor*. The disease is also known by the Latin names *Variola* or *Variola vera*, which is a derivative of the Latin *varius*, meaning spotted, or *varus*, meaning “pimple”. The term “smallpox” was first used in Europe in the 15th century to distinguish variola from the “great pox” (syphilis).

Smallpox localizes in small blood vessels of the skin and in the mouth and throat. In the skin, this results in a characteristic maculopapular rash, and later, raised fluid-filled blisters. *V. major* produces a more serious disease and has an overall mortality rate of 30–35%. *V. minor* causes a milder form of disease (also known as alastrim, cottonpox, milkpox, whitepox, and Cuban itch) which kills about 1% of its victims. Long-term complications of *V. major* infection include characteristic scars, commonly on the face, which occur in 65–85% of survivors. Blindness resulting from corneal ulceration and scarring, and limb deformities due to arthritis and osteomyelitis are less common complications, seen in about 2–5% of cases.

Smallpox is believed to have emerged in human populations about 10,000 BC. The disease killed an estimated 400,000 Europeans each year during the 18th century (including five reigning monarchs), and was responsible for a third of all blindness. Of all those infected, 20–60%—and over 80% of infected children—died from the disease.

During the 20th century, it is estimated that smallpox was responsible for 300–500 million deaths. In the early 1950s an estimated 50 million cases of smallpox occurred in the world each year. As recently as 1967, the World Health Organization estimated that 15 million people contracted the disease and that two million died in that year. After successful vaccination campaigns throughout the 19th and 20th centuries, the WHO certified the eradication of smallpox in December 1979. To this day, smallpox is the only human infectious disease to have been completely eradicated.

Cause

Smallpox is caused by infection with variola virus, which belongs to the genus Orthopoxvirus, the family Poxviridae, and subfamily chordopoxvirinae. Variola virus is a large brick-shaped virus measuring approximately 302 to 350 nanometers by 244 to 270 nm, with a single linear double stranded DNA genome 186 kilobase pairs (kbp) in size and containing a hairpin loop at each end. The two classic varieties of smallpox are variola major and variola minor. The closest viral relative is molluscum contagiosum, which, like smallpox, infects only humans. However, unlike variola species, molluscum infection is benign.

Four orthopoxviruses cause infection in humans: variola, vaccinia, cowpox, and monkeypox. Variola virus infects only humans in nature, although primates and other animals have been infected in a laboratory setting. Vaccinia, cowpox, and monkeypox viruses can infect both humans and other animals in nature. The lifecycle of poxviruses is complicated by having multiple infectious forms, with differing mechanisms of cell entry. Poxviruses are unique among DNA viruses in that they replicate in the cytoplasm of the cell rather than in the nucleus. In order to replicate, poxviruses produce a variety of specialized proteins not produced by other DNA viruses, the most important of which is a viral-associated DNA-dependent RNA polymerase. Both enveloped and unenveloped virions are infectious. The viral envelope is made of modified Golgi membranes containing viral-specific polypeptides, including hemagglutinin. Infection with either variola major or variola minor confers immunity against the other.

Evolution

Smallpox appears to have evolved from an African rodent-borne variola-like virus. The date of this evolution is uncertain at present and estimates vary between 16,000 and 68,000 years ago. The more severe form (variola major) originated in Asia between 400 and 1600 years ago. A second form –alastrim minor– found in West Africa and the Americas is thought to have evolved between 1,400 and 6,300 years ago. This clade gave rise to two subclades that diverged at least 800 years ago.

Transmission

Transmission of smallpox occurs through inhalation of airborne variola virus, usually droplets expressed from the oral, nasal, or pharyngeal mucosa of an infected person. It is transmitted from one person to another primarily through prolonged face-to-face contact with an infected person, usually within a distance of 6 feet, but can also be spread through direct contact with infected bodily fluids or contaminated objects (fomites) such as bedding or clothing. Rarely, smallpox has been spread by virus carried in the air in enclosed settings such as buildings, buses, and trains. The virus can cross the placenta, but the incidence of congenital smallpox is relatively low. Smallpox is not notably infectious in the prodromal period and viral shedding is usually delayed until the appearance of the rash, which is often accompanied by lesions in the mouth and pharynx. The virus can be transmitted throughout the course of the illness, but is most frequent during the first week of the rash, when most of the skin lesions are intact. Infectivity wanes in 7 to 10 days when scabs form over the lesions, but the infected person is contagious until the last smallpox scab falls off.

Smallpox is highly contagious, but generally spreads more slowly and less widely than some other viral diseases, perhaps because transmission requires close contact and occurs after the onset of the rash. The overall rate of infection is also affected by the short duration of the infectious stage. In temperate areas, the number of smallpox infections were highest during the winter and spring. In tropical areas, seasonal variation was less evident and the disease was present throughout the year. Age distribution of smallpox infections depends on acquired immunity. Vaccination immunity declines over time and is probably lost in all but the most recently vaccinated populations. Smallpox is not known to be transmitted by insects or animals and there is no asymptomatic carrier state.

Signs and Symptoms

There are two clinical forms of smallpox. Variola major is the severe and most common form of smallpox, with a more extensive rash and higher fever. There are four types of variola major smallpox based on the Rao classification: ordinary, modified, flat, and hemorrhagic. Historically, variola major has an overall fatality rate of about 30%; however, flat and hemorrhagic smallpox are usually fatal. In addition, a form called *variola sine eruptione* (smallpox without rash) is seen generally in vaccinated persons. This form is marked by a fever that occurs after the usual incubation period and can be confirmed only by antibody studies or, rarely, by virus isolation.

Variola minor is a less common presentation of smallpox, and a much less severe disease, with historical death rates of 1% or less. Subclinical (asymptomatic) infections with variola virus have also been noted, but are not believed to be common.

The incubation period between contraction and the first obvious symptoms of the disease is around 12 days. Once inhaled, variola virus invades the oropharyngeal (mouth and throat) or the respiratory mucosa, migrates to regional lymph nodes, and begins to multiply. In the initial growth phase the virus seems to move from cell to cell, but around the 12th day, lysis of many infected cells occurs and the virus is found in the bloodstream in large numbers (this is called *viremia*), and a second wave of multiplication occurs in the spleen, bone marrow, and lymph nodes.

The initial or prodromal symptoms are similar to other viral diseases such as influenza and the common cold: fever (at least 38.5 °C (101 °F)), muscle pain, malaise, headache, prostration, and as the digestive tract is commonly involved, nausea and vomiting and backache often occur. The prodrome, or preeruptive stage, usually lasts 2–4 days. By days 12–15 the first visible lesions—small reddish spots called *enanthem*—appear on mucous membranes of the mouth, tongue, palate, and throat, and temperature falls to near normal. These lesions rapidly enlarge and rupture, releasing large amounts of virus into the saliva.

Smallpox virus preferentially attacks skin cells, causing the characteristic pimples (called macules) associated with the disease. A rash develops on the skin 24 to 48 hours after lesions on the mucous membranes appear. Typically the macules first appear on the forehead, then rapidly spread to the whole face, proximal portions of extremities, the trunk, and lastly to distal portions of extremities. The process takes no more than 24 to 36 hours, after which no new lesions appear. At this point Variola major infection can take several very different courses.

Ordinary

Ninety percent or more of smallpox cases among unvaccinated persons are of the ordinary type. In this form of the disease, by the second day of the rash, the macules become raised *papules*. By the third or fourth day the papules fill with an opalescent fluid to become *vesicles*. This fluid becomes opaque and turbid within 24–48 hours, giving them the appearance of pustules; however, the so-called pustules are filled with tissue debris, not pus.

By the sixth or seventh day, all the skin lesions have become pustules. Between 7 and 10 days the pustules mature and reach their maximum size. The pustules are sharply raised, typically round, tense, and firm to the touch. The pustules are deeply embedded in the dermis, giving them the feel of a small bead in the skin. Fluid slowly leaks from the pustules, and by the end of the second week the pustules deflate, and start to dry up, forming crusts (or scabs). By day 16-20 scabs have formed over all the lesions, which have started to flake off, leaving de-pigmented scars.

Ordinary smallpox generally produces a *discrete* rash, in which the pustules stand out on the skin separately. The distribution of the rash is densest on the face; denser on the extremities than on the trunk; and on the extremities, denser on the distal parts than on the proximal. The palms of the hands and soles of the feet are involved in the majority of cases. In some cases, the blisters merge together into sheets, forming a *confluent* rash, which begin to detach the outer layers of skin from the underlying flesh Patients with confluent smallpox often remain ill even after scabs have formed over all the lesions. In one case series, the case-fatality rate in confluent smallpox was 62%.

Modified

Referring to the character of the eruption and the rapidity of its development, modified smallpox occurs mostly in previously vaccinated people. In this form the prodromal illness still occurs but may be less severe than in the ordinary type. There is usually no fever during evolution of the rash. The skin lesions tend to be fewer and evolve more quickly, are more superficial, and may not show the uniform characteristic of more typical smallpox. Modified smallpox is rarely, if ever, fatal. This form of variola major is more easily confused with chickenpox.

Malignant

In Malignant-type smallpox (also called flat smallpox) the lesions remain almost flush with the skin at the time when raised vesicles form in ordinary-type smallpox. It is unknown why some people develop this type of disease. Historically, malignant smallpox accounted for 5%–10% of cases, and the majority (72%) were in children. Malignant smallpox is accompanied by a severe prodromal phase that lasts 3–4 days, prolonged high fever, and severe symptoms of toxemia. The rash on the tongue and palate is usually extensive. The skin lesions mature very slowly and by the seventh or eighth day the lesions are flat and appear to be buried in the skin. Unlike ordinary-type smallpox, the vesicles contain very little fluid, are soft and velvety to the touch, and may contain hemorrhages. Malignant smallpox is nearly always fatal.

Hemorrhagic

Hemorrhagic smallpox is a severe form of smallpox that is accompanied by extensive bleeding into the skin, mucous membranes, and gastrointestinal tract. This form developed in perhaps 2% of infections and occurred mostly in adults. In hemorrhagic smallpox the skin does not blister, but remains smooth. Instead, bleeding occurs under the skin, making the skin look charred and black, hence this form of the disease is also known as black pox.

In the early, or fulminating form, hemorrhaging appears on the second or third day as sub-conjunctival bleeding turns the whites of the eyes deep red. Hemorrhagic smallpox also produces a dusky erythema, petechiae, and hemorrhages in the spleen, kidney, serosa, muscle, and, rarely, the epicardium, liver, testes, ovaries and bladder. Death often occurs suddenly between the fifth and seventh days of illness, when only a few insignificant skin lesions are present. A later form of the disease occurs in patients who survive for 8–10 days.

The hemorrhages appear in the early eruptive period, and the rash is flat and does not progress beyond the vesicular stage. Patients in the early stage of disease show a decrease in coagulation factors (e.g. platelets, prothrombin, and globulin) and an increase in circulating antithrombin. Patients in the late stage have significant thrombocytopenia; however, deficiency of coagulation factors is less severe. Some in the late stage also show increased antithrombin. This form of smallpox occurs in anywhere from 3–25% of fatal cases depending on the virulence of the smallpox strain. Hemorrhagic smallpox is usually fatal.

Diagnosis

The clinical definition of smallpox is an illness with acute onset of fever greater than 101°F (38.3°C) followed by a rash characterized by firm, deep seated vesicles or pustules in the same stage of development without other apparent cause. If a clinical case is observed, smallpox is confirmed using laboratory tests.

Microscopically, poxviruses produce characteristic cytoplasmic inclusions, the most important of which are known as Guarnieri bodies, and are the sites of viral replication. Guarnieri bodies are readily identified in skin biopsies stained with hematoxylin and eosin, and appear as pink blobs. They are found in virtually all poxvirus infections and the absence of Guarnieri bodies cannot be used to rule out smallpox. The diagnosis of an orthopoxvirus infection can also be made rapidly by electron microscopic examination of pustular fluid or scabs. However, all orthopoxviruses exhibit identical brick-shaped virions by electron microscopy.

Definitive laboratory identification of variola virus involves growing the virus on chorioallantoic membrane (part of a chicken embryo) and examining the resulting pock lesions under defined temperature conditions. Strains may be characterized by polymerase chain reaction (PCR) and restriction fragment length polymorphism (RFLP) analysis. Serologic tests and enzyme linked immunosorbent assays (ELISA), which measure variola virus-specific immunoglobulin and antigen have also been developed to assist in the diagnosis of infection.

Chickenpox was commonly confused with smallpox in the immediate post-eradication era. Chickenpox and smallpox can be distinguished by several methods. Unlike smallpox, chickenpox does not usually affect the palms and soles. Additionally, chickenpox pustules are of varying size due to variations in the timing of pustule eruption: smallpox pustules are all very nearly the same size since the viral effect progresses more uniformly. A variety of laboratory methods are available for detecting chickenpox in evaluation of suspected smallpox cases.

Whooping Cough

Pertussis, also known as the *whooping cough*, is a highly contagious disease caused by the bacterium *Bordetella pertussis*; it derived its origin from the "whoop" sound made from the inspiration of air after a cough; a similar, milder disease is caused by *B. parapertussis*. Although many medical sources describe the whoop as "high-pitched", this is generally the case with infected babies and children only, not adults.

Worldwide, there are 10–90 million pertussis cases and about 600,000 deaths per year. Despite generally high coverage with the DTP and DTaP vaccines, pertussis is one of the leading causes of vaccine-preventable deaths world-wide. Sixty percent of all cases occur in the Third World. Canada is the only rich, industrial nation in which pertussis is still commonplace, though Australia saw a large increase in cases during a 2008/09 outbreak.

Characterization

After a ten-day incubation period, pertussis in infants and young children is characterized initially by mild respiratory infection symptoms such as coughing, sneezing, runny nose (catarrhal stage). After one to three weeks, the cough changes character, with an increase of coughing followed by a respiratory "whoop" sound (paroxysmal stage). Coughing fits may be followed by vomiting and slight inner ear inflammation due to the sheer violence of the fit.

In severe cases, the vomiting induced by coughing fits can lead to malnutrition and dehydration as well as nose bleeds. The fits that do not occur on their own can also be triggered by yawning, stretching, laughing or yelling. Triggering fits gradually diminish over one to three months during the convalescent stage. Complications of the disease include pneumonia, encephalitis, pulmonary hypertension, and secondary bacterial superinfection.

Transmission and Diagnosis

Adults and adolescents are the primary reservoir for pertussis. Pertussis is spread by contact with airborne discharges from the mucous membranes of infected people, who are most contagious during the catarrhal stage.

Because the symptoms during the catarrhal stage are nonspecific, pertussis is usually not diagnosed until the appearance of the characteristic cough of the paroxysmal stage. Methods used in laboratory diagnosis include culturing of nasopharyngeall swabs on Bordet-Gengoul medium, polymerase chain reaction (PCR), immunofluorescence (DFA), and serological methods.

The bacteria can be recovered from the patient only during the first three weeks of illness, rendering culturing and DFA useless after this period, although PCR may have some limited usefulness for an additional three weeks. For most adults and adolescents, who often do not seek medical care until several weeks into their illness, serology is often used to determine whether antibody against pertussis toxin or another component of *B. pertussis* is present at high levels in the blood of the patient.

Treatment

Treatment with an effective antibiotic (erythromycin or azithromycin) shortens the infectious period but does not generally alter the outcome of the disease; however, when treatment is initiated during the catarrhal stage, symptoms may be less severe. Three macrolides (erythromycin, azithromycin and clarithromycin) are used in the U.S. for treatment of pertussis; trimethoprim-sulfamethoxazole is generally used when a macrolide is ineffective or is contraindicated.

Close contacts who receive appropriate antibiotics (*chemoprophylaxis*) during the 7–21 day incubation period may be protected from developing symptomatic disease. Close contacts are defined as anyone coming into contact with the respiratory secretions of an infected person in the 21 days before or after the infected person's cough began.

Isolation and Identification

B. pertussis was isolated in pure culture in 1906 by Jules Bordet and Octave Gengou, who also developed the first serology and vaccine. The complete B. pertussis genome of 4,086,186 base pairs was sequenced in 2002.

Vaccines

History of Pertussis Vaccine Development

Infection with pertussis induces immunity, but not lasting protective immunity, and a second attack is possible. Efforts to develop an inactivated whole-cell pertussis vaccine began soon after *B. pertussis* was grown in pure culture in 1906. In the 1920s Dr. Louis Sauer developed a vaccine for whooping cough at Evanston Hospital (Chicago, IL). In 1925, the Danish physician Thorvald Madsen was the first to test a whole-cell pertussis vaccine on a wide scale. He used the vaccine to control outbreaks in the Faroe Islands in the North Sea. In 1942, the American scientist Pearl Kendrick combined the whole-cell pertussis vaccine with diphtheria and tetanus toxoids to generate the first DTP combination vaccine. To minimize the frequent side effects caused by the pertussis component of the vaccine, the Japanese scientist Yuji Sato developed an acellular pertussis vaccine consisting of purified haemagglutinins (HAs: filamentous HA and leucocytosis-promoting-factor HA), which are secreted by *B. pertussis* into the culture medium. Sato's acellular pertussis vaccine was used in Japan since the autumn of 1981. Later versions of the acellular pertussis vaccine used in other countries consisted of additional defined components of *B. pertussis* and were often part of the DTaP combination vaccine.

Current Status of Pertussis Vaccines

Pertussis vaccines are highly effective, strongly recommended, and save many infant lives every year. Though the protection they offer lasts only a few years, they are given so that immunity lasts through childhood, the time of greatest exposure and greatest risk. The immunizations are given in combination with tetanus, diphtheria, polio and haemophilus influenzae type B immunizations, at ages 2, 3, and 4 months, and a later booster at 3 years and 4 months or soon after.

The short-term effectiveness of the vaccines and the presence of *B. pertussis* infection in adults and adolescents who may transmit the bacteria to infants have caused many in the medical field to call for booster immunizations at later ages. Although Canada, France, the U.S. and Germany now have approved booster shots for adolescents, adults, or both, other countries adhere to the tradition of discontinuing pertussis vaccination after the age of seven, from concerns that there are side effects associated with the first available "whole-cell" pertussis immunizations that tended to increase with age. The whole-cell vaccine is still used in poor countries, because it is cheaper than the newer and safer acellular formulation.

Whereas the immunity from infection or vaccination lasts only a few years, the discontinuation of booster vaccination in older persons caused the emergence of a large pool of older persons lacking immunity, followed by an increase of adult-onset pertussis that accelerated beginning in about 2004.

This burgeoning outbreak is predicted to increasingly infect adults and adolescents with debilitating cases, but poses even more serious public health dangers to newborns. As adolescent and adult cases surge, newborns are again at risk of exposure to pertussis circulating in adolescents or adults in the community before the infants' vaccinations can be completed.

The decision to resume vaccinating teens and adults reflects in part that the newer acellular vaccine, known as DTaP, has greatly reduced the incidence of adverse effects observed with the earlier "whole-cell" pertussis vaccine. An acellular vaccine preparation for adults and adolescents has been approved in Canada, Europe, and the United States. In the U.S., the Food and Drug Administration has authorized both the use of the vaccines Boostrix (GlaxoSmithKline) for 10-18 year olds in May 2005, with an expanded indication to age 64 in December 2008, and Adacel (Sanofi Pasteur) for 11-64 year olds in August 2005. These vaccines are recommended for all teens and adults within the indicated age ranges, except for those with a history of adverse reaction to the whole-cell pertussis vaccines. The most serious side-effects of traditional "whole-cell" pertussis immunizations were neurological: and included seizures and hypotonic episodes.

Whole-cell Pertussis Vaccine Controversy

Much of the controversy surrounding the DTP vaccine in the 1970s and 1980s related to the question of whether the whole-cell pertussis component caused permanent brain injury in rare cases. Although it was well-established that the pertussis component of the DTP vaccine accounted for most of the minor local and systemic side effects in many vaccinated infants, several published studies failed to show a causal relationship between administration of the DTP vaccine and permanent brain injury. However, criticism of these studies and well-publicized anecdotal reports of DTP-induced permanent disability and death gave rise to anti-DTP movements. In addition, a number of children suffered allergic reactions to the pertussis vaccination, including severe seizures. Despite this, doctors recommended the vaccine, and even threatened to report parents who refused to vaccinate their children.

By the late 1970s, publicity about adverse reactions and deaths following pertussis vaccination caused the immunization rate to fall in several countries, including Great Britain, Sweden, and Japan. In many cases, a dramatic increase in the incidence of pertussis followed. These developments led Yuji Sato to introduce a safer acellular version of the pertussis vaccine for Japan in 1981. Nevertheless, other countries continued to use the whole-cell DTP formulation.

In the United States, low profit margins and an increase in vaccine-related lawsuits led many manufacturers to stop producing the DTP vaccine by the early 1980s. In 1982, the television documentary "DTP: Vaccine Roulette" depicted the lives of children whose severe disabilities were blamed on the DTP vaccine. The negative publicity generated by the documentary led to a tremendous increase in the number of lawsuits filed against vaccine manufacturers. By 1985, manufacturers of vaccines had difficulty obtaining liability insurance. The price of the DTP vaccine skyrocketed, leading to shortages around the country. Only one manufacturer of the DPT vaccine remained in the U.S. by the end of 1985. To avert a vaccine crisis, Congress in 1986 passed the National Childhood Vaccine Injury Act (NCVIA), which established a federal no-fault system to compensate victims of injury caused by mandated vaccines. The majority of claims that have been filed through the NCVIA have been related to injuries allegedly caused by the whole-cell DTP vaccine. The acellular pertussis vaccine was approved in the United States in 1992 for use in the combination DTaP vaccine. Research has shown the acellular vaccine to be safer, with fewer reports of adverse effects. Although the whole-cell DTP vaccine is no longer used in the United States, it is still purchased by the World Health Organization and distributed to developing nations because of its much reduced cost compared to the acellular DTaP vaccine.

Epidemiology

Before vaccines, an average of 157 cases per 100,000 persons were reported in the U.S., with peaks reported every two to five years; more than 93% of reported cases occurred in children under 10 years of age. The actual incidence was likely much higher. After vaccinations were introduced in the 1940s, incidence fell dramatically to less than 1 per 100,000 by 1970. Incidence rates have increased somewhat since 1980. Pertussis is the only vaccine-preventable disease that is associated with increasing deaths in the U.S. The number of deaths increased from 4 in 1996 to 17 in 2001, almost all of which were infants under one year. Despite heavy vaccination efforts and universal health care, Canada remains as the only rich, industrialized nation in which pertussis is endemic, with 7,000 cases each year.

AIDS : Symptoms—Causes and Prevention

Acquired immune deficiency syndrome or acquired immunodeficiency syndrome (AIDS) is a disease of the human immune system caused by the human immunodeficiency virus (HIV).

This condition progressively reduces the effectiveness of the immune system and leaves individuals susceptible to opportunistic infections and tumors. HIV is transmitted through direct contact of a mucous membrane or the bloodstream with a bodily fluid containing HIV, such as blood, semen, vaginal fluid, preseminal fluid, and breast milk.

This transmission can involve anal, vaginal or oral sex, blood transfusion, contaminated hypodermic needles, exchange between mother and baby during pregnancy, childbirth, or breastfeeding, or other exposure to one of the above bodily fluids.

AIDS is now a pandemic. In 2007, it was estimated that 33.2 million people lived with the disease worldwide, and that AIDS had killed an estimated 2.1 million people, including 330,000 children. Over three-quarters of these deaths occurred in sub-Saharan Africa, retarding economic growth and destroying human capital.

Genetic research indicates that HIV originated in west-central Africa during the late nineteenth or early twentieth century. AIDS was first recognized by the U.S. Centers for Disease Control and Prevention in 1981 and its cause, HIV, identified in the early 1980s.

Although treatments for AIDS and HIV can slow the course of the disease, there is currently no vaccine or cure. Antiretroviral treatment reduces both the mortality and the morbidity of HIV infection, but these drugs are expensive and routine access to antiretroviral medication is not available in all countries. Due to the difficulty in treating HIV infection, preventing infection is a key aim in controlling the AIDS epidemic, with health organizations promoting safe sex and needle-exchange programmes in attempts to slow the spread of the virus.

Symptoms

The symptoms of AIDS are primarily the result of conditions that do not normally develop in individuals with healthy immune systems. Most of these conditions are infections caused by bacteria, viruses, fungi and parasites that are normally controlled by the elements of the immune system that HIV damages.

Opportunistic infections are common in people with AIDS. HIV affects nearly every organ system.

People with AIDS also have an increased risk of developing various cancers such as Kaposi's sarcoma, cervical cancer and cancers of the immune system known as lymphomas. Additionally, people with AIDS often have systemic symptoms of infection like fevers, sweats (particularly at night), swollen glands, chills, weakness, and weight loss. The specific opportunistic infections that AIDS patients develop depend in part on the prevalence of these infections in the geographic area in which the patient lives.

Pulmonary Infections

Pneumocystis pneumonia (originally known as *Pneumocystis carinii* pneumonia, and still abbreviated as PCP, which now stands for Pneumocystis pneumonia) is relatively rare in healthy, immunocompetent people, but common among HIV-infected individuals. It is caused by *Pneumocystis jirovecii*.

Before the advent of effective diagnosis, treatment and routine prophylaxis in Western countries, it was a common immediate cause of death. In developing countries, it is still one of the first indications of AIDS in untested individuals, although it does not generally occur unless the CD4 count is less than 200 cells per µL of blood.

Tuberculosis (TB) is unique among infections associated with HIV because it is transmissible to immunocompetent people via the respiratory route, is easily treatable once identified, may occur in early-stage HIV disease, and is preventable with drug therapy. However, multidrug resistance is a potentially serious problem.

Even though its incidence has declined because of the use of directly observed therapy and other improved practices in Western countries, this is not the case in developing countries where HIV is most prevalent. In early-stage HIV infection (CD4 count >300 cells per µL), TB typically presents as a pulmonary disease. In advanced HIV infection, TB often presents atypically with extrapulmonary (systemic) disease a common feature. Symptoms are usually constitutional and are not localized to one particular site, often affecting bone marrow, bone, urinary and gastrointestinal tracts, liver, regional lymph nodes, and the central nervous system.

Gastrointestinal Infections

Esophagitis is an inflammation of the lining of the lower end of the esophagus (gullet or swallowing tube leading to the stomach). In HIV infected individuals, this is normally due to fungal (candidiasis) or viral (herpes simplex-1 or cytomegalovirus) infections. In rare cases, it could be due to mycobacteria.

Unexplained chronic diarrhea in HIV infection is due to many possible causes, including common bacterial (*Salmonella*, *Shigella*, *Listeria* or *Campylobacter*) and parasitic infections; and uncommon opportunistic infections such as cryptosporidiosis, microsporidiosis, *Mycobacterium avium* complex (MAC) and viruses, astrovirus, adenovirus, rotavirus and cytomegalovirus, (the latter as a course of colitis).

In some cases, diarrhea may be a side effect of several drugs used to treat HIV, or it may simply accompany HIV infection, particularly during primary HIV infection. It may also be a side effect of antibiotics used to treat bacterial causes of diarrhea (common for *Clostridium difficile*). In the later stages of HIV infection, diarrhea is thought to be a reflection of changes in the way the intestinal tract absorbs nutrients, and may be an important component of HIV-related wasting.

Neurological and Psychiatric Involvement

HIV infection may lead to a variety of neuropsychiatric sequelae, either by infection of the now susceptible nervous system by organisms, or as a direct consequence of the illness itself.

Toxoplasmosis is a disease caused by the single-celled parasite called *Toxoplasma gondii*; it usually infects the brain, causing toxoplasma encephalitis, but it can also infect and cause disease in the eyes and lungs. Cryptococcal meningitis is an infection of the meninx (the membrane covering the brain and spinal cord) by the fungus *Cryptococcus neoformans*. It can cause fevers, headache, fatigue, nausea, and vomiting. Patients may also develop seizures and confusion; left untreated, it can be lethal.

Progressive multifocal leukoencephalopathy (PML) is a demyelinating disease, in which the gradual destruction of the myelin sheath covering the axons of nerve cells impairs the transmission of nerve impulses. It is caused by a virus called JC virus which occurs in 70% of the population in latent form, causing disease only when the immune system has been severely weakened, as is the case for AIDS patients. It progresses rapidly, usually causing death within months of diagnosis.

AIDS dementia complex (ADC) is a metabolic encephalopathy induced by HIV infection and fueled by immune activation of HIV infected brain macrophages and microglia These cells are productively infected by HIV and secrete neurotoxins of both host and viral origin. Specific neurological impairments are manifested by cognitive, behavioral, and motor abnormalities that occur after years of HIV infection and are associated with low CD4 T cell levels and high plasma viral loads.

Prevalence is 10–20% in Western countries but only 1–2% of HIV infections in India. This difference is possibly due to the HIV subtype in India. AIDS related mania is sometimes seen in patients with advanced HIV illness; it presents with more irritability and cognitive impairment and less euphoria than a manic episode associated with true bipolar disorder. Unlike the latter condition, it may have a more chronic course. This syndrome is less often seen with the advent of multi-drug therapy.

Tumors and Malignancies

Patients with HIV infection have substantially increased incidence of several cancers. This is primarily due to co-infection with an oncogenic DNA virus, especially Epstein-Barr virus (EBV), Kaposi's sarcoma-associated herpesvirus (KSHV), and human papillomavirus (HPV).

Kaposi's sarcoma (KS) is the most common tumor in HIV-infected patients. The appearance of this tumor in young homosexual men in 1981 was one of the first signals of the AIDS epidemic. Caused by a gammaherpes virus called Kaposi's sarcoma-associated herpes virus (KSHV), it often appears as purplish nodules on the skin, but can affect other organs, especially the mouth, gastrointestinal tract, and lungs.

High-grade B cell lymphomas such as Burkitt's lymphoma, Burkitt's-like lymphoma, diffuse large B-cell lymphoma (DLBCL), and primary central nervous system lymphoma present more often in HIV-infected patients. These particular cancers often foreshadow a poor prognosis. In some cases these lymphomas are AIDS-defining. Epstein-Barr virus (EBV) or KSHV cause many of these lymphomas.

Cervical cancer in HIV-infected women is considered AIDS-defining. It is caused by human papillomavirus (HPV).

In addition to the AIDS-defining tumors listed above, HIV-infected patients are at increased risk of certain other tumors, such as Hodgkin's disease and anal and rectal carcinomas. However, the incidence of many common tumors, such as breast cancer or colon cancer, does not increase in HIV-infected patients. In areas where HAART is extensively used to treat AIDS, the incidence of many AIDS-related malignancies has decreased, but at the same time malignant cancers overall have become the most common cause of death of HIV-infected patients.

Other Opportunistic Infections

AIDS patients often develop opportunistic infections that present with non-specific symptoms, especially low-grade fevers and weight loss. These include infection with *Mycobacterium avium-intracellulare* and cytomegalovirus (CMV). CMV can cause colitis, as described above, and CMV retinitis can cause blindness.

Penicilliosis due to *Penicillium marneffei* is now the third most common opportunistic infection (after extrapulmonary tuberculosis and cryptococcosis) in HIV-positive individuals within the endemic area of Southeast Asia.

Cause

AIDS is the most severe acceleration of infection with HIV. HIV is a retrovirus that primarily infects vital organs of the human immune system such as CD4 T cells (a subset of T cells), macrophages and dendritic cells. It directly and indirectly destroys CD4 T cells.

Once HIV has killed so many CD4 T cells that there are fewer than 200 of these cells per microliter (µL) of blood, cellular immunity is lost. Acute HIV infection progresses over time to clinical latent HIV infection and then to early symptomatic HIV infection and later to AIDS, which is identified either on the basis of the amount of CD4 T cells remaining in the blood, and/or the presence of certain infections, as noted above.

In the absence of antiretroviral therapy, the median time of progression from HIV infection to AIDS is nine to ten years, and the median survival time after developing AIDS is only 9.2 months. However, the rate of clinical disease progression varies widely between individuals, from two weeks up to 20 years.

Many factors affect the rate of progression. These include factors that influence the body's ability to defend against HIV such as the infected person's general immune function. Older people have weaker immune systems, and therefore have a greater risk of rapid disease progression than younger people.

Poor access to health care and the existence of coexisting infections such as tuborculosis also may predispose people to faster disease progression. The infected person's genetic inheritance plays an important role and some people are resistant to certain strains of HIV. An example of this is people with the homozygous CCR5-Ä32 variation are resistant to infection with certain strains of HIV. HIV is genetically variable and exists as different strains, which cause different rates of clinical disease progression.

Sexual Transmission

Sexual transmission occurs with the contact between sexual secretions of one person with the rectal, genital or oral mucous membranes of another. Unprotected receptive sexual acts are riskier than unprotected insertive sexual acts, and the risk for transmitting HIV through unprotected anal intercourse is greater than the risk from vaginal intercourse or oral sex.

However, oral sex is not entirely safe, as HIV can be transmitted through both insertive and receptive oral sex. Sexual assault greatly increases the risk of HIV transmission as condoms are rarely employed and physical trauma to the vagina occurs frequently, facilitating the transmission of HIV.

Other sexually transmitted infections (STI) increase the risk of HIV transmission and infection, because they cause the disruption of the normal epithelial barrier by genital ulceration and/or microulceration; and by accumulation of pools of HIV-susceptible or HIV-infected cells (lymphocytes and macrophages) in semen and vaginal secretions. Epidemiological studies from sub-Saharan Africa, Europe and North America suggest that genital ulcers, such as those caused by syphilis and/or chancroid, increase the risk of becoming infected with HIV by about fourfold. There is also a significant although lesser increase in risk from STIs such as gonorrhea, chlamydia and trichomoniasis, which all cause local accumulations of lymphocytes and macrophages.

Transmission of HIV depends on the infectiousness of the index case and the susceptibility of the uninfected partner. Infectivity seems to vary during the course of illness and is not constant between individuals. An undetectable plasma viral load does not necessarily indicate a low viral load in the seminal liquid or genital secretions.

However, each 10-fold increase in the level of HIV in the blood is associated with an 81% increased rate of HIV transmission. Women are more susceptible to HIV-1 infection due to hormonal changes, vaginal microbial ecology and physiology, and a higher prevalence of sexually transmitted diseases.

People who have been infected with one strain of HIV can still be infected later on in their lives by other, more virulent strains.

Infection is unlikely in a single encounter. High rates of infection have been linked to a pattern of overlapping long-term sexual relationships. This allows the virus to quickly spread to multiple partners who in turn infect their partners. A pattern of serial monogamy or occasional casual encounters is associated with lower rates of infection.

HIV spreads readily through heterosexual sex in Africa, but less so elsewhere. One possibility being researched is that schistosomiasis, which affects up to 50 per cent of women in parts of Africa, damages the lining of the vagina.

Exposure to Blood-borne Pathogens

This transmission route is particularly relevant to intravenous drug users, hemophiliacs and recipients of blood transfusions and blood products. Sharing and reusing syringes contaminated with HIV-infected blood represents a major risk for infection with HIV.

Needle sharing is the cause of one third of all new HIV-infections in North America, China, and Eastern Europe. The risk of being infected with HIV from a single prick with a needle that has been used on an HIV-infected person is thought to be about 1 in 150 (see table above). Post-exposure prophylaxis with anti-HIV drugs can further reduce this risk.

This route can also affect people who give and receive tattoos and piercings. Universal precautions are frequently not followed in both sub-Saharan Africa and much of Asia because of both a shortage of supplies and inadequate training.

The WHO estimates that approximately 2.5% of all HIV infections in sub-Saharan Africa are transmitted through unsafe healthcare injections. Because of this, the United Nations General Assembly has urged the nations of the world to implement precautions to prevent HIV transmission by health workers.

The risk of transmitting HIV to blood transfusion recipients is extremely low in developed countries where improved donor selection and HIV screening is performed. However, according to the WHO, the overwhelming majority of the world's population does not have access to safe blood and between 5% and 10% of the world's HIV infections come from transfusion of infected blood and blood products.

Perinatal Transmission

The transmission of the virus from the mother to the child can occur *in utero* during the last weeks of pregnancy and at childbirth. In the absence of treatment, the transmission rate between a mother and her child during pregnancy, labour and delivery is 25%. However, when the mother takes antiretroviral therapy and gives birth by caesarean section, the rate of transmission is just 1%. The risk of infection is influenced by the viral load of the mother at birth, with the higher the viral load, the higher the risk. Breastfeeding also increases the risk of transmission by about 4 %.

Misconceptions

A number of misconceptions have arisen surrounding HIV/AIDS. Three of the most common are that AIDS can spread through casual contact, that sexual intercourse with a virgin will cure AIDS, and that HIV can infect only homosexual men and drug users. Other misconceptions are that any act of anal intercourse between gay men can lead to AIDS infection, and that open discussion of homosexuality and HIV in schools will lead to increased rates of homosexuality and AIDS.

Common Athletic Injuries

Below are just a few of the injuries most commonly experienced by sports participants. Provided is a brief summary of the injury, possible causes that result in that injury, as well as signs and symptoms to expect when experiencing that particular injury.

Strains

Muscle strains are one of the more common injuries experienced by individuals playing sports. Having a basic understanding of the structural make-up, cause of injury, and appropriate treatment of muscle strains can help an athlete return to the playing field efficiently and safely.

Description: Muscle strains refers to damage that can occur to a muscle or its attaching tendons. Muscle damage can be in the form of tearing (part or all) of the muscle fibers and the tendons attached to the muscle. The tearing of the muscle can also damage small blood vessels, causing local bleeding (bruising) and pain.

Cause of Injury: Strains or pulls can be caused by various mechanisms such as overstretching, overstressing, a violent contraction against heavy resistance, a strength imbalance between muscles, or an abnormal muscle contraction.

Signs & Symptoms

Grade I: Most common type of sprain. It results in a mild stretching of the anterior talofibular ligament. Mild pain and disability occur. Athlete is able to walk on ankle with minimal impairment. Signs are point tenderness and swelling over this ligament with no joint laxity.

Grade II: This indicates the possibility of a complete tear of the talofibular ligament and a stretch or tear of the calcaneofibular ligament. Athlete usually hears or feels a pop or snap on the outside of the ankle. There is moderate pain and disability and bearing weight on ankle is difficult. This injury degree can produce a persistently unstable ankle that recurrently becomes sprained and later develops into traumatic arthritis.

Grade III: These injuries are relatively uncommon in sports. This classification indicates that the ankle joint has slid partly out of joint but slid back in. This is called subluxation. Injury to all three key lateral (outside) ankle ligaments is suspected along with damage to the joint itself. Pain is felt over the outside ankle bone (lateral malleolus). Bearing weight on the ankle is impossible due to pain and swelling. Immediate bruising maybe present around the ankle.

Sprain

A sprain (from the French *espraindre*-to wring) is an injury which occurs to ligaments caused by being stretched beyond their normal capacity and possibly torn. Muscular tears caused in the same manner are referred to as a strain. In cases where either ligament or muscle tissue is torn, immobilization and surgical repair may be necessary.

Degrees

Although some signs and symptoms can be used to assess the severity of a sprain, the most definitive method is with the use of Magnetic Resonance Imaging (MRI). Sprains are graded in five degrees.

- The *first* degree is only a minor tear or stretch of a ligament.
- The *second* degree is a tear of a ligament, which is usually followed by pain or swelling
- The *third* degree is a complete rupture.
- The *fourth* degree breaks the ligament, along with some small bones if severe enough, and requires surgery to repair.
- The *fifth* degree tears all the ligaments and actually breaks all the surrounding bones; sometimes cannot be repaired and results in amputation.

Joints Involved

Although any joint can experience a sprain, some of the more common include:

- the ankle. It is the most common, and has been said that sprains such as serious ankle sprains are more painful and take longer to heal than actually breaking the bones in that area.
- the knee. Perhaps one of the more talked about sprains is that to the anterior cruciate ligament (ACL) of the knee. This is a disabling sprain common to athletes, especially in basketball, football, pole vaulting, and judo. See Anterior cruciate ligament injury.
- the fingers.
- the wrist.
- the toes.

Treatment

The first modality for a sprain can be remembered using the acronym R.I.C.E.

- *Rest:* The sprain should be rested. No additional force should be applied on site of the sprain. If, for example, the sprain were an ankle sprain, then walking should be kept to a minimum.
- *Ice:* Ice should be applied immediately to the sprain to minimize swelling and ease pain. It can be applied for 20-30 minutes at a time, 3-4 times a day. Ice can be combined with a wrapping to minimize swelling and provide support.
- *Compression:* Dressings, bandages, or ace-wraps should be used to immobilize the sprain and provide support.
- *Elevation:* Keeping the sprained joint elevated above heart level will also help to minimize swelling.

Ice and compression (cold compression therapy) will not completely stop swelling and pain, but will help to minimize them as the sprain begins to heal itself. Careful management of swelling is critical to the healing process as additional fluid may pool in the sprained area.

Contusion

Contusion a form of traumatic brain injury, is a bruise of the brain tissue. Like bruises in other tissues, cerebral contusion can be associated with multiple microhemorrhages, small blood vessel leaks into brain tissue. Contusion occurs in 20–30% of severe head injuries. A cerebral laceration is a similar injury except that, according to their respective definitions, the pia-arachnoid membranes are torn over the site of injury in laceration and are not torn in contusion. The injury can cause a decline in mental function in the long term and in the emergency setting may result in brain herniation, a life-threatening condition in which parts of the brain are squeezed past parts of the skull. Thus treatment aims to prevent dangerous rises in intracranial pressure, the pressure within the skull.

Contusions are likely to heal on their own without medical intervention.

- Signs and symptoms
- Causes
- Features
- Multiple petechial hemorrhages
- Treatment
- References

Signs and Symptoms

Contusion can present with weakness, lack of motor coordination, numbness, aphasia, and memory and cognitive problems. Signs depend on the contusion's location in the brain.

Causes

Often caused by a blow to the head, contusions commonly occur in coup or contre-coup injuries. In coup injuries, the brain is injured directly under the area of impact, while in contrecoup injuries it is injured on the side opposite the impact.

Contusions occur primarily in the cortical tissue, especially under the site of impact or in areas of the brain located near sharp ridges on the inside of the skull. The brain may be contused when it collides with bony protuberances on the inside surface of the skull. The protuberances are located on the inside of the skull under the frontal and temporal lobes and on the roof of the ocular orbit. Thus, the tips of the frontal and temporal lobes located near the bony ridges in the skull are areas where contusions frequently occur and are most severe. For this reason, attention, emotional and memory problems, which are associated with damage to frontal and temporal lobes, are much more common in head trauma survivors than are syndromes associated with damage to other areas of the brain.

Features

Contusions, which are frequently associated with edema, are especially likely to cause increases in intracranial pressure (ICP) and concomitant crushing of delicate brain tissue.

Contusions typically form in a wedge-shape with the widest part in the outermost part of the brain.

The distinction between contusion and intracerebral hemorrhage is blurry because both involve bleeding within the brain tissue; however, an arbitrary cutoff exists that the injury is a contusion if two thirds or less of the tissue involved is blood and a hemorrhage otherwise.

The contusion may cause swelling of the surrounding brain tissue, which may be irritated by toxins released in the contusion. The swelling is worst at around four to six days after the injury.

Extensive contusion associated with subdural hematoma is called burst lobe. Cases of a burst frontal or temporal lobe are associated with high mortality and morbidity.

Old or remote contusions are associated with resorption of the injured tissue, resulting in various degrees of cavitation, in addition to the presence of a golden-yellow discoloration due to residual hemosiderin. These remote contusions are often referred to as *plaque jaune* or yellow plaque.

Multiple Petechial Hemorrhages

Numerous small contusions from broken capillaries that occur in grey matter under the cortex are called multiple petechial hemorrhages or multifocal hemorrhagic contusion. Caused by shearing injuries at the time of impact, these contusions occur especially at the junction between grey and white matter and in the upper brain stem, basal ganglia, thalamus and areas near the third ventricle.

The hemorrhages can occur as the result of brain herniation, which can cause arteries to tear and bleed. A type of diffuse brain injury, multiple petechial hemorrhages are not always visible using current imaging techniques like CT and MRI scans. This may be the case even if the injury is quite severe, though these may show up days after the injury. Hemorrhages may be larger than in normal contusions if the injury is quite severe. This type of injury has a poor prognosis if the patient is comatose, even with no apparent causes for the coma.

Treatment

Since cerebral swelling presents a danger to the patient, treatment of cerebral contusion aims to prevent swelling. Measures to avoid swelling include prevention of hypotension (low blood pressure), hyponatremia (insufficient sodium), and hypercapnia (excess carbon dioxide in the blood). Due to the danger of increased intracranial pressure, surgery may be necessary to reduce it. People with cerebral contusion may require intensive care and close monitoring.

Laceration

Laceration is a chest injury in which lung tissue is torn or cut. An injury that is potentially more serious than pulmonary contusion, pulmonary laceration involves disruption of the architecture of the lung, while pulmonary contusion does not. Pulmonary laceration is commonly caused by penetrating trauma but may also result from forces involved in blunt trauma such as shear stress. A cavity filled with blood, air, or both can form. The injury is diagnosed when collections of air or fluid are found on a CT scan of the chest. Surgery may be required to stitch the laceration, to drain blood, or even to remove injured parts of the lung. The injury commonly heals quickly with few problems if it is given proper treatment; however it may be associated with scarring of the lung or other complications.

Causes

Pulmonary laceration is a common result of penetrating trauma but may also be caused by blunt trauma; broken ribs may perforate the lung, or the tissue may be torn due to shearing forces that result from different rates of acceleration or deceleration of different tissues of the lung. Violent compression of the chest can cause lacerations by rupturing or shearing the lung tissue. Pulmonary laceration may result from blunt and penetrating forces that occur in the same injury and may be associated with pulmonary contusion. Lacerations of the lung tissue can also occur by compression of the alveoli agaist the ribs or spine. As with contusions, pulmonary lacerations usually occur near solid structures in the chest such as ribs. Pulmonary laceration is suspected when rib fractures are present.

Classification

In 1988, a group led by R.B. Wagner divided pulmonary lacerations into four types based on the manner in which the person was injured and indications found on a CT scan. In type 1 lacerations, which occur in the mid lung area, the air-filled lung bursts as a result of sudden compression of the chest. Also called compression-rupture lacerations, type 1 are the most common type and usually occur in a central location of the lung. They tend to be large, ranging in size from 2–8 cm. The shearing stress in type 2 results when the lower chest is suddenly compressed and the lower lung is suddenly moved across the vertebral bodies. Type 2, also called compression-shear, tends to occur near the spine and have an elongated shape. Type 2 lacerations usually occur in younger people with more flexible chests. Type 3, which are caused by punctures from fractured ribs, occur in the area near the chest wall underlying the broken rib. Also called rib penetration lacerations, type 3 lacerations tend to be small and accompanied by pneumothorax. Commonly, more than one type 3 laceration will occur. Type 4, also called adhesion tears, occur in cases where a pleuropulmonary adhesion had formed prior to the injury, in which the chest wall is suddenly fractured or pushed inwards. They occur in the subpleural area and result from shearing forces at sites of transpleural adhesion.

Pathophysiology

A pulmonary laceration can cause air to leak out of the lacerated lung and into the pleural space, if the laceration goes through to it. Pulmonary laceration invariably results in pneumothorax (due to torn airways), hemothorax (due to torn blood vessels), or a hemopneumothorax (with both blood and air in the chest cavity). Unlike hemothoraces that occur due to pulmonary contusion, those due to lung laceration may be large and long lasting. However, the lungs do not usually bleed very much because the blood vessels involved are small and the pressure within them is low. Therefore, pneumothorax is usually more of a problem than hemothorax. A pneumothorax may form or be turned into a tension pneumothorax by mechanical ventilation, which may force air out of the tear in the lung.

The laceration may also close up by itself, which can cause it to trap blood and potentially form a cyst or hematoma. Because the lung is elastic, the tear forms a round cyst called a *traumatic air cyst* that may be filled with air, blood, or both and that usually shrinks over a period of weeks or months. Lacerations that are filled with air are called pneumatoceles, and those that are filled with blood are called pulmonary hematomas. In some cases, both pneumatoceles and hematomas exist in the same injured lung. A pneumatocele can become enlarged, for example when the patient is mechanically ventilated or has acute respiratory distress syndrome, in which case it may not go away for months. Pulmonary hematomas take longer to heal than simple pneumatoceles and commonly leave the lungs scarred.

Over time, the walls of lung lacerations tend to grow thicker due to edema and bleeding at the edges.

Diagnosis

Pulmonary laceration may not be visible using chest X-ray because an associated pulmonary contusion or hemorrhage may mask it. As the lung contusion clears (usually within two to four days), lacerations begin to become visible on chest X-ray. CT scanning is more sensitive and better at detecting pulmonary laceration than X-rays are, and often reveals multiple lacerations in cases where chest X-ray showed only a contusion. Before CT scanning was widely available, pulmonary laceration was considered unusual because it was not common to find with X-ray alone. On a CT scan, pulmonary lacerations show up in a contused area of the lung, typically appearing as cavities filled with air or fluid that usually have a round or ovoid shape due to the lung's elasticity.

Hematomas appear on chest radiographs as smooth masses that are round or ovoid in shape. Like lacerations, hematomas may initially be hidden on X-ray by lung contusions, but they become more apparent as the contusion begins to heal. Pneumatoceles have a similar shape to that of hematomas but have thin, smooth walls. Lacerations may be filled completely with blood, completely with air, or partially with both. Lacerations filled with both blood and air display a distinctive air-fluid level. A single laceration may occur by itself, or many may be present, creating an appearance like Swiss cheese in the radiography of the lung.

Pulmonary laceration is usually accompanied by hemoptysis (coughing up blood or of blood-stained sputum).

Thoracoscopy may be used in both diagnosis and treatment of pulmonary laceration.

A healing laceration may resemble a pulmonary nodule on radiographs, but unlike pulmonary nodules, lacerations decrease in size over time on radiographs.

Treatment

As with other chest injuries such as pulmonary contusion, hemothorax, and pneumothorax, pulmonary laceration can often be treated with just supplemental oxygen, ventilation, and drainage of fluids from the chest cavity. A thoracostomy tube can be used to remove blood and air from the chest cavity. About 5% of cases require surgery, called thoracotomy. Thoracotomy is especially likely to be needed if a lung fails to re-expand; if pneumothorax, bleeding, or coughing up blood persist; or in order to remove clotted blood from a homothorax. Surgical treatment includes suturing, stapling, oversewing, and wedging out of the laceration. Occasionally, surgeons must perform a lobectomy, in which a lobe of the lung is removed, or a pneumonectomy, in which an entire lung is removed.

Prognosis

Full recovery is common with proper treatment. Pulmonary laceration usually heals quickly after a chest tube is inserted and is usually not associated with major long-term problems. Pulmonary lacerations usually heal within three to five weeks, and lacerations filled with air will commonly heal within one to three weeks but on occasion take longer. However, the injury often takes weeks or months to heal, and the lung may be scarred. Small pulmonary lacerations frequently heal by themselves if material is removed from the pleural space, but surgery may be required for larger lacerations that do not heal properly or that bleed.

Complications

Complications are not common but include infection, pulmonary abscess, and bronchopleural fistula (a fistula between the pleural space and the bronchial tree). A bronchopleural fistula results when there is a communication between the laceration, a bronchiole, and the pleura; it can cause air to leak into the pleural space despite the placement of a chest tube. The laceration can also enlarge, as may occur when the injury creates a valve that allows air to enter the laceration, progressively expanding it.

One complication, air embolism, in which air enters the bloodstream, is potentially fatal, especially when it occurs on the left side of the heart. Air can enter the circulatory system through a damaged vein in the injured chest and can travel to any organ; it is especially deadly in the heart or brain. Positive pressure ventilation can cause pulmonary embolism by forcing air out of injured lungs and into blood vessels.

Fracture

A fracture is the (local) separation of an object or material into two, or more, pieces under the action of stress.

The word *fracture* is often applied to bones of living creatures, or to crystals or crystalline materials, such as gemstones or metal. Sometimes, in crystalline materials, individual crystals fracture without the body actually separating into two or more pieces. Depending on the substance which is fractured, a fracture reduces strength (most substances) or inhibits transmission of light (optical crystals).

A detailed understanding of how fracture occurs in materials may be assisted by the study of fracture mechanics.

Types of Fracture

Brittle Fracture

In *brittle fracture*, no apparent plastic deformation takes place before fracture. In brittle crystalline materials, fracture can occur by *cleavage* as the result of tensile stress acting normal to crystallographic planes with low bonding (cleavage planes). In amorphous solids, by contrast, the lack of a crystalline structure results in a conchoidal fracture, with cracks proceeding normal to the applied tension.

The theoretical strength of a crystalline material is (roughly) where:-

E is the Young's modulus of the material,

a is the surface energy, and

r_o is the equilibrium distance between atomic centers.

On the other hand, a crack introduces a stress concentration modeled by

(For sharp cracks)

where:-

o applied is the loading stress,

a is half the length of the crack, and

n is the radius of curvature at the crack tip.

Putting these two equations together, we get

Looking closely, we can see that sharp cracks (small ñ) and large defects (large *a*) both lower the fracture strength of the material.

Recently, scientists have discovered supersonic fracture, the phenomenon of crack motion faster than the speed of sound in a material. This phenomenon was recently also verified by experiment of fracture in rubber-like materials.

Ductile Fracture

In *ductile fracture*, extensive plastic deformation takes place before fracture. Many ductile metals, especially materials with high purity, can sustain very large deformation of 50–100% or more strain before fracture under favorable loading condition and environmental condition. The strain at which the fracture happens is controlled by the purity of the materials. At room temperature, pure iron can undergo deformation up to 100% strain before breaking, while cast iron or high-carbon steels can barely sustain 3% of strain. Because ductile rupture involves a high degree of plastic deformation, the fracture behavior of a propagating crack as modeled above changes fundamentally. Some of the energy from stress concentrations at the crack tips is dissipated by plastic deformation before the crack actually propagates. The basic steps sample of smallest cross-sectional area), void formation, void coalescence (also known as crack formation), crack propagation, and failure, often resulting in a cup-and-cone shaped failure surface.

Crack Separation Modes

There are three ways of applying a force to enable a crack to propagate:

- *Mode I Crack* – Opening mode (a tensile stress normal to the plane of the crack)
- *Mode II Crack* – Sliding mode (a shear stress acting parallel to the plane of the crack and perpendicular to the crack front)
- *Mode III Crack* – Tearing mode (a shear stress acting parallel to the plane of the crack and parallel to the crack front)

Bone Fracture

A bone fracture (sometimes abbreviated FRX or Fx, F_x, or #) is a medical condition in which a bone is cracked but not broken; it is a break in the continuity of the bone. While many fractures are the result of high force impact or stress, bone fracture can also occur as a result of certain medical conditions that weaken the bones, such as osteoporosis, certain types of cancer, or osteogenesis imperfecta, where the fracture is then termed pathological fracture. Although broken bone and bone break are common colloquialisms for a bone fracture, *break* is not a formal orthopedic term.

Classification Systems

Orthopedic: In orthopedic medicine, fractures are classified in various ways.

- *Closed* fractures are those in which the skin is intact, while *open* (compound) fractures involve wounds that communicate with the fracture, or where fracture hematoma is exposed, and may thus expose bone to contamination. Open injuries carry a higher risk of infection; they require antibiotic treatment and usually urgent surgical treatment (debridement). This involves removal of all dirt, contamination, and dead tissue.
- *Simple* fractures are fractures that only occur along one line, splitting the bone into two pieces, while *multi-fragmentary* fractures (formerly called *comminuted*) involve the bone splitting into multiple pieces. A simple, closed fracture is much easier to treat and has a much better prognosis than an open, comminuted fracture.

Other considerations in fracture care are displacement (fracture gap) and angulation. If angulation or displacement is large, *reduction* (manipulation) of the bone may be required and, in adults, frequently requires surgical care. These injuries may take longer to heal than injuries without displacement or angulation.

Another type of bone fracture is a *compression fracture*. It usually occurs in the vertebrae, for example when the front portion of a vertebra in the spine collapses due to osteoporosis (a medical condition which causes bones to become brittle and susceptible to fracture, with or without trauma).

Other types of fracture are:

- *Complete Fracture*-A fracture in which bone fragments separate completely.
- *Incomplete Fracture*-A fracture in which the bone fragments are still partially joined.
- *Linear Fracture*-A fracture that is parallel to the bone's long axis.
- *Transverse Fracture*-A fracture that is at a right angle to the bone's long axis.

- *Oblique Fracture*-A fracture that is diagonal to a bone's long axis.
- *Spiral Fracture*-A fracture where at least one part of the bone has been twisted.
- *Compacted Fracture*-A fracture caused when bone fragments are driven into each other.

OTA Classification

The Orthopaedic Trauma Association, an association for Orthopaedic surgeons, devised an elaborate classification system to describe the injury accurately and guide treatment. There are five parts to the code:

- Bone: Description of a fracture starts by naming the bone:

(1) Humerus, (2) Radius/Ulna, (3) Femur, (4) Tibia/Fibula, (5) Spine, (6) Pelvis, (24) Carpus, (25) Metacarpals, (26) Phalanx (Hand), (72) Talus, (73) Calcaneus, (74) Navicular, (75) Cuneiform, (76) Cuboid, (80) LisFranc, (81) Metatarsals, (82) Phalanx (Foot), (45) Patella, (06) Clavicle, (09) Scapula,

- *Location:* The part of the bone involved (e.g. shaft of the femur): proximal, diaphyseal, distal, malleolar.
- *Type:* It is important to note whether the fracture is simple or multifragmentary and whether it is closed or open: A=simple fracture, B=wedge fracture, C=complex fracture
- *Group:* The geometry of the fracture is also described by terms such as transverse, oblique, spiral, or segmental.
- *Subgroup:* Other features of the fracture are described in terms of displacement, angulation and shortening. A stable fracture is one which is likely to stay in a good (functional) position while it heals; an unstable one is likely to shorten, angulate or rotate before healing and lead to poor function in the long term.

Other Classification Systems

There are other systems used to classify different types of bone fractures:

- "Neer classification": humerus
- "Denis classification": spine
- "Seinsheimer's Classification": femur
- "Frykman classification": radius and ulna

Pain

Bone tissue itself doesn't contain nociceptors. Still, bone fracture is very painful, for several reasons:

- Breaking in the continuity of the periosteum, with or without similar discontinuity in endosteum, as both contain multiple nociceptors.
- Edema of nearby soft tissues caused by bleeding of torn periosteal blood vessels evokes pressure pain.
- Muscle spasms trying to hold bone fragments in place

Bone Healing

The natural process of healing a fracture starts when the injured bone and surrounding tissues bleed, forming what's called fracture Hematoma. The blood coagulates to form a blood clot situated between the broken fragments. Within a few days blood vessels grow into the jelly-like matrix of the blood clot. The new blood vessels bring phagocytes to the area, which gradually remove the non-viable material. The blood vessels also bring fibroblasts in the walls of the vessels and these multiply and produce collagen fibres. In this way the blood clot is replaced by a matrix of collagen. Collagen's rubbery consistency allows bone fragments to move only a small amount unless severe or persistent force is applied.

At this stage, some of the fibroblasts begin to lay down bone matrix (calcium hydroxyapatite) in the form of insoluble crystals. This mineralization of the collagen matrix stiffens it and transforms it into bone. In fact, bone *is* a mineralized collagen matrix; if the mineral is dissolved out of bone, it becomes rubbery. Healing bone callus is on average sufficiently mineralized to show up on X-ray within 6 weeks in adults and less in children. This initial "woven" bone does not have the strong mechanical properties of mature bone. By a process of remodeling, the woven bone is replaced by mature "lamellar" bone. The whole process can take up to 18 months, but in adults the strength of the healing bone is usually 80% of normal by 3 months after the injury.

Several factors can help or hinder the bone healing process. For example, any form of nicotine hinders the process of bone healing, and adequate nutrition (including calcium intake) will help the bone healing process. Weight-bearing stress on bone, after the bone has healed sufficiently to bear the weight, also builds bone strength. The bone shards can also embed in the muscle causing great pain. Although there are theoretical concerns about NSAIDs slowing the rate of healing, there is not enough evidence to warrant withholding this type analgesic.

Treatment

First aid for fractures includes stabilizing the break with a splint in order to prevent movement of the injured part, which could sever blood vessels and cause further tissue damage. Waxed cardboard splints are inexpensive, lightweight, waterproof and strong. Compound fractures are treated as open wounds in addition to fractures.

At the hospital, closed fractures are diagnosed by taking an X-ray photograph of the injury.

Since bone healing is a natural process which will most often occur, fracture treatment aims to ensure the best possible *function* of the injured part after healing. Bone fractures are typically treated by restoring the fractured pieces of bone to their natural positions (if necessary), and maintaining those positions while the bone heals. Often, a physician will align the bone, called reduction, in good position and verify the improved alignment with an X-ray. This process is extremely painful without anesthesia, about as painful as breaking the bone itself. To this end, a fractured limb is usually immobilized with a plaster or fiberglass cast or splint which holds the bones in position and immobilizes the joints above and below the fracture. When the initial post-fracture edema or swelling goes down, the fracture may be placed in a removable brace or orthosis. If being treated with surgery, surgical nails, screws, plates and wires are used to hold the fractured bone together more directly.

Alternatively, fractured bones may be treated by the Ilizarov method which is a form of external fixator.

Occasionally smaller bones, such as toes, may be treated without the cast, by buddy wrapping them, which serves a similar function to making a cast. By allowing only limited movement, fixation helps preserve anatomical alignment while enabling callus formation, towards the target of achieving union.

Surgical methods of treating fractures have their own risks and benefits, but usually surgery is done only if conservative treatment has failed or is very likely to fail. With some fractures such as hip fractures (usually caused by osteoporosis or Osteogenesis Imperfecta), surgery is offered routinely, because the complications of non-operative treatment include deep vein thrombosis (DVT) and pulmonary embolism, which are more dangerous than surgery. When a joint surface is damaged by a fracture, surgery is also commonly recommended to make an accurate anatomical reduction and restore the smoothness of the joint. Infection is especially dangerous in bones, due to their limited blood flow. Bone tissue is predominantly extracellular matrix, rather than living cells, and the few blood vessels needed to support this low metabolism are only able to bring a limited number of immune cells to an injury to fight infection. For this reason, open fractures and osteotomies call for very careful antiseptic procedures and prophylactic antibiotics.

Sometimes bones are reinforced with metal, but these fracture implants must be designed and installed with care. *Stress shielding* occurs when plates or screws carry too large of a portion of the bone's load, causing atrophy. This problem is reduced, but not eliminated, by the use of low-modulus materials, including titanium and its alloys. The heat generated by the friction of installing hardware can easily accumulate and damage bone tissue, reducing the strength of the connections. If dissimilar metals are installed in contact with one another (i.e., a titanium plate with cobalt-chromium alloy or stainless steel screws), galvanic corrosion will result. The metal ions produced can damage the bone locally and may cause systemic effects as well.

In Children

In children, whose bones are still developing, there are risks of either a growth plate injury or a greenstick fracture.

- A greenstick fracture occurs due to mechanical failure on the tension side. That is, Since the bone is not as brittle as it would be in an adult, It does not completely fracture, but rather exhibits bowing without complete disruption of the bone's cortex in the surface opposite the applied force.
- Growth plate injuries, as in Salter-Harris fractures, require careful treatment and accurate reduction to make sure that the bone continues to grow normally.
- Plastic deformation of the bone, in which the bone permanently bends but does not break, is also possible in children. These injuries may require an osteotomy (bone cut) to realign the bone if it is fixed and cannot be realigned by closed methods.
- Certain fractures are known to occur mainly in pediatric age group, as fracture clavicle & supracondylar fracture of Humerus.

Dislocation

What is a Dislocation?

A dislocation occurs when extreme force is put on a ligament, allowing the ends of two connected bones to separate. Ligaments are flexible bands of fibrous tissue that connect various bones and cartilage. Ligaments also bind the bones in a joint together. Stress on joint ligaments can lead to dislocation of the joint. The hip and shoulder joints, for example, are called "ball and socket" joints. Extreme force on the ligaments in these joints can cause the head of the bone (ball) to partially or completely come out of the socket.

Illustration of Types of Joints

The most commonly dislocated joint is the shoulder.

Dislocations are uncommon in younger children because their growth plates (area of bone growth located in the ends of long bones) are weaker than the muscles or tendons; instead, children are more prone to a fracture than a dislocation.

What are the Symptoms of a Dislocation?

The following are the most common symptoms of a dislocation. However, each child may experience symptoms differently. Symptoms may include:

- pain in the injured area
- swelling in the injured area
- difficulty using or moving the injured area in a normal manner
- deformity of the dislocated area
- warmth, bruising, or redness in the injured area

The symptoms of a dislocation may resemble other medical conditions. Always consult your child's physician for a diagnosis.

How is a Dislocation Diagnosed?

The physician makes the diagnosis with a physical examination. During the examination, the physician obtains a complete medical history of the child and asks how the injury occurred.

Diagnostic procedures may help to evaluate the problem. Diagnostic procedures may include:

- *X-ray*-a diagnostic test which uses invisible electromagnetic energy beams to produce images of internal tissues, bones, and organs onto film.
- *Magnetic Resonance Imaging (MRI)*-a diagnostic procedure that uses a combination of large magnets, radiofrequencies, and a computer to produce detailed images of organs and structures within the body.

Treatment for Dislocation

Specific treatment for a dislocation will be determined by your child's physician based on:

- your child's age, overall health, and medical history
- the extent of the injury
- the type of injury

- your child's tolerance for specific medications, procedures, or therapies
- expectations for the course of the condition
- your opinion or preference

All dislocations require immediate medical attention since fractures can also occur with dislocations.

Initial treatment of a dislocation includes R.I.C.E. (rest, ice, compression, and elevation). Dislocations may reduce spontaneously, meaning the bone ends may go back into place by themselves. However, for those dislocations that do not go back into place, your child's physician will need to place the joint back into its proper position so it will heal. Your child will receive sedation to help him/her remain comfortable before the procedure. Sedation will also help the muscles around the dislocated joint relax, so the joint can be put back into place more easily.

Your child's physician may recommend any of the following to help reduce the dislocation or promote healing afterwards:

- *Splint/cast*-immobilizes the dislocated area to promote alignment and healing; protects the injured area from motion or use.
- medication (for pain control)
- *Traction*-the application of a force to stretch certain parts of the body in a specific direction. Traction consists or pulleys, strings, weights, and a metal frame attached over or on the bed. The purpose of traction is to stretch the muscles and tendons around the bone ends to help reduce the dislocation.
- surgery (especially for reoccurring dislocations or if a muscle, tendon, or ligament is badly torn)

Additional recommendations may include

- activity restrictions (while the dislocation heals)
- crutches/wheelchair (to enable your child to move around during healing)
- physical therapy (to stretch and strengthen the injured muscles, ligaments, and tendons)

Long-term Outlook after a Dislocation

While dislocations are rare in younger children, they do occur more frequently among adolescents. It is important that the child adhere to the activity restrictions and/or stretching and strengthening rehabilitation programmes to prevent re-injury.

First Aid—Need and Importance of First Aid

First aid is the provision of initial care for an illness or injury. It is usually performed by a lay person to a sick or injured casualty until definitive medical treatment can be accessed. Certain self-limiting illnesses or minor injuries may not require further medical care past the first aid intervention. It generally consists of a series of simple and, in some cases, potentially life-saving techniques that an individual can be trained to perform with minimal equipment.

While first aid can also be performed on animals, the term generally refers to care of human patients.

History

The earliest instances of recorded first aid were provided by religious knights, such as the Knights Hospitaller, formed in the 11th century, providing care to pilgrims and knights, and training other knights in how to treat common battlefield injuries. The practice of first aid fell largely in to disuse during the High Middle Ages, and organized societies were not seen again until in 1859 Henry Dunant organized local villagers to help victims of the Battle of Solferino, including the provision of first aid. Four years later, four nations met in Geneva and formed the organization which has grown into the Red Cross, with a key stated aim of “aid to sick and wounded soldiers in the field”. This was followed by the formation of St. John Ambulance in 1877, based on the principles of the Knights Hospitaller, to teach first aid, and numerous other organization joined them, with the term first aid first coined in 1878 as civilian ambulance services spread as a combination of ‘first treatment’ and ‘national aid’ in large railway centres and mining districts as well as with police forces. First aid training began to spread through the empire through organisations such as St John, often starting, as in the UK, with high risk activities such as ports and railways.

Many developments in first aid and many other medical techniques have been driven by wars, such as in the case of the American Civil War, which prompted Clara Barton to organize the American Red Cross. Today, there are several groups that promote first aid, such as the military and the Scouting movement. New techniques and equipment have helped make today's first aid simple and effective.

Aims

The key aims of first aid can be summarised in three key points:

- *Preserve life*-the overriding aim of all medical care, including first aid, is to save lives
- *Prevent further harm*-also sometimes called prevent the condition from worsening, this covers both external factors, such as moving a patient away from any cause of harm, and applying first aid techniques to prevent worsening of the condition, such as applying pressure to stop a bleed becoming dangerous.
- *Promote recovery*-first aid also involves trying to start the recovery process from the illness or injury, and in some cases might involve completing a treatment, such as in the case of applying a plaster to a small wound.

First aid training also involves the prevention of initial injury and responder safety, and the treatment phases.

Key Skills

Certain skills are considered essential to the provision of first aid and are taught ubiquitously. Particularly, the "ABC"s of first aid, which focus on critical life-saving intervention, must be rendered before treatment of less serious injuries. ABC stands for *Airway*, *Breathing*, and *Circulation*. Attention must first be brought to the airway to ensure it is clear. Obstruction (choking) is a life-threatening emergency. Following evaluation of the airway, a first aid attendant would determine adequacy of breathing and provide rescue breathing if necessary. Assessment of circulation is now not usually carried out for patients who are not breathing, with first aiders now trained to go straight to chest compressions (and thus providing artificial circulation) but pulse checks may be done on less serious patients.

Some organizations add a fourth step of "D" for *Deadly bleeding* or *Defibrillation*, while others consider this as part of the *Circulation* step. Variations on techniques to evaluate and maintain the ABCs depend on the skill level of the first aider. Once the ABCs are secured, first aiders can begin additional treatments, as required. Some organizations teach the same order of priority using the "3Bs": *Breathing*, *Bleeding*, and *Bones* (or "4Bs": *Breathing*, *Bleeding*, *Brain*, and *Bones*). While the ABCs and 3Bs are taught to be performed sequentially, certain conditions may require the consideration of two steps simultaneously. This includes the provision of both artificial respiration and chest compressions to someone who is not breathing and has no pulse, and the consideration of cervical spine injuries when ensuring an open airway.

Preserving Life

In order to preserve life, all persons require to have an open airway-a clear passage where air can move in through the mouth or nose through the pharynx and down in to the lungs, without obstruction. Conscious people will maintain their own airway automatically, but those who are unconscious (with a GCS of less than 8) may be unable to maintain a patent airway, as the part of the brain which autonomously controls in normal situations may not be functioning.

If the patient was breathing, a first aider would normally then place them in the recovery position, with the patient leant over on their side, which also has the effect of clearing the tongue from the pharynx. It also avoids a common cause of death in unconscious patients, which is choking on regurgitated stomach contents.

The airway can also become blocked through a foreign object becoming lodged in the pharynx or larynx, commonly called choking. The first aider will be taught to deal with this through a combination of 'back slaps' and 'abdominal thrusts'.

Once the airway has been opened, the first aider would assess to see if the patient is breathing. If there is no breathing, or the patient is not breathing normally, such as agonal breathing, the first aider would undertake what is probably the most recognized first aid procedure-Cardiopulmonary resuscitation or CPR, which involves breathing for the patient, and manually massaging the heart to promote blood flow around the body.

Promoting Recovery

The first aider is also likely to be trained in dealing with injuries such as cuts, grazes or broken bones. They may be able to deal with the situation in its entirety (a small adhesive bandage on a paper cut), or may be required to maintain the condition of something like a broken bone, until the next stage of definitive care (usually an ambulance) arrives.

The Importance of First Aid

If your friend has an accident then the first person there will be the first aider or the person who will help her until others get there. First aid is about using your commonsense in ways that will keep your friend safe without doing harm to her.

Until emergency help arrives, try to control bleeding. If possible, first put on rubber or latex gloves before touching any blood. If these are not available, a clean plastic bag can be used to cover your hands. It is important not to come in contact with blood because of the health risks. If finger or hand pressure is inadequate to control bleeding, place a thick pad of clean cloth or bandage directly over the wound, and hold in place with a belt, bandage, neckties or cloth strips. Take care not to stop the circulation to the rest of the limb. For injuries where a tie cannot be used, such as to the groin, back, chest, head and neck, place a thick pad of clean cloth or bandage directly over the wound and control the bleeding with finger or hand pressure. If bones are not broken, raise the bleeding part higher than the rest of the body. If the injury is extensive, the victim may go into shock and should be treated for it.

Control severe bleeding by applying firm pressure to the wound using a clean, dry dressing and raise it above the level of the heart. Lay the person down, reassure them, keep them warm and loosen tight clothing. Safety is an awareness of your surroundings and a healthy fear of unstable situations. By its very nature, an emergency is an unstable situation. If everything were truly under control, nothing bad would've happened in the first place. If, for example, you see a person struck by a car in a crosswalk, do not rush headlong into the street to see if they're injured. You will no doubt find yourself lying next to them after being struck by the next car barreling down the road. For getting them to do something that may have been on their 'To do' list for years! Most people know that it would be a good idea to take a first aid course, but sometimes life gets in the way and it is hard to find the time. However, people usually feel happy and relieved once they have learned some lifesaving skills and it improves their confidence and self esteem. If you host a course, you are going to feel great for having had such a positive influence on your family, friends and co-workers!

You can purchase supplies for your travel first aid kit at drug stores, or buy a prearranged kit online. Many travel first aid kits cost under $10. Don't be afraid to personalize purchased travel first aid kits with any additional supplies like you or you family might need. For example, include a plastic bag with a mild solution of soap and water, along with paper towels for a quick and inexpensive way to wash sticky hands.

It is important to have a first aid kit is because they enable someone who is injured, to be quickly treated with basic first aid, before they can be properly treated at the local hospital. Therefore in an emergency situation, it is recommended someone knows where the nearest first aid kit is located and how to use the contents within it.

Why do I Need to Know First Aid?

Saving Lives: In the time it takes to read this page, you could learn enough first aid to save a life.

A blocked airway can kill someone in three to four minutes, but it can take more than eight minutes for an ambulance to arrive. So a simple procedure such as opening someone's airway can save their life while they're waiting for emergency medical help.

The latest government figures, from 2002, estimate 2.7 million people in the UK went to A&E because of an accident in their home.

Of these, 910,000 were aged under 16.

Sadly, almost 4,000 people in England and Wales died because of accidents in or around their home in 2004, according to the Office for National Statistics.

This means you're more likely to give first aid to someone you know than a stranger. Knowing what to do will allow you to react rapidly if an accident does happen.

Top Ten Home Accidents and Injuries

1. Falls (1,248,000)
2. Strikes and collisions (530,000)
3. Cuts and tears (230,000)
4. Foreign bodies (128,000)
5. Acute overexertion, for example moving furniture (90,000)
6. Burns, scalds (84,000)
7. Pinching or crushing injuries (79,000)
8. Bites, stings (72,000)
9. Puncture wounds (54,000)
10. Suspected poisonings (33,000)

What Not to Do?

There are many misconceptions surrounding first aid, some of which can cause serious harm.

Top Ten First Aid Misconceptions

1. You should put butter or cream on a burn. The only thing you should put on a burn is cold water-keep the butter for cooking.

2. If you can't move a limb, it must be broken/If you can move a limb, it can't be broken. The only accurate way to diagnose a broken limb is to x-ray it.
3. The best way to treat bleeding is to put the wound under a tap. If you put a bleeding wound under a tap you wash away the body's clotting agents and make it bleed more.
4. Nosebleeds are best treated by putting the head back. If you put the head back during a nosebleed, all the blood goes down the back of the airway.
5. A tourniquet is the best way to treat serious bleeding. It's harmful to stop the blood flow to a limb for more than 10-15 minutes.
6. If someone has swallowed a poison you should make them sick. If you make someone sick by putting your fingers in their mouth, the vomit may block their airway.
7. If you perform CPR on someone who has a pulse you can damage their heart. The evidence is that it isn't dangerous to do chest compressions on a casualty with a pulse.
8. You need lots of training to do first aid. You don't-what you mostly need is common sense. You can learn enough first aid in ten minutes to save someone's life.
9. You need lots of expensive equipment to do first aid. You don't need any equipment to do first aid, there are lots of ways to improvise anything you need.

UNIT-VI

Posture, Meaning and Definition

Meaning of Posture

Posture: The carriage of the body as a whole, the attitude of the body, or the position of the limbs (the arms and legs).

"Postural" pertains to the posture or position. For example, postural hypotension is a drop in blood pressure (hypotension) due to a change in body position (a change in posture) when a person moves to a more vertical position: from sitting to standing or from lying down to sitting or standing.

The root of the word "posture" is the Latin verb "ponere" meaning "to put or place." The past participle "positus" gave the noun "positura" that travelled via France to England in the 16th century as "posture."

Posture and Body Alignment

Poor posture was thought to be an important contributing factor in the development of scoliosis in the early 19th century in the U.S. Posture training was one of the primary treatments for scoliosis in that era. It fell out of favour in the later years of the 19th century as bracing and surgery became the preferred treatment of orthopedic doctors.

Posture correction training did help me personally to improve my scoliotic curves, and a couple of recent papers suggest it has been beneficial in other cases of scoliosis, too. My physical therapist constantly stressed the importance of proper posture and body alignment to me, similar to the methods described in my antique medical books. Today we call it "ergonomics" and "body alignment", but the basic premise of posture training seems to have remained the same for the last 100 years. Perhaps posture training is a lost art.

In any case, proper posture is thought to have many benefits besides scoliosis prevention and treatment, and no downside risks of which I am aware. The bottom line is that good posture won't hurt you, by keeping the muscles of the rib cage balanced it may help people to breathe better and reduce muscle tension, and according to a majority of the older medical text books and a couple of more recent studies, it *may* even help your scoliosis.

Postural Defects and Prevention

Posture can be defined as the relationship of the parts of the body to the line of the center of gravity. The posture is a gauge of mechanical efficiency of the neuromusculoskeletal system in the erect position.

Development of Posture

In the uterus the fetus is almost invariably in a position of flexion, with the convex curve of the spine lying against the curve of the uterine wall. The head, arms, and legs of the fetus are flexed on the torso.

The entire fetus lies suspended in the amniotic fluid, which has a specific gravity similar to that of the fetus. Following birth the development of posture is affected by constant forces exerted by gravity.

The newborn holds his shoulders, elbows, hips, and knees in flexion, with his limbs slightly bowed and rotated inward. Fifteen to thirty degrees of flexion contracture of the knee is a normal physical finding.

The infant lies in a nearly horizontal position, unable to support his head or trunk. In either the prone or the supine position, gravitational force is exerted on a horizontal plane and tends to unroll the "coiling" that was previously assumed within the uterus.

The rate of development of muscle strength varies in the different parts of the body.

When the infant is in a horizontal position, the hip flexors, the anterior muscles of the neck, and the abdominal muscles are stretched and used minimally, whereas the extensors of the neck, back, and thigh are relaxed and are the first to increase their motor power.

When the child is able to support his head and begins to sit up, the weight of the head, combined with the persistent flexion attitude of the hips and the associated of the pelvis on the spine, produces a long convex curve of the entire spine.

In the prestanding stage, this total convex curve of the back is normal.

When the child begins to stand and walk, the extensor muscles of the back, neck, and hips are well developed and the ine is usually straight.

the upright position, the force of gravity is exerted in a ve cal direction, causing an exaggerated lumbar lordosis and a protuberant abdomen. With further growth and development, the child improves his stance and becomes more agile in walking and running.

Normal Posture

The posture of each person has characteristics that are uniquely his. Various factors affecting posture are:

Bony Contours: The shape of the vertebrae may be modified by diseases such as tuberculosis or Scheuermann's disease, which produce dorsal kyphosis.

Ligaments: The degree of ligamentous laxity varies in different individuals, giving rise to looseness or tautness of the joints. The spine is composed of many joints, and is itself dependent upon the articulation inferior to it, such as those of the feet, knees, and hips.

Fascial and Musculotendinous Tautness: Tautness of soft-tissue structures, especially the fascia lata, hamstrings, anterior hip capsule, and pectorals, affect posture.

Muscle Strength: Particularly important is the strength of the gluteus maximus, abdominal erector spinae, and scapular adductor muscles.

Pelvic Inclination: The pelvis is the base upon which the vertebral column rests. Any change in its inclination will cause a corresponding change in the position of the fifth lumbar vertebra in relation to the sacrum, which in turn alters the posture of the entire spine. Inclination of the pelvis is ordinarily controlled by the muscles about the hip.

Pelvic inclination is increased by contraction of the extensors of the hip, i.e., the glutei, hamstrings, and the posterior portion of the hip adductors, and it is decreased by contraction of hip flexors. Motion of the vertebral column is greatest in the lumbar region; in the thoracic spine, however, rotation is of considerable magnitude, but flexion and extension are limited.

The muscles of respiration (the diaphragm and intercostals) produce a secondary effect on posture, as there is some extension of the dorsal spine with each inspiration.

In normal posture the body weight is carried forward on the balls of the feet, the lower limbs are straight with the hips and knees in neutral extension, the pelvic inclination is about 60 degrees to the vertical, the abdomen is retracted, the shoulders are level and flat, and the head is held erect.

The line of the center of gravity of the body passes from the mastoid process to the cervicodorsal junction, crossing the bodies of the vertebrae at the dorsolumbar junction, and falling just anterior to the sacro-iliac articulation and slightly posterior to the hip joint; it passes through the anterior knee joint and terminates at the front of the talus in the ankle.

Gradation of Posture

Posture can be classified into four grades:

A. Excellent or almost perfect posture

B. Good, but not ideal posture

C. Poor, but not the worst possible posture

D. Bad and very possibly symptom-producing posture

In excellent (A) posture, the head and shoulder are balanced over the pelvis, hips, and ankles, with the head erect and the chin held in. The sternum is the part of the body farthest forward, the abdomen is drawn in and flat, and the spinal curves are within normal limits.

In bad (D) posture, the head is held forward to a marked degree, the chest is depressed, the abdomen is completely relaxed and protuberant, the spinal curves are exaggerated, and the shoulders are held behind the pelvis.

Treatment of Postural Defects

Poor posture in children should be observed, and corrective measures taken to increase the strength of the back so that it will be less susceptible in adult life to fatigue, back strain, and injury.

Children rarely complain of backache from poor posture.

Treatment consists of passive and active exercises

Exercises to increase the motor strength of the key muscles affecting posture are also helpful.

The most important is the pelvic tilt. The patient is instructed to decrease the pelvic inclination by use of the abdominal and gluteus maximus muscles. Initially, he performs the pelvic tilt exercise in a supine position, then standing against the wall.

Postural exercises should be carried out until the individual is able to maintain the correct posture naturally. The patient should continue the exercises until they become part of his normal stance and gait.

Food and Nutrition

The Government of India adopted the National Nutrition Policy under the aegis of Department of Women and Child Development in 1993.

As per the orders of the Prime Minister, the Food and Nutrition Board infrastructure comprising of a technical wing at the Centre, 4 Regional Offices and Quality Control Laboratories at Delhi, Mumbai, Kolkata and Chennai and 43

Community Food and Nutrition Extension Units (CFNEUs) located in 29 States/UTs (list annexed) was transferred from Ministry of Food to the Department of Women and Child Development on 1 April, 1993 with a view to serve better the objectives of the National Nutrition Policy.

FNB is primarily engaged in Nutrition Education and Training Activities, Mass Awareness Campaigns, Promotion of Infant and Young Child Nutrition and Follow Up Action on instruments of National Nutrition Policy. A para on each is as under:

Nutrition Education and Training

- The CFNEUs organise five-day Training of Trainers (TOT) courses for orienting CDPOs, medical officers, senior supervisors, LHVs etc on various aspects of nutrition. These master trainers in turn organise two-day Orientation Training Courses for the grassroot level functionaries particularly of ICDS and health besides volunteers from the community.
- Five-day training course in Home Scale Preservation of Fruits and Vegetables and Nutrition is organised for housewives and adolescent girls to promote consumption of fruits and vegetables, the richest source of micronutrients, fibre and anti-oxidants. This also serves as an income generation activity for the participants.
- The staff of CFNEU inspects 11/6 anganwadies per month for supplementary feeding as well as nutrition and health education components. The visit is also utilised to impart nutrition information to the AWW and community.

Mass Awareness Campaigns

FNB celebrates annual nutrition events namely National Nutrition Week (1-7 September), World Breastfeeding Week (1-7 August), World Food Day (16 October), Global Iodine Deficiency Disorders Prevention Day (21 October), Universal Children's Day (14 November) in collaboration with State Governments, National Institutes and field agencies through out the country with a view to intensify awareness generation on nutritional issues. These events are organised on specific themes. The theme of the National Nutrition Week (1-7 September, 2006) was 'Nutrition Literacy'. The theme of World Breastfeeding Week (1-7 August, 2006) was "The IMS Act: Making It Known to People". Nutrition advocacy and awareness generation is intensified during these events utilising all channels of communication. Some of the special programmes organised to celebrate these events included the following:

Advertisement campaign (during 2006) –

- o 2 half page (1 colored ad on 1.8.2006 and 1 Black & white on 7.8.2006) advertisements during the World Breastfeeding Week.
- o 2 half page (1 colored ad on 1.9.2006 and 1 black & white on 7.9.2006) advertisements during National Nutrition Week.
- o One half page colour advertisement on 2 October on the eve of Integrated Child Development Nutrition (ICDS).
- o One half page colored advertisement on World Food Day on the theme 'Invest in Agriculture for Food Security' highlighting the importance of diversified diet for better nutrition, health and development.
- o Half page black and white advertisement on Global Iodine Deficiency Disorders Prevention Day highlighting the importance of consumption of iodised salt in our daily diet.
    - State level workshops in 29 States/UTs during the World Breastfeeding Week as well as National Nutrition Week.
    - Special awareness generation programmes like Orientation Training Course, community meetings, camps, essay competitions, healthy baby shows etc, during these events.
    - Broadcast and telecast of audio and video spots & Radio sponsored programmes on nutrition of infants, adolescent girls, micronutrient malnutrition control etc.

- Mobilization of the State machinery through D.O. letters of the Secretary (WCD), GOI for creating nutritional awareness on these events.

Mass Media Communication

Development of educational and training material on nutrition has been one of the important activities of FNB Headquarters. Some of the important publications include Handbook on Integrated Nutrition Education, Guidelines for Management of Grade I and II Malnutrition, Wall Hanger on Nutrition of Pregnant Women, Posters on Child's Health, Girl Child, Nursing Mothers, Complementary Feeding, Instant Food Mixes, Iodised Salt, folders on mother's milk, green leafy vegetables, fruits and vegetables for vitality, stickers for school children, National Plan of Action on Nutrition, Task Force Report on Micronutrients, India Nutrition Profile 1998 giving disaggregated picture of malnutrition upto district level from 18 States/UTs. The printed publicity material is produced in Hindi, English and 16 regional languages and distributed widely through DAVP.

A Wall Calendar on Nutrition for the year 2006 on the theme 'Promote Nutrition of Children and Women and Accelerate the Pace of National Development' was printed in Hindi and English with nutrition messages appearing on all the 12 sheets. These were disseminated to the Women & Child Development and Health infrastructure with a view to create nutritional awareness among the functionaries as well as the community.

A number of posters/charts on nutrition of infants, girl child, pregnant and lactating mothers and iodine deficiency disorders have been printed in 16 regional languages including North Eastern and disseminated widely.

Some of the audio-video software is as under:

- A set of 27 short films on Nutrition titled "*Poshan aur Rashtra Nirman*" have been developed and produced in the North East Regional languages, Bengali, Hindi and English. These films have been converted into a set of 7 CDs and have been provided to all State

Secretaries incharge of WCD, H&FW, Education, Training Institutions, NIPCCD and its regional centres, MLTC etc for field publicity..

- A 30 episode Radio programme on "Poshan aur Swasthya" in 20 languages was re-broadcast with effect from August 2006.
- Nine audio jingles on infant, young child and adolescent nutrition in regional languages. These were broadcast through primary channels during August-September 2004 and 2005.
- Eight video spots on nutrition telecast during February-March 2005.
- Films on *Poshan Bagiya*, infant feeding etc.
- FNB sponsored a programme on *Khel Khel Mein Badlo Duniya* giving Nutrition messages, to Petroleum Conservation Research Association (PCRA), was telecast from 1 to 15 January 2006 through National Channel of Doordarshan.
- 3 video spots on Infant and Young Child Feeding telecast during January-February 2006 on DD1 at prime time.
- Three video and audio spots on deficiencies of Vitamin A, Iodine and Iron in the country have been produced in Hindi, English and 12 regional languages and are being broadcast/telecast w.e.f. 14 November, 2006.

Infant and Young Child Nutrition

Infant and Young Child Nutrition which is of utmost importance in the lives of human beings has been focused through intensified information, education and communication and protecting the norms for breastfeeding and complementary feeding at international fora namely Codex Committee on Nutrition and Foods for Special Dietary Uses, Codex Alimentarius Commission and World Health Assembly.

A land mark decision to protect, promote and support breastfeeding was taken in 54 World Health Assembly in 2001 giving rise to a Global Public Health recommendation for exclusive breastfeeding for first six months of life, complementary feeding with home based safe and nutritious foods to start at six months of age and continued breastfeeding upto the age two years and beyond. This Global Public Health recommendation has honoured India's traditional wisdom of breastfeeding for first six months and complementary feeding starting thereafter through a ceremony called *annaprashan* and continuing breastfeeding for more than two years.

The 55 World Health Assembly adopted a Global Strategy on Infant and Young Child Nutrition recognizing the importance of nutrition of women through out their life cycle for ensuring optimum nutrition of the child. The inter-generational cycle of malnutrition perpetuated by the poor nutritional status of the girl child was also recognised.The Food and Nutrition Board had developed *National Guidelines on Infant and Young Child Feeding*. The Guidelines in Hindi and English have been distributed to various concerned partners like Health and Family Welfare, Medical and Home Science Colleges, Training Institutions for Nutrition and Health, State Departments of WCD and Health, and field infrastructure of FNB and ICDS. The 2 edition of National Guidelines on Infant and Young Child Feeding was released on 17 May, 2006.

The Chief secretaries and State Secretaries in charge of Women & Child Development were requested to draw up action plans and mobilize the State Machinery for implementation of the Guidelines. The Guidelines are being translated into Regional languages to reach the same to remote corners of the country.

Follow Up Action on National Nutrition Policy :

- Intersectoral Coordination with key partners was intensified with:
  - o Health and Family Welfare for reimposing ban on sale of non-iodised salt.
  - o Food and Public Distribution for including iodised salt under TPDS, fortifying wheat flour with iron and folic acid and distribution through PDS.
  - o Elementary Education and Literacy for provision of a Nutritionist at the district level for Mid Day

Meal programme, use of iodized salt only in the Mid Day Meal Programme.

- o ICMR, MHFW for expediting action on double fortified salt.
- • Expert Consultations on important issues like IYCF, Micronutrient malnutrition, nutrition monitoring and surveillance, vitamin etc organised and the decisions communicated to State Secretaries (WCD) for implementation.
- • Nutrition Advocacy of policy makers:
- o Through D.O. letters to Chief Secretaries and State Secretaries (WCD).
- o Organising Regional Consultation Meets on Nutrition. Five such Meets have been organised for North-Eastern (Shillong), Western (Pune), Eastern (Bhubaneswar), Northern (Chandigarh) and Central (Bhopal) Regions with active involvement of senior policy makers from WCD, Health, Food, Education and Panchayati Raj and, professional bodies, Home Science and Medical Colleges, NGOs and international organisations.

Food Analysis and Standardisation

FNB has four Quality Control Laboratories at Delhi, Mumbai, Calcutta and Chennai for chemical analysis of processed fruit, and vegetable products as well as various supplementary foods used in feeding programmes. The samples of the supplementary foods used in ICDS and Mid-Day Meal Programme are received from the State Departments of Social Welfare and Women & Child Development for analysis.

FNB renders technical expertise for food standardisation through various Committees like Codex, Bureau of Indian Standards, Food and Development Panel of Ministry of Defense.

Balanced Diet

Carbohydrates: Carbohydrates are the most important source of energy. They contain the elements Carbon, Hydrogen and Oxygen. The first part of the name "carbo-" means that they contain Carbon. The second part of the name "-hydr-" means that they contain Hydrogen. The third part of the name "-ate-" means that they contain Oxygen. In all carbohydrates the ratio of Hydrogen atoms to Oxygen atoms is 2:1 just like water.

We obtain most of our carbohydrate in the form of starch. This is found in potato, rice, spaghetti, yams, bread and cereals. Our digestive system turns all this starch into another carbohydrate called glucose. Glucose is carried around the body in the blood and is used by our tissues as a source of energy. (See my pages on respiration and balanced chemical equations.) Any glucose in our food is absorbed without the need for digestion. We also get some of our carbohydrate in the form of sucrose; this is the sugar which we put in our tea and coffee (three heaped spoonfuls for me!). Both sucrose and glucose are sugars, but sucrose molecules are too big to get into the blood, so the digestive system turns it into glucose. When we use glucose in tissue respiration we need Oxygen. This process produces Carbon Dioxide and water and releases energy for other processes.

Proteins

Proteins are required for growth and repair. Proteins contain Carbon, Hydrogen, Oxygen, Nitrogen and sometimes Sulphur. Proteins are very large molecules, so they cannot get directly into our blood; they must be turned into amino-acids by the digestive system. There are over 20 different amino-acids. Our bodies can turn the amino-acids back into protein. When our cells do this they have to put the amino-acids together in the correct order. There are many millions of possible combinations or sequences of amino-acids; it is our DNA which contains the information about how to make proteins. Our cells get their amino-acids from the blood. Now try my Biuret test in the Virtual Laboratory.

Proteins can also be used as a source of energy. When excess amino-acids are removed from the body the Nitrogen is excreted as a chemical called urea. The liver makes urea and the kidney puts the urea into our urine.

Fats

Like carbohydrates, fats contain the elements Carbon, Hydrogen and Oxygen. Fats are used as a source of energy: they are also stored beneath the skin helping to insulate us against the cold. Do not think that by avoiding fat in your diet you will stay thin and elegant! If you eat too much carbohydrate and protein, you will convert some of it into fat, so you will put on weight. You must balance the amount of energy containing foods with the amount of energy that you use when you take exercise.

You must have some fat in your diet because it contains fat soluble vitamins.

Vitamins

Vitamins are only required in very small quantities. There is no chemical similarity between these chemicals; the similarity between them is entirely biological.

Vitamin A: good for your eyes.

Vitamin B: about 12 different chemicals.

Vitamin C: needed for your body to repair itself.

Vitamin D: can be made in your skin, needed for absorption of Calcium.

Vitamin E: the nice one-reproduction?

Mineral Salts

These are also needed in small quantities, but we need more of these than we need of vitamins.

Iron: required to make haemoglobin.

Calcium: required for healthy teeth, bones and muscles.

Sodium: all cells need this, especially nerve cells.

Iodine: used to make a hormone called thyroxin.

Fibre

We do not // can not digest cellulose. This is a carbohydrate used by plants to make their cell walls. It is also called roughage. If you do not eat foods materials which contain fibre you might end up with problems of the colon and rectum. The muscles of you digestive system mix food with the digestive juices and push food along the intestines by peristalsis; if there is no fibre in your diet these movements cannot work properly.

A Balanced Diet

You must have carbohydrate, protein, fat, vitamins, minerals salts and fibre in the correct proportions. If there is not enough protein, you will not be able to grow properly and you will not be able to repair yourself i.e. wounds will not heal properly. If you do not have enough energy containing foods you will feel very tired, you will not have enough energy. If you have too much energy containing foods you will become overweight. If you think that you are overweight you might try taking more exercise to "burn off" some of the excess food which you ate at you last meal.

Malnutrition

Malnutrition is a general term for a medical condition caused by an improper or inadequate diet and nutrition.

According to the World Health Organization, hunger and malnutrition are the single gravest threats to the world's public health and malnutrition is by far the biggest contributor to child mortality, present in half of all cases.

In addition to infant mortality risks, lifelong malnutrition can begin *in utero* and is typically associated with the mother's stature (associated with her childhood nutritional status), her nutritional status prior to conception, and diarrheal disease, intestinal parasites, and/or respiratory infection status. Multiple studies have shown that nutritional status of adults is substantially influenced by their nutritional experience from conception through early childhood. Even if individuals have had adequate nutrition from childhood on, their health outcomes are still impacted.

Causes of Malnutrition

Sociopolitical: In the late eighteenth and early nineteenth century, the English economist Thomas Malthus noted how increases in food production were likely to occur along a slow arithmetic progression due to the law of diminishing returns while population growth follows much faster, geometric progressions. His theory argued that this lag in productivity caused food shortages, that it would lead to famines worldwide as humans surpassed the carrying capacity of the land, and that it would create checks on socio-cultural systems in the forms of poverty and misery as humans would earn and live off of just enough to subsist and survive. This Malthusian argument has long since been refuted on several grounds but has nonetheless served as a backdrop for understanding of the causes of malnutrition.

The actual causes of malnutrition can be varied and complex and are difficult to encapsulate in a single theory. Certainly, as Malthus suggests, lack of agricultural productivity combined with increases in population can cause and are often correlated to malnutrition. Over-cultivation, overgrazing, and deforestation lead to desertification or otherwise impoverished soils that can not support crops or cattle for subsistence agriculture but this scenario only accounts for malnutrition in certain, specific instances and does not consider larger social issues such as the influence of political inequality. Further, malnutrition can stem from impacts of natural disasters, from the results of conflict and war, as an impact of the HIV/AIDS pandemic as a consequence of other health issues such as diarrheal disease or chronic illness from lack of education regarding proper nutrition, or from countless other potential factors.

Various scales of analysis also have to be considered in order to determine the sociopolitical causes of malnutrition. For example, the population of a community may be at risk if it lacks health-related services, but on a smaller scale certain households or individuals may be at even higher risk due to differences in income levels, access to land, or levels of education. Also within the household, there may be differences in levels of malnutrition between men and women, and these differences have been shown to vary significantly from one region to another with problem areas showing relative deprivation of women. Children and the elderly tend to be especially susceptible.

Approximately 27 percent of children under 5 in developing world are malnourished, and in these developing countries, malnutrition claims about half of the 10 million deaths each year of children under 5.

Often the consequences of malnutrition exacerbate its causes and form a vicious downward spiral. For example, in cases of malnourishment, lack of sufficient nutrients can weaken the immune system and invite infectious disease, and by compromising digestive function, many of these diseases can intensify malnutrition. In communities or areas that lack access to safe drinking water, these additional health risks present a critical problem. Lower energy and impaired function of the brain also represent the downward spiral of malnutrition as victims are less able to perform the tasks they need to in order to acquire food, earn an income, or gain an education.

Since the time of Malthus, various new theories and approaches have developed for understanding the truly complex mechanisms and underlying causes of malnutrition. Most famous among recent theorists is the Indian economist and philosopher Amartya Sen whose breakthrough 1981 book *Poverty and Famines: An Essay on Entitlement and Deprivation* went beyond the Malthusian argument that lack of food production led to hunger and demonstrated that malnutrition and famine were more related to problems of food distribution A person's entitlements, according to Sen, are "commodity bundles that a person in society can command using the totality of rights and opportunities that he or she faces," (p.8) and famine can then be described as a collapse of entitlements for a certain segment of society and the failure of the state to protect those entitlements.

South Asia

According to the Global Hunger Index, South Asia has the highest child malnutrition rate of world's regions. India contributes to about 5.6 million child deaths every year, more than half the world's total. The 2006 report mentioned that "the low status of women in South Asian countries and their lack of nutritional knowledge are important determinants of high prevalence of underweight children in the region" and was concerned that South Asia has "inadequate feeding and caring practices for young children".

Half of children in India are underweight, one of the highest rates in the world and nearly double the rate of Sub-Saharan Africa.

Malnutrition in Developed Nations

Childhood malnutrition is generally thought of as being limited to developing countries, but although most malnutrition occurs there, it is also an ongoing presence in developed nations. For example, in the United States of America, one out of every six children is at risk of hunger. A study, based on 2005-2007 data from the U.S. Census Bureau and the Agriculture Department, shows that an estimated 3.5 million children under the age of five are at risk of hunger in the United States. In developed countries, this persistent hunger problem is not due to lack of food or food programmes, but is largely due to an underutilization of existing programmes designed to address the issue, such as food stamps or school meals. Many citizens of rich countries such as the United States of America attach stigmas to food programmes or otherwise discourage their use. In the USA, only 60% of those eligible for the food stamp programme actually receive benefits.

Effects

Mortality Due to Malnutrition:

- On the average, a person dies every second as a result of hunger-4000 every hour-100 000 each day-36 million each year-58 % of all deaths (2001-2004 estimates).
- On the average, a child dies every 5 seconds as a result of hunger-700 every hour-16 000 each day-6 million each year-60% of all child deaths (2002-2008 estimates).

According to the World Health Organization, hunger is the gravest single threat to the world's public health. According to Jean Ziegler (the United Nations Special Rapporteur on the Right to Food for 2000 to March 2008), mortality due to malnutrition accounted for 58% of the total mortality in 2006:

"In the world, approximately 62 millions people, all causes of death combined, die each year. One in twelve people worldwide are malnourished. In 2006, more than 36 millions died of hunger or diseases due to deficiencies in micronutrients". The World Health Organization estimates that one-third of the world is well-fed, one-third is under-fed and one-third is starving.

Hunger and malnutrition have an even bigger impact on children's health than was previously thought. According to the World Health Organization, malnutrition is by far the biggest contributor to child mortality, present in half of all cases. Underweight births and inter-uterine growth restrictions cause 2.2 million child deaths a year. Poor or non-existent breastfeeding causes another 1.4 million. Other deficiencies, such as lack of vitamin A or zinc, for example, account for 1 million. According to The Lancet, malnutrition in the first two years is irreversible. Malnourished children grow up with worse health and lower educational achievements. Their own children also tend to be smaller. Hunger was previously seen as something that exacerbates the problems of diseases such as measles, pneumonia and diarrhea. But malnutrition actually causes diseases as well, and can be fatal in its own right. This is the impact The Lancet seeks to identify.

Children are not only affected by the consequences of malnourishment, but the societies they live in suffer as well. Both severe and moderate cases of malnutrition have a significant impact on the outcomes children face for the remainder of their lives and are also a cause of severe illnesses leading to growth retardation both physical and mental, and possibly death. The risk of death is not limited to only those who suffer from severe forms of malnutrition, though the risk of death is higher among severely malnourished children. Considering the elevated risks of mortality among children that are associated with moderate forms of malnutrition, combined with a high prevalence worldwide, it would seem more appropriate to distinguish that the deaths of children as a result of malnourishment is attributable to moderate, rather than severe conditions of malnutrition. Another factor that largely keeps malnutrition from being properly treated is a lack of education in many developing countries. This lack of education allows cultures of superstitions to persist. For example, in some cases in China, breast-feeding started at a very late stage. As such, there is an increasing wide effort to implement an access for education about proper feeding methods.

Biological Effects

An extended period of malnutrition can result in starvation or deficiency diseases such as scurvy. Malnutrition increases the risk of infection and infectious disease; for example, it is a major risk factor in the onset of active tuberculosis.

Malnutrition appears to increase activity and movement in many animals-for example an experiment on spiders showed increased activity and predation in starved spiders, resulting in larger weight gain. This pattern is seen in many animals, including humans while sleeping. It even occurs in rats with their cerebral cortex or stomachs completely removed. Increased activity on hamster wheels occurred when rats were deprived not only of food, but also water or B vitamins such as thiamine This response may increase the animal's chance of finding food, though it has also been speculated the emigration response relieves pressure on the home population.

Responses to Malnutrition

Societal responses to malnutrition vary depending upon which factor one subscribes to as the primary cause of hunger and malnutrition. While most responses are targeted to address undernutrition, there are several that also respond to overnutrition.

If the principal cause of malnutrition is that humans have populated the earth (or a specific geographic region) beyond its carrying capacity, then a restricted population size is the solution. This is an argument that is espoused by people of both liberal and conservative persuasions. In the late 1700's, Thomas Malthus originally argued that nothing could be done as only natural disasters could check population growth, but he later included the possibility of voluntary limits through "moral restraint." More recently, Robert Chapman suggests that an intervention through government policies is a necessary ingredient of curtailing global population growth. Garret Hardin takes an anti-immigration, isolationist approach arguing that "...all sovereign states must accept the responsibility of solving their population problems in their own territories." Hardin also asserts that immigration acts as a sort of pressure release valve which allows countries to continue to ignore solving their population problems.

Others, Amartya Sen among them, argue that other social and economic factors, such as declining wages, unemployment, rising food prices, and poor food-distribution systems, rather than population numbers per se, lead to malnutrition and in severe cases famine. For Sen, "no matter how a famine is caused, methods of breaking it call for a large supply of food in the public distribution system. This applies not only to organizing rationing and control, but also to undertaking work programmes and other methods of increasing purchasing power for those hit by shifts in exchange entitlements in a general inflationary situation."

One suggested policy framework to resolve access issues is termed food sovereignty, the right of peoples to define their own food, agriculture, livestock, and fisheries systems in contrast to having food largely subjected to international market forces. Food First is one of the primary think tanks working to build support for food sovereignty.

One policy adopted in recent decades to alleviate world malnutrition is direct humanitarian aid in the form of food. For the rich donor countries, this is a way to reduce domestic excess supply created by domestic agricultural subsidies, stabilizing farm prices in rich countries, even if the cost of supplying the food to its final beneficiaries is high. Food aid may be provided for short-term emergencies (natural disasters or human-made like war) or in the form of a long-term programme for an extended period. For recipient countries, emergency food aid is welcome, though aid in cash may also be welcome because the food may often be purchased locally in zones not affected by the emergency, thus benefitting local farmers. Long-term foreign food aid has been criticized as discouraging local production and distorting markets.

Neoliberals advocate for an increasing role of the free market. The World Bank itself claims to be part of the solution to malnutrition, asserting that the best way for countries to succeed in breaking the cycle of poverty and malnutrition is to build export-led economies that will give them the financial means to buy foodstuffs on the world market.

There are several different technical approaches in combating under-nutrition including nutritional education and medical nutrition which consists of micro-nutrient supplementation, immunizations and food fortifications. Nutritional education is a preventative measure that focuses on raising awareness on what foods are necessary for the body to gain the nutrients needed to function.

In recent years many foods, such as Spirulina and peanut butter, have been developed or refined for mass-production in hopes of combating malnutrition and its effects. Foodstuffs are usually selected that allow the supplementing of the required daily 2000kcal, as well as the requirements in proteïn and other micro-nutrients. These allow the curing of protein-energy malnutrition. See Spirulina and Plumpy'nut for more on these efforts.

Of them Spirulina deserves a special mention as not only they were the first life forms that originated on the Earth but have been a traditional foods for human beings in many ancient civilizations such as Mayan, Aztecs and the Kingdom of Chad among others.] The United Nations World Food Conference of 1974 declared Spirulina as 'the best food for the future.' Because of its tremendous nutritional benefits, cost effectiveness and practical applications such as ready harvest every 24 hours make Spirulina a potent tool to eradicate malnutrition. The Intergovernmental Institution for the use of Micro-algae Spirulina Against Malnutrition,IIMSAM, that was formed by many United Nations Member States and based in New York, strives to make Spirulina a key driver to eradicate malnutrition, achieve food security and bridge the health divide with a special priority for the developing and the least developed countries.

Vitamins and Deficiency Diseases

A vitamin is an organic compound required as a nutrient in tiny amounts by an organism. A compound is called a vitamin when it cannot be synthesized in sufficient quantities by an organism, and must be obtained from the diet. Thus, the term is conditional both on the circumstances and the particular organism. For example, ascorbic acid functions as vitamin C for some animals but not others, and vitamins D and K are required in the human diet only in certain circumstances. The term *vitamin* does not include other essential nutrients such as dietary minerals, essential fatty acids, or essential amino acids, nor does it encompass the large number of other nutrients that promote health but are otherwise required less often.

Vitamins are classified by their biological and chemical activity, not their structure. Thus, each "vitamin" may refer to several *vitamer* compounds that all show the biological activity associated with a particular vitamin. Such a set of chemicals are grouped under an alphabetized vitamin "generic descriptor" title, such as "vitamin A," which includes the compounds retinal, retinol, and many carotenoids. Vitamers are often inter-converted in the body.

Vitamins have diverse biochemical functions, including function as hormones (e.g. vitamin D), antioxidants (e.g. vitamin E), and mediators of cell signaling and regulators of cell and tissue growth and differentiation (e.g. vitamin A). The largest number of vitamins (e.g. B complex vitamins) function as precursors for enzyme cofactor bio-molecules (coenzymes), that help act as catalysts and substrates in metabolism. When acting as part of a catalyst, vitamins are bound to enzymes and are called prosthetic groups. For example, biotin is part of enzymes involved in making fatty acids. Vitamins also act as coenzymes to carry chemical groups between enzymes. For example, folic acid carries various forms of carbon group – methyl, formyl and methylene-in the cell. Although these roles in assisting enzyme reactions are vitamins' best-known function, the other vitamin functions are equally important.

Until the 1900s, vitamins were obtained solely through food intake, and changes in diet (which, for example, could occur during a particular growing season) can alter the types and amounts of vitamins ingested. Vitamins have been produced as commodity chemicals and made widely available as inexpensive pills for several decades, allowing supplementation of the dietary intake.

Vitamin and Mineral Deficiency Diseases

Throughout mankind's history vitamin and mineral deficiencies have been two of the primary causes of disease in both man and animal. Deficiency diseases were documented as early as 1500 B.C. in the Ebers papyrus and in early Roman and Greek writings. In the early days of world exploration by European nations, when long periods were spent at sea, deficiency diseases ravaged many seafaring crews.

According to nutrition experts, and documented by testimony on the Congressional Record (see excerpts below), a wide variety of diseases are caused by or exacerbated by vitamin and mineral deficiencies. Mineral deficiency diseases can be attributed to the following: heart disease and heart attacks to deficiency of selenium, copper and calcium, strokes and ruptured aortic aneurysm to deficiency of copper, arthritis and bone diseases to a deficiency of calcium and boron, mental depression and hyperactivity to a deficiency of calcium, hypoglycemia and fatigue to a deficiency of chromium and vanadium, blood problems to a deficiency of iron, neurological irregularities to a deficiency of potassium and magnesium, and a lack of bacterial resistance to a deficiency of sulfur. Vitamin deficiency diseases can be attributed to the following: scurvy to vitamin C deficiency, neurological development problems and pernicious anemia to vitamin B 12 deficiency, rickets and joint disorders to vitamin D deficiency, cancer and cataracts to vitamin E deficiency, numerous metabolic problems to various vitamin deficiencies and the list goes on.

Much of the world's mass food producing soils, have long been depleted of the necessary nutrients required to life a long, healthy, and disease free life, making it necessary to augment our diets with those missing nutrients. As bio-chemical creatures, we are quite literally "what we consume" and if the foods consumed don't contain the minerals and vitamins we require, we will sooner or later, have to deal with the consequences of malnutrition. Keep in mind that the classic picture of malnutrition showing a starving child in India or Africa is not the same picture of malnutrition that we should be seeing in the industrialized and technological world of the 21st century. Today's picture would have to include, not only the overweight and obese, but the trim, muscular, and seemingly fit athlete.

Our farmer and rancher friends have understood for many decades that to have viable agricultural operations, you must have healthy, disease free animals. This is primarily accomplished by supplementing into their feed the vitamins and minerals that are not already there. Veterinarians and farmers know that when animals exhibit what is called cribbiting and pica, where they chew fence posts, barn doors, metal troughs, tin cans, etc.; they are vitamin and mineral deficient. The simple cure is adding supplements to their diet.

Mankind experiences the same symptoms, but we may call it snacking or having the munchies. Much of the problem of obesity in the developed nations is a direct result of vitamin and mineral deficiencies, which can cause a constant craving for those nutrients that aren't getting in their diets. Therefore you have people always hungry because their bodies are demanding nutrition that they aren't getting. Most readily available foods supply loads of calories, but little real nutrition in the form of vitamins and minerals required to sustain a healthy living being.

The sad reality is that human medicine has for the most part focused on treating symptoms of disease rather than on the prevention of deficiency disease. Strangely enough, animal health care hasn't generally followed the same flawed path as human health care, because the reality of any viable agricultural operation is that you must have healthy and disease free animals to have a profitable operation. Farmers and ranchers have understood for many decades and even centuries that this is primarily accomplished by supplementing into the feed of their livestock the vitamins and minerals that may not already be there. But there is hope; people healthcare is moving slowly but surely in that same direction.

This material is intended only as information and should not be used to replace the expertise of medical professionals. When looking for medical help, we believe it best to consult those who practice not only the more conventional methods of medicine, but also whose first consideration are the nutritional deficiency aspects of disease treatment.

Following are excerpts from the 2nd Session of the 74th Congressional Record:

> *"Our physical well-being is more directly dependent upon minerals we take into our system than upon calories or vitamins, or upon precise proportions of starch, protein or carbohydrates we consume."*
>
> *"Do you know that most of us today are suffering from certain dangerous diet deficiencies which cannot be remedied until depleted soils from which our food comes are brought into proper mineral balance?"*
>
> *"The alarming fact is that foods (fruits, vegetables, and grains) now being raised on millions of acres of land that no longer contain enough of certain minerals are starving us-no matter how much of them we eat. No man of today can eat enough fruits and vegetables to supply his system with the minerals he requires for perfect health because his stomach isn't big enough to hold them."*

The truth is that our foods vary enormously in [nutritional] value, and some of them aren't worth eating as food ..."

> *"Laboratory tests prove that the fruits, the vegetables, the grains, the eggs and even the milk and the meats of today are not what they were a few generations ago (which doubtless explains how our forefathers thrived on a selection of foods that would starve us today!)"*
>
> *"It is bad news to learn from our leading authorities that 99% of the American people are deficient in these minerals, and that a marked deficiency in any one of the more important minerals actually results in disease.*

Any upset of the balance, any considerable lack of one or another element, however microscopic the body requirement may be, and we sicken, suffer, and shorten our lives."

"We know that vitamins are complex chemical substances which are indispensable to nutrition, and that each of them is of importance for normal function of some special structure of the body. Disorder and disease result from any vitamin [or mineral] deficiency. It is not commonly realized, however, that vitamins control the body's appropriation of minerals, and in the absence of minerals they have no function to perform. Lacking vitamins, the system can make some use of minerals, but lacking minerals, vitamins are useless."

Deficiency Diseases

Deficiency Diseases, disorders caused by lack of specific essential substances such as vitamins, minerals, or amino acids. More broadly, the term applies to conditions in which the essential substances are present but not absorbed, or in which the organism fails to produce a natural and essential substance (*see* Hormone). Such diseases as beriberi, scurvy, pellagra, and rickets are caused by lack of particular vitamins, and recovery is dramatically prompt when adequate quantities of the vitamins are supplied in the diet. Certain types of anemia may be caused by a dietary lack of iron in usable form. At least ten amino acids, ten minerals, and ten vitamins are indispensable nutritional elements in the human diet, and the absence of any one causes a specific deficiency disease.

Diet for Obesity and Under Weight

Most often, being underweight is a sign of an accompanying disorder.

This disorder must first be dealt with in order to bring your weight back to normal. In addition, to this treatment, physical activity may need to be modified and psychological counseling may be required. After the treatment of the primary disorder is successful, nutritional support may be provided along with dietary changes.

Dietary Management

The objectives of dietary modification are to restore the body to its normal weight, rebuild tissue and store nutrients, and maintain the desirable body weight.

Energy: A nutritious high energy diet providing calories over and above the body's requirement will result in weight gain. An increase of about 500-1000 Cal per day can result in a weight gain of approximately one kilogram per week.

Protein: A liberal intake of high quality protein will help in building up of muscle tissue. A daily protein intake of two grams per kilogram of body weight will be required. For example, if your body weight is 60 kg, you require 75-120 g protein.

Carbohydrates: A high carbohydrate intake is also necessary to meet the energy requirements of a malnourished body. The bulk of the diet, however, should not be increased as it cuts down food intake. Avoid taking more fiber than is necessary fcr regular bowel movement.

Fats: Fats aid in the weight gain process, but they should only be used in amounts that can be tolerated. Emulsified fats like butter, cream etc. are better tolerated by the body.

Minerals and Vitamins: These must be provided in sufficient amounts in order to counter for nutritional deficiencies.

Diet and Feeding Pattern: The amount of food intake cannot be substantially increased all of a sudden. The amount of food at each meal and the frequency of meals should be increased gradually. The calorie density of the foods can be increased, without increasing bulk, by using more sugar, jam, butter, cream, oil, and nuts. To increase the protein content of the diet, milk powder, cheese, cottage cheese, and protein concentrates can be added to liquid milk, and other beverages and soups.

Obesity-overeating-weight loss Diets-other Weight Issues...

Weight loss diets that work? Let's see ... "I can't stand women who can't get back to their original figure after having children." That seemed like a ridiculous thing to say but somehow this throw-away comment fell onto fertile ground. Six months later – a starvation diet. It was easy enough. A week later, and 10 pounds were gone.

Then, a few years later, another innocuous remark, by another person. Another man, to be precise – quite likely, that's important: "125 pounds? Well, you don't need to weigh more." It was probably forgotten the moment he turned back to his newspaper. And so it went, for years and years. Weight gain, weight loss, diets, exercising – a decade-long spiral.

Moments of emotional upheaval suggested food (and weight gain) just as those male voices suggested weight loss. And the food tasted good, the fullness in the stomach was reassuring, the slightly drugged feeling was a wonderful escape, the heaviness gave the feeling of groundedness that seemed otherwise so elusive. Then there were the occasional fantastic weight loss experiences!

But the spiral went up and up. This is what happens with yoyo dieting. Lose 10 pounds, gain 15. Lose 20 pounds, gain 30. Lose 30 pounds ... you get the picture. It's not just about losing weight but how to lose weight and keep it off.

When we analyze this little story, we see a number of things. Of course, they are not the only elements, and many of these elements are intricately intertwined. At any rate, looking at these elements can help untangle the web of obesity.

Expectations. Our culture is obsessed with weight and how much a person "should" weigh. Here's a question. If you are reasonably healthy and fit, how much does your weight matter? There is a saying, "scales are for fish". Let's not let the scales dictate how we feel about our bodies.

Self esteem/self worth. So much of our self worth is tied up in what other people say about us (or worse yet, what we imagine they say about us). Even unimportant little comments can throw us for a loop if we already feel insecure in a certain area.

For example, if I already feel insecure in my feminity or sexuality, a comment about my body shape by an important man in my life can inflict a wound that may fester for a long time.

Dieting: Weight loss diets don't work for yoyo dieters. Dieting certainly works for some people, for example for the person who overdoes it a bit on Christmas and then goes on a diet to lose five pounds – and those five pounds stay off. Diets don't work for most people with chronic weight problems. They need a lifestyle change.

Emotional Eating: Being angry or lonely can trigger the desire to eat. Sadness, excitement, boredom, fear, resentments add to the list of triggers. Literally any feeling at all can be the reason to grab those chips, a couple of donuts, the bag of cookies, a chocolate bar, or bring on yet another trip to the fridge. Eating can simply be a response to emotions – a sort of companion – or it can be used to mask those feelings. Food can be a drug, a form of self medication.

The Physical Experience of Eating: What can I say – food just tastes and feels good, and if something tastes and feels good, it's natural to want more of it. Pretty much everyone knows the experience of eating more than necessary. But for the overeater, it just doesn't stop. There is often an actual inability – learned or "wired in the brain" – to understand and react to the cues of hunger and fullness. It's like a car alarm that never goes off, or one that can't be turned off.

The Weight: The experience of being a "weighty person" is more reassuring than most people would think. One feels like a "person of substance", someone who can't be pushed around. The weight feels like insulation – it's harder to get hurt when there is an armour for protection.

So .... if you recognize yourself in any of this and you want a change in your life, what are some of your options?

Another Weight Loss Diet: There is a slim possibility that you haven't tried the right diet yet. If you need to try that again, make sure you use one that you can see yourself following for a long time. The more variety that diet has, the greater the chance it'll work. Says diet expert M.L. Dansiger, "The key to success is finding a diet plan that you can stick to".

Psychotherapy/counselling: As mentioned above, overeating may be connected to psychological issues such as low self esteem. Many people with weight problems have suffered abuse as children. A good counsellor can help sort out these problems. Just having someone listen to some things that have been kept hidden for a long time can be the beginning of weight release. If you feel that counselling might help, get in touch with me and we'll see what we can do. You can also go to the American Psychological Association for more information.

Overeaters Anonymous: Similar to Alcoholics Anonymous, these are support groups of peers who "have been there, done that, got the t-shirt". You can find people there who have struggled with their weight and successfully kept it off for many years. Many people find that underneath their eating problem is a "living problem". While by no means religious, Overeaters Anonymous is a spiritual approach.

> *... and, last not least: men and weight issues. We seem to think that women are the only ones who struggle with weight. There are lots of men who have weight issues, too. Because of cultural factors, these tend to be hidden– with the result that usually, men are very isolated around their weight issues. First of all, there are probably more women who are overweight, and second, men find it much, much harder to come together for support around such problems. Stay tuned for a section on men and weight issues.*

Weight Gain Diets

It is not a good idea of Increasing intake of junk foods and fatty foods to gain weight. You should be eating calorie dense yet nutritious food. Your calorie intake should come from foods that are healthy for you. The weight gaining diet should include high protein foods, high carbohydrate foods and healthy fats. Include these in your diet.

Example of Weight Gain Diet

Breakfast: Banana and milk or banana shake or smoothie, whole-grain toast, fruits, granola, nuts. Eat more fruit and drink less juice.

Do not give milk mixed with ghee to your child. It is not healthy.

Lunch: Roti/chapatti/wholegrain bread, rice, green vegetables, paneer (cottage cheese), dal, chickpeas (chole), black-eyed beans (lobia), rajma, whole wheat pudding (dalia), etc.

Dinner: Similar to lunch

In-between Meals: fruit, sandwich, yogurt (curd), milk, cheese, salad.

Avoid deep fried snacks like samosa, pakodas, bhujia etc.

Avoid fast foods including donut.

Weight Gain Tips : How to Gain Weight

Weight gain is as difficult as losing it, if you are naturally thin. Gaining weight is a problem for many people. They complain that they can't put on any weight.

Following are some tips to follow to gain weight. You will take some time to gain the weight you need, but be patient.

1. Consume more calories than you burn. Choose healthy foods to add calories.

   Drink healthy beverages to add calories.
2. Eat healthy food frequently, 5-6 times a day-3 larger meals and 3 smaller meals alternately. Separate them by at least 3 hours so you can digest each meal fully. Don't go without food for 5-6 hours after having a major meal.

   For example, if you wish to consume 3000 calories a day, you may eat 3 larger meals of about 650 calories and 3 smaller meals of about 450 calories.
3. Have a balanced diet.
4. Exercise regularly for healthy weight gain. Some thin people think that exercise is not good for them. This is not true, it keeps the metabolism high. Remember that eating alone is not sufficient. You don't want to gain fat but lean mass, so exercise is important.

Resistance training exercises will help to increase your muscle mass, which in turn will increase your metabolism. Learn to distinguish between weight gaining exercises and weight loss exercises.

Note that if you do not get enough amino acids during exercise, the existing muscle may break down. Amino acids come from protein rich foods.

Weight Gaining Foods

5. Protein is the key for the muscle mass. Without adequate protein, muscle gain is not possible because weight training demand for amino acids (which comes from protein).

You should daily eat about 2.2g of protein per kilogram (1g per pound) of your weight. For example, if you are 50kg (110pound), then you should eat 50x2.2=111g of protein spread over 5-6 meals in the day. Include high protein foods in your diet. Your protein intake should be from foods rather than from supplements.

Good sources of protein: whey, fish, dairy products (low fat variety), meats, unroasted nuts and seeds (almonds, pumpkin seeds, sesame seeds, sunflower seeds).

Milk is one of the best muscle foods.

The milk contains two high quality proteins, about 80 percent whey and 20 percent casein. Whey is quickly broken down into amino acids and absorbed into the bloodstream. Whey is very good to consume after workout. Casein is digested more slowly and provides the body with a steady supply of protein for a longer period of time.

Milk Nutrition

6. *Healthy Fats:* Avoid fatty foods. Most mothers, especially in India give too much ghee or butter to their children, thinking they will gain weight fast. But ghee is mostly saturated fat which is not a healthy fat for any body. Healthy fats are monounsaturated and polyunsaturated fats and omega-3 essential fatty acids.

Good Fats: cold pressed oils (olive, sunflower, linseed, canola, best cooking oil)

7. Complex carbohydrates is also needed.
8. Some people think that drinking beer helps gain weight. But it is not true, it accumulates in your abdomen, making it fatty.
9. Don't take protein supplements. Consult your doctor for protein supplements.

UNIT-VII

Yoga and Exercise

Yoga : Meaning and Definition

The word Yoga comes from the Sanskrit root 'yuj' which means 'to join'. Yoga is the science that teaches us the method of uniting the individual soul with the Supreme Soul, of merging the individual will in the Cosmic Will. To live in God, to commune with God is Yoga. Yoga is life in God, life in perfection, peace, lasting happiness and eternal Bliss. Life in God brings eternal Bliss. Yoga shows you the way, unites you with God, and makes you perfect and Immortal.

The meaning of the Sanskrit term: 'a state of union with the Divine; or an experience of oneness with the great Reality'. Yoga means to direct your mind towards God, to realise your oneness with the Divine Consciousness. It implies any effort that the soul may make in its endeavor to attain God. Yoga makes available to you the scientific method for approaching God. All the techniques, which eventually bestow upon the practitioner the experience of Divine Consciousness, may also be designated by the one word 'Yoga'.

If you define Yoga in the simplest term, it is the steady movement of the individual soul towards the Supreme Soul. Yoga is a steady ascent to the Divine. Yoga and Vedanta are universal in their scope. They are the property of all mankind. Yoga uses a technique by which you overcome the bondage of body through restraining your senses, mastering your mind, and controlling your thoughts and desires. Going beyond them, you reach the inner depth of your all-perfect and divine being.

Yoga is a path that leads up to the state of supreme blessedness and peace. Its practices constitute the techniques for the purification and preparation of human consciousness for entering into the experience of the supreme blissful Divine Reality.

Yoga is an exact science. The science of Yoga makes a study of man himself and declares that he is a triune being:

a) Firstly, with a gross and bestial nature;
b) secondly, endowed with reason but full of impurity;
c) thirdly, with all-pure and all-perfect divine nature which lies deep within.

1) The foremost feature in the yogic pattern of life is the process of purifying the lower nature. Purity is the foundation of yogic life. One has to be rooted in goodness, purity, truth and selflessness. Half of the process of Yoga is in thus getting perfectly established in ideal moral conduct. Yoga transforms one's lower nature into the Divine nature. Yoga shows how to overcome the imperfections of the lower nature and how to gain complete mastery over the mind and senses. Yoga is elimination of the negative traits of the animal nature through purification and refinement.

2) Yoga tells you not to be deluded by these passing objects which are perishable and therefore temporary. Yoga is a process of controlling the animal nature and eliminating the negative traits of that animal nature, and purifying and refining your psychological nature, so that the mind, the thoughts and sentiments are now directed towards the Supreme Divine Reality, and ultimately awakening the sleeping Divinity within. It is giving an upward trend to your psychological nature, to your emotions, sentiments and reasoning processes.

3) Man is essentially all-perfect. Yoga is the technique of attaining Divine Perfection and Immortality. Yoga is the art and science of divesting and directing

your entire human personality potential beyond your present state of sorrow, restlessness, isolation and fear into a higher state of Consciousness characterised by bliss, peace, fullness and fearlessness. Thus unfolding this awakened Divinity and trying to enter into an experience of radiant, unfolded and awakened Consciousness and to become established in this Consciousness of perennial Bliss, peace and blessedness is Yoga. Yoga is to awaken the sleeping Divinity within, to unfold it and make it radiantly manifest in your thought, word and deed, and enter into an experience of the all-perfect divine nature, and abide in Bliss and Peace.

Definition of Yoga

The word "yoga" comes from the Sanskrit root yuj, which means "to join" or "to yoke".

Yoga is a practical aid, not a religion. Yoga is an ancient art based on a harmonizing system of development for the body, mind, and spirit. The continued practice of yoga will lead you to a sense of peace and well-being, and also a feeling of being at one with their environment.

The practice of yoga makes the body strong and flexible, it also improves the functioning of the respiratory, circulatory, digestive, and hormonal systems. Yoga brings about emotional stability and clarity of mind.

In the practice of Yoga the ultimate aim is one of *self-development and self-realization.*

Extra Information

Think of this practice as being the means and tools to realign and rebalance your vehicle (body) on a regular basis. You take control and you can then become your body mechanic instead of having to pay someone else to do it (medical professionals). Because your body is finely tuned you will find that your chances for injuries and illnesses will drop as you are in a much more attuned state.

You don't want for something major to happen to you before you decide to do something about it. That's reactive behavior and that's going to set you back big time, all you have to do is take action now.

Prevention and care is by far the best medicine there is.

It all comes down to balance.

Getting Older

For most people getting old is a decision they make whether they know it or not. It basically comes down to the saying-Use it or lose it! Old age and the associated illnesses that come with it are big business, so therefore people in the western world especially are not encouraged to look after themselves. Everyone is worth more in the health business when they are sick.

Yoga Definition

Yoga is a Sanskrit word derived from the Sanskrit root "yuj" which means to connect, join or balance.

The most important thing, however, is that Yoga-with its entire applications and implications-is a powerful means to an end. The ultimate end of all human pursuits is "Moksha." Moksha is freedom from all bondage; freedom from insecurities; freedom from the clutches of desires; freedom from the sense of limitations and inadequacy; freedom from all that thwarts us on our divine journey in life. In other words, the end of all human pursuits is everlasting peace, happiness and a sense of fulfillment. This is possible with steady and prolonged sincere practice of Yoga. It activates a process of cleansing and purification of mind, which in turn, prepares us for the dawning of Self-knowledge. Yoga means this connection; this knowledge that removes the impurities and the veil of ignorance that keeps us strangers to ourselves.

Yoga should never be mistaken for any other mode of exercise, which is operational only on a physical level.

Yoga is a way of life; it is not removed from it. We do not need to feel disappointed or frustrated considering our limitations with regard to physical health; shape and size of the body; lack of time; lack of space or unavailability of a teacher. Yoga, in fact, is the means to overcome all these problems. Yoga includes every aspect of life. Yoga touches everything in life. All healing methods and meditations are part and parcel of Yoga. Yoga is like the sun itself, which brightens everything that comes into contact with it.

Definition: Yoga is usually defined as union: union between the limited self and the Divine Self. The aim of Yoga is not really to unite us with anything for we are already united. It is to help us realize our identity with the Divine Self, to make us know and tune into our intrinsic nature.

There are many definitions of Yoga, which apply to all levels of existence and awareness. At the physical level, we need to harmonize the functions of different organs, muscles and nerves so that they do not hamper or oppose each other. Disharmony in various body parts and systems brings about inefficiency and lethargy or clumsiness. Moreover, it manifests in diseases in the body.

In this context we can define Yoga as physical harmony & health and mental balance & peace.

The Bhagwad Gita, a very widely known classical text on Yoga, gives various definitions of Yoga.

1. Yoga is equanimity of mind in success and failure.
2. Yoga is discretion in work.
3. Yoga is the remover of misery and destroyer of pain.
4. Yoga is the supreme secret of life.
5. Yoga is serenity.
6. Yoga is the giver of infinite happiness. Patañjali, the author of the classical Yoga text, The Yoga Sutras, defines Yoga as, "complete control over patterns or modifications of the mind."

The Structure of Yoga:

The various branches of Yoga could be, for practical purposes, classified into five basic groups:

- *Jnana Yoga:* the Yoga committed to inquiry.
- *Karma Yoga:* the Yoga committed to selfless service and Dharma.

- *Bhakti Yoga:* the Yoga devoted to love and devotion to God.
- *Raja Yoga:* the Yoga committed to introspection and contemplation.
- *Hatha Yoga:* the Yoga devoted to the discipline of the body and the balance of the mental, physical and subtle forces of the body through the practice of asana and pranayama.

Iyengar Yoga is the name given to the Yoga of those who follow the practice and teachings of Yogacharya B.K.S. Iyengar, the world's greatest living master of Hatha Yoga. It is Ashtanga Yoga, a practice which embraces the 8 limbs of Yoga (yama, niyama, asana, pranayama, pratyahara, dharana, dhyana and samadhi). The emphasis is on the integrity of practice in asana and pranayama through concentration on alignment, creation of strength and flexibility and availability of the asana and/or pranayama to the practitioner by demonstration, verbal instruction and use of props.

There is an inherent therapeutic aspect as well as a body-mind-breath component in the practice due to this emphasis.

The Eight Limbs of Yoga

The practice of yoga is an art and science dedicated to creating union between body, mind and spirit. Its objective is to assist the practitioner in using the breath and body to foster an awareness of ourselves as individualized beings intimately connected to the unified whole of creation.

In short it is about making balance and creating equanimity so as to live in peace, good health and harmony with the greater whole. This art of right living was perfected and practiced in India thousands of years ago and the foundations of yoga philosophy were written down in *The Yoga Sutra* of Patanjali, approximately 200 AD. This sacred text describes the inner workings of the mind and provides an eight-step blueprint for controlling its restlessness so as to enjoying lasting peace.

The core of Patanjali's *Yoga Sutra* is an eight-limbed path that forms the structural framework for yoga practice. Upon practicing all eight limbs of the path it becomes self-evident that no one element is elevated over another in a hierarchical order. Each is part of a holistic focus which eventually brings completeness to the individual as they find their connectivity to the divine. Because we are all uniquely individual a person can emphasize one branch and then move on to another as they round out their understanding.

In brief the eight limbs, or steps to yoga, are as follows:

1. *Yama :* Universal morality
2. *Niyama :* Personal observances
3. *Asanas :* Body postures
4. *Pranayama :* Breathing exercises, and control of prana
5. *Pratyahara :* Control of the senses
6. *Dharana :* Concentration and cultivating inner perceptual awareness
7. *Dhyana :* Devotion, Meditation on the Divine
8. *Samadhi :* Union with the Divine

The first two limbs that Patanjali describes are the fundamental ethical precepts called yamas, and the niyamas. These can also be looked at as universal morality and personal observances. Yamas and niyamas are the suggestions given on how we should deal with people around us and our attitude toward ourselves. The attitude we have toward things and people outside ourselves is *yama*, how we relate to ourselves inwardly is *niyama*. Both are mostly concerned with how we use our energy in relationship to others and to ourselves.

The *yamas* are broken down into five "wise characteristics." Rather than a list of dos and don'ts, "they tell us that our fundamental nature is compassionate, generous, honest and peaceful." They are as follows:

Yamas (Universal Morality)

Ahimsa–Compassion for All Living Things: The word ahimsa literally mean not to injure or show cruelty to any creature or any person in any way whatsoever. Ahimsa is, however, more than just lack of violence as adapted in yoga. It means kindness, friendliness, and thoughtful consideration of other people and things. It also has to do with our duties and responsibilities too. Ahimsa implies that in every situation we should adopt a considerate attitude and do no harm.

Satya–Commitment to Truthfulness: Satya means "to speak the truth," yet it is not always desirable to speak the truth on all occasions, for it could harm someone unnecessarily. We have to consider what we say, how we say it, and in what way it could affect others. If speaking the truth has negative consequences for another, then it is better to say nothing. Satya should never come into conflict with our efforts to behave with ahimsa. This precept is based on the understanding that honest communication and action form the bedrock of any healthy relationship, community, or government, and that deliberate deception, exaggerations, and mistruths harm others.

Asteya-Non-stealing: Steya means "to steal"; asteya is the opposite-to take nothing that does not belong to us. This also means that if we are in a situation where someone entrusts something to us or confides in us, we do not take advantage of him or her. Non-stealing includes not only taking what belongs to another without permission, but also using something for a different purpose to that intended, or beyond the time permitted by its owner. The practice of asteya implies not taking anything that has not been freely given. This includes fostering a consciousness of how we ask for others' time for inconsiderate behavior demanding another's attention when not freely given is, in effect, stealing.

Brahmacharya-Sense Control: Brahmacharya is used mostly in the sense of abstinence, particularly in relationship to sexual activity. Brahmacharya suggests that we should form relationships that foster our understanding of the highest truths. Brahmacharya does not necessarily imply celibacy. Rather, it means responsible behavior with respect to our goal of moving toward the truth. Practicing brahmacharya means that we use our sexual energy to regenerate our connection to our spiritual self. It also means that we don't use this energy in any way that might harm others.

Aparigraha-Neutralizing the Desire to Acquire and Hoard Wealth: Aparigraha means to take only what is necessary, and not to take advantage of a situation or act greedy. We should only take what we have earned; if we take more, we are exploiting someone else. The yogi feels that the collection or hoarding of things implies a lack of faith in God and in himself to provide for his future. Aparigraha also implies letting go of our attachments to things and an understanding that impermanence and change are the only constants.

The Yoga Sutra describes what happens when these five behaviors outlined above become part of a person's daily life. Thus, the yamas are the moral virtues which, if attended to, purify human nature and contribute to health and happiness of society.

Niyama (Personal Observances)

Niyama means "rules" or "laws." These are the rules prescribed for personal observance. Like the yamas, the five niyamas are not exercises or actions to be simply studied. They represent far more than an attitude. Compared with the yamas, the niyamas are more intimate and personal. They refer to the attitude we adopt toward ourselves as we create a code for living soulfully

***Sauca-Purity*:** The first niyama is sauca, meaning purity and cleanliness. Sauca has both an inner and an outer aspect. Outer cleanliness simply means keeping ourselves clean. Inner cleanliness has as much to do with the healthy, free functioning of our bodily organs as with the clarity of our mind. Practicing asanas or pranayama are essential means for attending to this inner sauca. Asanas tones the entire body and removes toxins while pranayama cleanses our lungs, oxygenates our blood and purifies our nerves. "But more important than the physical cleansing of the body is the cleansing of the mind of its disturbing emotions like hatred, passion, anger, lust, greed, delusion and pride."

Santosa-Contentment: Another niyama is santosa, modesty and the feeling of being content with what we have. To be at peace within and content with one's lifestyle finding contentment even while experiencing life's difficulties for life becomes a process of growth through all kinds of circumstances.

We should accept that there is a purpose for everything-yoga calls it karma – and we cultivate contentment 'to accept what happens'. It means being happy with what we have rather than being unhappy about what we don't have.

Tapas–Disciplined Use of Our Energy: Tapas refers to the activity of keeping the body fit or to confront and handle the inner urges without outer show. Literally it means to heat the body and, by so doing, to cleanse it. Behind the notion of tapas lies the idea we can direct our energy to enthusiastically engage life and achieve our ultimate goal of creating union with the Divine. Tapas helps us burn up all the desires that stand in our way of this goal. Another form of tapas is paying attention to what we eat. Attention to body posture, attention to eating habits, attention to breathing patterns-these are all tapas.

Svadhyaya–Self-study: The fourth niyama is svadhyaya. Sva means "self' adhyaya means "inquiry" or "examination". Any activity that cultivates self-reflective consciousness can be considered svadhyaya. It means to intentionally find self-awareness in all our activities and efforts, even to the point of welcoming and accepting our limitations. It teaches us to be centered and non-reactive to the dualities, to burn out unwanted and self-destructive tendencies.

Isvarapranidhana-Celebration of the Spiritual: Isvarapranidhana means "to lay all your actions at the feet of God." It is the contemplation on God (Isvara) in order to become attuned to god and god's will. It is the recognition that the spiritual suffuses everything and through our attention and care we can attune ourselves with our role as part of the Creator. The practice requires that we set aside some time each day to recognize that there is some omnipresent force larger than ourselves that is guiding and directing the course of our lives.

Asanas (Body postures)

Asana is the practice of physical postures. It is the most commonly known aspect of yoga for those unfamiliar with the other seven limbs of Patanjali's *Yoga Sutra*. The practice of moving the body into postures has widespread benefits; of these the most underlying are improved health, strength, balance and flexibility. On a deeper level the practice of asana, which means "staying" or "abiding" in Sanskrit, is used as a tool to calm the mind and move into the inner essence of being. The challenge of poses offers the practitioner the opportunity to explore and control all aspects of their emotions, concentration, intent, faith, and unity between the physical and the ethereal body.

Indeed, using asanas to challenge and open the physical body acts as a binding agent to bring one in harmony with all the unseen elements of their being, the forces that shape our lives through our responses to the physical world. Asana then becomes a way of exploring our mental attitudes and strengthening our will as we learn to release and move into the state of grace that comes from creating balance between our material world and spiritual experience.

As one practices asana it fosters a quieting of the mind, thus it becomes both a preparation for meditation and a meditation sufficient in and of itself. Releasing to the flow and inner strength that one develops brings about a profound grounding spirituality in the body. The physicality of the yoga postures becomes a vehicle to expand the consciousness that pervades our every aspect of our body.

The key to fostering this expansion of awareness and consciousness begins with the control of breath, the fourth limb–Pranayama. Patanjali suggests that the asana and the pranayama practices will bring about the desired state of health; the control of breath and bodily posture will harmonize the flow of energy in the organism, thus creating a fertile field for the evolution of the spirit. "This down-to-earth, flesh-and-bones practice is simply one of the most direct and expedient ways to meet yourself. ... This limb of yoga practice reattaches us to our body. In reattaching ourselves to our bodies we reattach ourselves to the responsibility of living a life guided by the undeniable wisdom of our body." To this B.K.S. Iyengar adds: "The needs of the body are the needs of the divine spirit which lives through the body. The yogi does not look heaven-ward to find God for he know that He is within."

Pranayama (Breath Control)

Pranayama is the measuring, control, and directing of the breath. Pranayama controls the energy (prana) within the organism, in order to restore and maintain health and to promote evolution. When the in-flowing breath is neutralized or joined with the out-flowing breath, then perfect relaxation and balance of body activities are realized. In yoga, we are concerned with balancing the flows of vital forces, then directing them inward to the chakra system and upward to the crown chakra.

Pranayama, or breathing technique, is very important in yoga. It goes hand in hand with the asana or pose. In the *Yoga Sutra*, the practices of pranayama and asana are considered to be the highest form of purification and self discipline for the mind and the body, respectively. The practices produce the actual physical sensation of heat, called tapas, or the inner fire of purification. It is taught that this heat is part of the process of purifying the nadis, or subtle nerve channels of the body. This allows a more healthful state to be experienced and allows the mind to become more calm. As the yogi follows the proper rhythmic patterns of slow deep breathing "the patterns strengthen the respiratory system, soothe the nervous system and reduce craving. As desires and cravings diminish, the mind is set free and becomes a fit vehicle for concentration."

Pratyahara (Control of the Senses)

Pratyahara means drawing back or retreat. The word *ahara* means "nourishment"; pratyahara translates as "to withdraw oneself from that which nourishes the senses." In yoga, the term pratyahara implies withdrawal of the senses from attachment to external objects. It can then be seen as the practice of non-attachment to sensorial distractions as we constantly return to the path of self realization and achievement of internal peace. It means our senses stop living off the things that stimulate; the senses no longer depend on these stimulants and are not fed by them any more.

In pratyahara we sever this link between mind and senses, and the senses withdraw. When the senses are no longer tied to external sources, the result is restraint or pratyahara. Now that the vital forces are flowing back to the Source within, one can concentrate without being distracted by externals or the temptation to cognize externals.

Pratyahara occurs almost automatically when we meditate because we are so absorbed in the object of meditation. Precisely because the mind is so focused, the senses follow it; it is not happening the other way around.

No longer functioning in their usual manner, the senses become extraordinarily sharp. Under normal circumstances the senses become our masters rather than being our servants. The senses entice us to develop cravings for all sorts of things. In pratyahara the opposite occurs: when we have to eat we eat, but not because we have a craving for food. In pratyahara we try to put the senses in their proper place, but not cut them out of our actions entirely.

Much of our emotional imbalance are our own creation. A person who is influenced by outside events and sensations can never achieve the inner peace and tranquility. This is because he or she will waste much mental and physical energy in trying to suppress unwanted sensations and to heighten other sensations. This will eventually result in a physical or mental imbalance, and will, in most instances, result in illness.

Patanjali says that the above process is at the root of human unhappiness and uneasiness. When people seek out yoga, hoping to find that inner peace which is so evasive, they find that it was theirs all along. In a sense, yoga is nothing more than a process which enables us to stop and look at the processes of our own minds; only in this way can we understand the nature of happiness and unhappiness, and thus transcend them both.

Dharana (Concentration and cultivating inner perceptual awareness)

Dharana means "immovable concentration of the mind". The essential idea is to hold the concentration or focus of attention in one direction. "When the body has been tempered by asanas, when the mind has been refined by the fire of pranayama and when the senses have been brought under control by pratyahara, the sadhaka (seeker) reaches the sixth stage, dharana. Here he is concentrated wholly on a single point or on a task in which he is completely engrossed. The mind has to be stilled in order to achieve this state of complete absorption."

In dharana we create the conditions for the mind to focus its attention in one direction instead of going out in many different directions. Deep contemplation and reflection can create the right conditions, and the focus on this one point that we have chosen becomes more intense. We encourage one particular activity of the mind and, the more intense it becomes, the more the other activities of the mind fall away.

The objective in dharana is to steady the mind by focusing its attention upon some stable entity. The particular object selected has nothing to do with the general purpose, which is to stop the mind from wandering-through memories, dreams, or reflective thought-by deliberately holding it single-mindedly upon some apparently static object.

B.K.S. Iyengar states that the objective is to achieve the mental state where the mind, intellect, and ego are "all restrained and all these faculties are offered to the Lord for His use and in His service. Here there is no feeling of 'I' and 'mine'."

When the mind has become purified by yoga practices, it becomes able to focus efficiently on one subject or point of experience. Now we can unleash the great potential for inner healing.

Dhyana (Devotion, Meditation on the Divine)

Dhyana means worship, or profound and abstract religious meditation. It is perfect contemplation. It involves concentration upon a point of focus with the intention of knowing the truth about it. The concept holds that when one focuses their mind in concentration on an object the mind is transformed into the shape of the object. Hence, when one focuses on the divine they become more reflective of it and they know their true nature. "His body, breath, senses, mind, reason and ego are all integrated in the object of his contemplation–the Universal Spirit."

During dhyana, the consciousness is further unified by combining clear insights into distinctions between objects and between the subtle layers of perception. "We learn to differentiate between the mind of the perceiver, the means of perception, and the objects perceived, between words, their meanings, and ideas, and between all the levels of evolution of nature."

As we fine-tune our concentration and become more aware of the nature of reality we perceive that the world is unreal. "The only reality is the universal self, or God, which is veiled by Maya (the illusory power). As the veils are lifted, the mind becomes clearer. Unhappiness and fear–even the fear of death–vanishes. This state of freedom, or Moksha, is the goal of Yoga. It can be reached by constant enquiry into the nature of things." Meditation becomes our tool to see things clearly and perceive reality beyond the illusions that cloud our mind.

Samadhi (Union with the Divine)

The final step in the eight-fold path of Yoga is the attainment of Samadhi. Samadhi means "to bring together, to merge." In the state of samadhi the body and senses are at rest, as if asleep, yet the faculty of mind and reason are alert, as if awake; one goes beyond consciousness. During samadhi, we realize what it is to be an identity without differences, and how a liberated soul can enjoy pure awareness of this pure identity. The conscious mind drops back into that unconscious oblivion from which it first emerged.

Thus, samadhi refers to union or true Yoga. There is an ending to the separation that is created by the "I" and "mine" of our illusory perceptions of reality. The mind does not distinguish between self and non-self, or between the object contemplated and the process of contemplation. The mind and the intellect have stopped and there is only the experience of consciousness, truth and unutterable joy.

The achievement of samadhi is a difficult task. For this reason the *Yoga Sutra* suggests the practice of asanas and pranayama as preparation for dharana, because these influence mental activities and create space in the crowded schedule of the mind. Once dharana has occurred, dhyana and samadhi can follow.

These eight steps of yoga indicate a logical pathway that leads to the attainment of physical, ethical, emotional, and psycho-spiritual health. Yoga does not seek to change the individual; rather, it allows the natural state of total health and integration in each of us to become a reality.

Need and Importance of Yoga

Yoga Benefits: The most important benefit of yoga is physical and mental therapy. The aging process, which is largely an artificial condition, caused mainly by autointoxication or self-poisoning, can be slowed down by practicing yoga. By keeping the body clean, flexible and well lubricated, we can significantly reduce the catabolic process of cell deterioration. To get the maximum benefits of yoga one has to combine the practices of yogasanas, pranayama and meditation.

Regular practice of asanas, pranayama and meditation can help such diverse ailments such as diabetes, blood pressure, digestive disorders, arthritis, arteriosclerosis, chronic fatigue, asthma, varicose veins and heart conditions. Laboratory tests have proved the yogi's increased abilities of consciously controlling autonomic or involuntary functions, such as temperature, heartbeat and blood pressure. Research into the effects of yogic practices on HIV is currently underway with promising results.

According to medical scientists, yoga therapy is successful because of the balance created in the nervous and endocrine systems which directly influences all the other systems and organs of the body. Yoga acts both as a curative and preventive therapy. The very essence of yoga lies in attaining mental peace, improved concentration powers, a relaxed state of living and harmony in relationships.

Through the practice of yoga, we become aware of the interconnectedness between our emotional, mental and physical levels. Gradually this awareness leads to an understanding of the more subtle areas of existence. The ultimate goal of yoga is to make it possible for you to be able to fuse together the gross material (annamaya), physical (pranamaya), mental (manomaya), intellectual (vijnanamaya) and spiritual (anandamaya) levels within your being.

Physiological Benefits

Physicians and scientists are discovering brand new health benefits of yoga everyday. Studies show it can relieve the symptoms of several common and potentially life-threatening illnesses such as arthritis, arteriosclerosis, chronic fatigue, diabetes, AIDS, asthma and obesity.

Asthma

Studies conducted at yoga institutions in India have reported impressive success in improving asthma. It has also been proved that asthma attacks can usually be prevented by yoga methods without resorting to drugs. Physicians have found that the addition of improved concentration abilities and yogic meditation together with the practice of simple postures and pranayama makes treatment more effective. Yoga practice also results in greater reduction in anxiety scores than drug therapy. Doctors believe that yoga practice helps patients by enabling them to gain access to their own internal experience and increased self-awareness.

Respiration Problems

Patients who practice yoga have a better chance of gaining the ability to control their breathing problems. With the help of yogic breathing exercises, it is possible to control an attack of severe shortness of breath without having to seek medical help. Various studies have confirmed the beneficial effects of yoga for patients with respiratory problems.

High Blood Pressure

The relaxation and exercise components of yoga have a major role to play in the treatment and prevention of high blood pressure (hypertension). A combination of biofeedback and yogic breathing and relaxation techniques has been found to lower blood pressure and reduce the need for high blood pressure medication in people suffering from it.

Pain Management

Yoga is believed to reduce pain by helping the brain's pain center regulate the gate-controlling mechanism located in the spinal cord and the secretion of natural painkillers in the body. Breathing exercises used in yoga can also reduce pain. Because muscles tend to relax when you exhale, lengthening the time of exhalation can help produce relaxation and reduce tension. Awareness of breathing helps to achieve calmer, slower respiration and aid in relaxation and pain management.

Yoga's inclusion of relaxation techniques and meditation can also help reduce pain. Part of the effectiveness of yoga in reducing pain is due to its focus on self-awareness. This self-awareness can have a protective effect and allow for early preventive action.

Back Pain

Back pain is the most common reason to seek medical attention. Yoga has consistently been used to cure and prevent back pain by enhancing strength and flexibility. Both acute and long-term stress can lead to muscle tension and exacerbate back problems.

Arthritis

Yoga's gentle exercises designed to provide relief to needed joints had been Yoga's slow-motion movements and gentle pressures reach deep into troubled joints. In addition, the easy stretches in conjunction with deep breathing exercises relieve the tension that binds up the muscles and further tightens the joints. Yoga is exercise and relaxation rolled into one-the perfect anti-arthritis formula.

Weight Reduction

Regular yoga practice can help in weight management. Firstly, some of the asanas stimulate sluggish glands to increase their hormonal secretions. The thyroid gland, especially, has a big effect on our weight because it affects body metabolism. There are several asanas, such as the shoulder stand and the fish posture, which are specific for the thyroid gland. Fat metabolism is also increased, so fat is converted to muscle and energy. This means that, as well as losing fat, you will have better muscle tone and a higher vitality level.

Yogic practices that reduce anxiety tend to reduce anxious eating. In addition, yoga deep breathing increases the oxygen intake to the body cells, including the fat cells. This causes increased oxidation or burning up of fat cells. Yogic exercises induce more continuous and deeper breathing which gradually burns, sometimes forcefully, many of the calories already ingested.

Psychological Benefits

Regular yoga practice creates mental clarity and calmness, increases body awareness, relieves chronic stress patterns, relaxes the mind, centers attention and sharpens concentration.

Self-Awareness

Yoga strives to increase self-awareness on both a physical and psychological level. Patients who study yoga learn to induce relaxation and then to use the technique whenever pain appears. Practicing yoga can provide chronic pain sufferers with useful tools to actively cope with their pain and help counter feelings of helplessness and depression.

Mental Performance

A common technique used in yoga is breathing through one nostril at a time. Electroencephalogram (EEG) studies of the electrical impulses of the brain have shown that breathing through one nostril results in increased activity on the opposite side of the brain. Some experts suggest that the regular practice of breathing through one nostril may help improve communication between the right and left side of the brain. Studies have also shown that this increased brain activity is associated with better performance and doctors even suggest that yoga can enhance cognitive performance.

Mood Change and Vitality

Mental health and physical energy are difficult to quantify, but virtually everyone who participates in yoga over a period of time reports a positive effect on outlook and energy level.

Yogic stretching and breathing exercises have been seen to result in an invigorating effect on both mental and physical energy and improved mood.

Spiritual Benefits

When you achieve the yogic spirit, you can begin knowing yourself at peace. The value of discovering one‘s self and of enjoying one‘s self as is, begins a journey into being rather than doing. Life can then be lived practicing “ yoga off the mat”.

Pride

Pride, and especially anxiety about pride, is something which Hatha Yoga seeks to diminish or eliminate. To one who has been dejected because he cannot do his work properly when he becomes tired, irritable, or haggard, any degree of refreshment may be accompanied by additional degrees of self-respect. Furthermore, one who has benefited from yoga may be moved to help his friends who are obviously in need, he may instruct others and be rewarded with appreciation due a to teacher. But if one succeeds in achieving skill which provides health and self-confidence, one may justly raise his self-esteem simply by observing himself living the improved results as an achieved fact.

Knowledge

Yogic theory and practice lead to increased self-knowledge. This knowledge is not merely that of the practical kind relating to techniques, but especially of a spiritual sort pertaining to grasping something about the nature of the self at rest.

Knowing the self at rest, at peace, as a being rather than merely as an agent or doer, is a genuine kind of knowledge which usually gets lost in the rush of activities and push of desires. The value of discovering one‘s self and of enjoying one‘s self as it is, rather than as it is going to be, is indeed a value as well as a kind of knowledge.

Importance of Yoga

The importance of yoga and it’s role in healing and preventing various disorders has been developed over centuries of research and experience.They have been found to be extremely effective.It is important to have a proper yoga mat.Please visit Yoga Mats in order to have a safer and and more convinient mat.

Major role of yoga is to:

Increase the flexibility of body and preving formation of energy blocks which leads to a healthier body.

Massage the internal organs of the body and the rarely stimulated parts such as the thyroid gland.

help obese people to loose extra fat and weight which is one of the major causes of illness.

it can heal various health disorders such as back ache,arthritis etc and even stammering.

it imroves systemic circulation of blood through out the body and there by increase of oxygen to tissues.

improves gastrointestinal tract(stimulates secretions in hypo conditions)

prevents protien loud on kidney

improves psychology and patient has a more positive attitude towards life.

Yoga Practice for Enhancing Body and Mind

More significantly, yoga is considered as an all in one practice. There are many different types of yoga exercises and a variety of exercises with different health benefits of yoga.

These exercise choices can be stopped whenever you start practicing yoga.

- Weight training for strength
- Cardiovascular health through jogging or aerobics
- Tai Chi for increasing a sense of balance and synchronization
- Flexibility and strength can be increased with stretching exercises
- Meditation for peace of mind and relaxation

Yoga is above stretching and relaxation techniques, it's the ideal challenge for body and mind.

Who Should Practice Toga?

Yoga can be practiced by anyone from the range of people who presently find no physical exercise at all to the range of Olympic athletes. People of all age groups can practice yoga. Knowing the effects of yoga on physical, mental and spiritual aspects, yoga is being practiced by millions of people all over the world.

Purna yoga also called integral yoga, is a careful alignment of your body while you hold poses, and directs to growth physically, emotionally, and mentally. In particular, yoga needs concentration, determination, and practice. If your aim is to recuperate vigor, health, and feel stronger and younger, then assumes yoga as your exercise of choice. However, if you are in search of a quick fix or just temporary relief of the symptoms, then it is better to look at another form of exercise.

If you desire for a programme that acquires more challenging as you move forward, that can begin despite of the condition your body is in, and if you are in search of a type of exercise that is balanced, then yoga may be the best for you.

After making yoga as a choice of exercise, you can start on the lookout for yoga classes, but it is more important for you to become familiar with the different types of yoga, so as to ask about the types of yoga you are interested in when you consult a yoga instructor.

Consider that there are numerous different types and styles of yoga that have been developed over the years. So, you can select your yoga practice according to your fitness level. Thus, the practice of yoga can assure you all the benefit from the discipline, breathing techniques and the physical exercise you get in yoga practices.

Practice of Yoga and Physical Exercise

According to a report by the Himalayan Academy's Hinduism Today publication, a schism has occurred between Christians and Hindus in the former Soviet Republic of Slovakia ("Slovakia"). The situation revolves around a simple question: "Is Yoga a Hindu religious practice or physical exercise?"

In this particular incident, the question arose when a variant of Swami Maheshwarananda's "Yoga in Daily Life" programme was considered for introduction into Slovakia's school system. According to the *Hinduism Today* report, the plan was to offer the class to help alleviate back pain in the students. However, critics of the programme have suggested the exercise is much more than a simple substitute for Tylenol.

Apparently, after hearing about this initiative, both Protestant and Catholic Christians sent a clear message – this is not just exercise, it is Hinduism. Bishop Ivan Osusky of the Evangelical Church of Augsburg Confession commented, "Yoga is not [merely] gymnastics. It leads to individualism, which further leads to belief in reincarnation. It is an onslaught of Hinduism" ("Slovakia"). Slovakia's Catholic Bishops also protested with a strongly worded communique.

Christian Apologist Robert M. Bowman, Jr., of the Institute for the Development of Evangelical Apologetics, seems to agree with the Bishops. In an article for Apologetics Index Bowman argues against Yoga, saying "Does yoga conflict with my religion? You betcha. [...] Anything that encourages people to believe that spiritual fulfillment can be attained in any religion [...] conflicts with my belief that without Jesus Christ people of all religions (even Christianity!) are lost."

Milan Ftacnik, Slovak's Minister of Education, disagrees, instead siding with the Swami. The Hinduism Today coverage quotes Ftacnik as saying, "Yoga has existed here for decades and we have not become a Hindu country. Catholics, Baptists, Hindus or Muslims can practice yoga." The article notes that Ftacnik does not belong to an organized religion.

At the very least, even the defenders of Yoga must admit that its core purpose is religious in nature. According to Lewis Hopfe and Mark Woodward, "Yoga basically follows the Sankhya system, viewing the world as a dualism and teaching that one should attempt to yoke or join the individual spirit to god, the atman, to Brahman." The tome also notes "The main feature of Yoga is meditation. Meditation is necessary even for the gods if they are to find release from the cycle of birth, death, and rebirth" (96-97).

Perhaps the real issue occurs in that the clash is between Christianity, which historically rejects pluralistic acceptance of other religions' beliefs and practices, and Hinduism, which as one Swami put it, "believe[s] not only in universal tolerance, but [... also] accept[s] all religions as true" (71). From the Hindu's perspective, then, it may seem harmless for Christians to participate in Yoga even if it does have religious overtones, perhaps leaving Hindus to wonder what the problem is.

For now, it seems that connection will delay any introduction of Yoga into Slovak classrooms. After the Christian Democratic Movement threatened to cease support for the ruling coalition government, the administration backed off on the programme. Should they choose to renew their push for the programme, it will no doubt cause the question of Hinduism's ties to Yoga to be considered much more deeply then previously. With Yoga's popularity in many nations, including the United States, the results of this debate should prove to have far reaching effects beyond the small CIS nation.

Different Types of Yoga

Ananda Yoga: Ananda Yoga classes focus on gentle postures designed to move the energy up to the brain and prepare the body for meditation. Classes also focus on proper body alignment and controlled breathing.

Anusara Yoga is a relatively new form of yoga (1997), which pairs strict principles of alignment with a playful spirit. Postures can be challenging, but the real message of Anusara is to open your heart and strive to connect with the divine in yourself and others.

Ashtanga (or Astanga) Yoga is the name given to the system of yoga taught by Sri K. Pattabhi Jois. This style of yoga is physically demanding as it involves synchronizing breathing with progressive and continuous series of postures-a process producing intense internal heat and a profuse, purifying sweat that detoxifies muscles and organs. The result is improved circulation, flexibility, stamina, a light and strong body, and a calm mind. Ashtanga is an athletic yoga practice and is not for beginners.

Bikram Yoga is the method of yoga that is a comprehensive workout that includes all the components of fitness: muscular strength, muscular endurance, cardiovascular flexibility and weight loss. The founder, Bikram Choudhury, was a gold medal Olympic weight lifter in 1963 and is a disciple of Bishnu Ghosh, brother of Paramahansa Yogananda, (Autobiography of a Yogi). One of the unusual but most beneficial aspects of Bikram's yoga practice is the 95-105 degree temperature which promotes more flexibility, detoxification, and prevention of injuries. This is the only yoga style that specializes in using the heated environment.

Hatha is an easy-to-learn basic form of yoga that has become very popular in the United States. Hatha Yoga is the foundation of all Yoga styles. It incorporates Asanas (postures), Pranayama (regulated breathing), meditation (Dharana & Dhyana) and kundalini (Laya Yoga) into a complete system that can be used to achieve enlightenment or self-realization. It has become very popular in America as source of exercise and stress management. The ideal way to practice the Hatha Yoga poses (asanas) is to approach the practice session in a calm, meditative mood. Sit quietly for a few moments, then begin the series, slowly, with control and grace, being inwardly aware as the body performs the various poses selected for the practice session. Do not overdo the asanas or try to compete with others. Take it easy and enjoy.

Integral Yoga: This traditional type of yoga combines postures, breathing exercises, selfless service, meditation, chanting, prayer, and self-inquiry.

ISHTA: Developed by South African teacher Mani Finger and popularized in the States by his son Alan, ISHTA (Integral Science of Hatha and Tantric Arts) focuses on opening energy channels throughout the body with postures, visualizations, and meditation.

Iyengar Yoga, developed by yoga master B.K.S. Iyengar more than 60 years ago, promotes strength, flexibility, endurance, and balance through coordinated breathing and poses that require precise body alignment. The poses are generally held longer than in other styles of yoga. In Iyengar, you slowly move into a pose, hold it for a minute or so, and then rest for a few breaths before stretching into another. Equipment like cushions, blankets, straps, and blocks to help the less flexible also distinguishes Iyengar from other types of yoga.

Although Iyengar incorporates the traditional postures, or asanas, that make up the broader category of hatha yoga, the cushions and other props revolutionized yoga by enabling everyone — even the elderly, sick, and disabled — to practice. Because of its slow pace, attention to detail, and use of props, Iyengar yoga can be especially good if you're recovering from an injury. Iyengar is still one of the most popular types of yoga taught today.

Jivamukti Yoga: Developed in 1986 by Sharon Gannon and David Life, the Jivamukti Yoga method expresses the spiritual and ethical aspects of the practice of yoga that have been disregarded or devalued in contemporary times. It is a vigorous and challenging asana form with an emphasis on scriptural study, Sanskrit chanting, vegetarianism, non-violence, meditation, devotion to God and the role that music and listening play in the practice of yoga. Life and Gannon currently operate a popular yoga studio in New York City.

Kali Ray TriYoga: A series of flowing, dancelike movements was developed by Kali Ray in 1980. The practice also incorporates pranayama (breathing exercises) and meditation. Kali Ray runs the TriYoga Center in Santa Cruz, California.

Kripalu is called the yoga of consciousness. This gentle, introspective practice urges practitioners to hold poses to explore and release emotional and spiritual blockages. Goal-oriented striving is discouraged and precise alignment is not as important as in some other traditions. There are three stages in Kripalu yoga. Stage One focuses on learning the postures and exploring your bodies abilities. Stage Two involves holding the postures for an extended time, developing concentration and inner awareness. Stage Three is like a meditation in motion in which the movement from one posture to another arises unconsciously and spontaneously.

Kundalini practice concentrates on awakening the energy at the base of the spine and drawing it upward. In addition to postures, a typical class will also include chanting, meditation, and breathing exercises. Power Yoga is essentially yoga with brawn. It's the American interpretation of ashtanga yoga, a discipline that combines stretching, strength training, and meditative breathing. But power yoga takes ashtanga one step further. Many of the poses (also called postures or their Sanskrit name, asanas) resemble basic calisthenics — push-ups and handstands, toe touches and side bends — but the key to power yoga's sweat-producing, muscle-building power is the pace. Instead of pausing between poses as you would in traditional yoga, each move flows into the next, making it an intense aerobic workout.

Restorative Yoga: In a restorative yoga class you'll spend long periods of time lying on blocks, blankets and bolsters-passively allowing muscles to relax.

Sivananda Yoga: Like Integral Yoga, this traditional type of yoga combines postures, breathing, dietary restrictions, chanting, scriptural study, and meditation. The popular TV yoga teacher Lilias got her start practicing Sivananda Yoga.

Svaroopa Yoga: New students find this a very approachable style, often beginning in chair poses that are comfortable. Promotes healing and transformation.

Viniyoga: This is commonly used as a therapeutic practice for people who have suffered injuries or are recovering from surgery. It is a gentle, healing practice that is tailored to each person's body type and needs as they grow and change.

Vinyasa: Focuses on coordination of breath and movement and it is a very physically active form of yoga. It began with Krishnamacharya who later passed it on to Pattabhi Jois.

White Lotus Yoga: A modified Ashtanga practice developed by Ganga White which is combined with breathwork and meditation.

Exerciese Types : Aerobic Exercise

Aerobic exercise refers to exercise that involves or improves oxygen consumption by the body. Aerobic means "with oxygen", and refers to the use of oxygen in the body's metabolic or energy-generating process.

Many types of exercise are aerobic, and by definition are performed at moderate levels of intensity for extended periods of time. To obtain the best results, an aerobic exercise session involves a warming up period, followed by at least 20 minutes of moderate to intense exercise involving large muscle groups, and a cooling down period at the end.

History

Both the term and the specific exercise method were developed by Kenneth H. Cooper, M.D., an exercise physiologist, and Col. Pauline Potts, a physical therapist, both in the United States Air Force. Dr. Cooper, an avowed exercise enthusiast, was personally and professionally puzzled about why some people with excellent muscular strength were still prone to poor performance at tasks such as long-distance running, swimming, and bicycling. He began measuring systematic human performance using a bicycle ergometer, and began measuring sustained performance in terms of a person's ability to use oxygen. His groundbreaking book, *Aerobics*, was published in 1968, and included scientific exercise programmes using running, walking, swimming and bicycling. The book came at a fortuitous historical moment, when increasing weakness and inactivity in the general population was causing a perceived need for increased exercise. It became a bestseller. Cooper's data provided the scientific baseline for almost all modern aerobics programmes, most of which are based on oxygen-consumption equivalency.

Aerobic versus Anaerobic Exercise

Aerobic exercise and fitness can be contrasted with anaerobic exercise, of which strength training and weight training are the most salient examples. The two types of exercise differ by the duration and intensity of muscular contractions involved, as well as by how energy is generated within the muscle. Initially during aerobic exercise, glycogen is broken down to produce glucose, which is then broken down using oxygen to generate energy. In the absence of these carbohydrates, fat metabolism is initiated instead. The latter is a slow process, and is accompanied by a decline in performance level. This gradual switch to fat as fuel is a major cause of what marathon runners call "hitting the wall". Anaerobic exercise, in contrast, refers to the initial phase of exercise, or to any short burst of intense exertion, in which the glycogen or sugar is consumed without oxygen, and is a far less efficient process. Operating anaerobically, an untrained 400 meter sprinter may "hit the wall" short of the full distance.

Aerobic exercise comprises innumerable forms. In general, it is performed at a moderate level of intensity over a relatively long period of time. For example, running a long distance at a moderate pace is an aerobic exercise, but sprinting is not. Playing singles tennis, with near-continuous motion, is generally considered aerobic activity, while golf or two person team tennis, with brief bursts of activity punctuated by more frequent breaks, may not be predominantly aerobic. Some sports are thus inherently "aerobic", while other aerobic exercises, such as fartlek training or aerobic dance classes, are designed specifically to improve aerobic capacity and fitness.

Among the recognized benefits of doing regular aerobic exercise are:

- Strengthening the muscles involved in respiration, to facilitate the flow of air in and out of the lungs
- Strengthening and enlarging the heart muscle, to improve its pumping efficiency and reduce the resting heart rate, known as aerobic conditioning
- Toning muscles throughout the body
- Improving circulation efficiency and reducing blood pressure
- Increasing the total number of red blood cells in the body, facilitating transport of oxygen
- Improved mental health, including reducing stress and lowering the incidence of depression

As a result, aerobic exercise can reduce the risk of death due to cardiovascular problems. In addition, high-impact aerobic activities (such as jogging or jumping rope) can stimulate bone growth, as well as reducing the risk of osteoporosis for both men and women. In addition to the health benefits of aerobic exercise, there are numerous performance benefits:

- Increased storage of energy molecules such as fats and carbohydrates within the muscles, allowing for increased endurance
- Neovascularization of the muscle sarcomeres to increase blood flow through the muscles
- Increasing speed at which aerobic metabolism is activated within muscles, allowing a greater portion of energy for intense exercise to be generated aerobically
- Improving the ability of muscles to use fats during exercise, preserving intramuscular glycogen
- Enhancing the speed at which muscles recover from high intensity exercise

"Aerobics" is a particular form of aerobic exercise. Aerobics classes generally involve rapid stepping patterns, performed to music with cues provided by an instructor. This type of aerobic activity became quite popular in the United States after the 1970 publication of *The New Aerobics* by Dr. Kenneth H. Cooper, and went through a brief period of intense popularity in the 1980s, when many celebrities (such as Jane Fonda and Richard Simmons) produced videos or created television shows promoting this type of aerobic exercise. Group exercise aerobics can be divided into two major types: freestyle aerobics and pre-choreographed aerobics.

Aerobic Capacity

'Aerobic capacity' describes the functional capacity of the cardiorespiratory system, (the heart, lungs and blood vessels). Aerobic capacity is defined as the maximum amount of oxygen the body can use during a specified period, usually during intense exercise. It is a function both of cardiorespiratory performance and the maximum ability to remove and utilize oxygen from circulating blood. To measure maximal aerobic capacity, an exercise physiologist or physician will perform a VO_2 max test, in which a subject will undergo progressively more strenuous exercise on a treadmill, from an easy walk through to exhaustion. The individual is typically connected to a respirometer to measure oxygen consumption, and the speed is increased incrementally over a fixed duration of time. The higher the measured cardiorespiratory endurance level, the more oxygen has been transported to and used by exercising muscles, and the higher the level of intensity at which the individual can exercise.

More simply stated, the higher the aerobic capacity, the higher the level of aerobic fitness. The Cooper and multi-stage fitness tests can also be used to assess functional aerobic capacity for particular jobs or activities.

The degree to which aerobic capacity can be improved by exercise varies very widely in the human population: while the average response to training is an approximately 17% increase in VO_2max, in any population there are "high responders" who may as much as double their capacity, and "low responders" who will see little or no benefit from training. Studies indicate that approximately 10% of otherwise healthy individuals cannot improve their aerobic capacity with exercise at all. The degree of an individual's responsiveness is highly heritable, suggesting that this trait is genetically determined.

Criticisms

When overall fitness is an occupational requirement, as it is for athletes, soldiers, and police and fire personnel, aerobic exercise alone may not provide a well balanced exercise programme. In particular, muscular strength, especially upper-body muscular strength, may be neglected. Also, the metabolic pathways involved in anaerobic metabolism (glycolysis and lactic acid fermentation) that generate energy during high intensity, low duration tasks, such as sprinting, are not exercised at peak aerobic exercise levels. Aerobic exercise remains however a valuable component of a balanced exercise programme and is good for cardiovascular health.

Some persons suffer repetitive stress injuries with some forms of aerobics, and then must choose less injurious, "low-impact" forms of aerobics, or lengthen the gap between bouts of exercise to allow for greater recovery.

Aerobics does not increase the basal metabolic rate as much as some forms of weight-training (which builds muscle mass), and may therefore be less effective at reducing obesity. Further, higher intensity exercise, such as High-intensity interval training (HIIT), increases the resting metabolic rate (RMR) in the 24 hours following high intensity exercise, ultimately burning more calories than lower intensity exercise; low intensity exercise burns more calories during the exercise, but fewer afterwards. Aerobic activity is also used by individuals with anorexia as a means of suppressing appetite, since aerobic exercise increases sugar and fatty acids in the blood by stimulating tissues to release their energy stores. While there is some support for exercising while hungry as a means of tapping into fat stores, most evidence is equivocal. In addition, performance can be impaired by lack of nutrients, which will reduce training effects.

Commercial Success

Aerobic exercise has long been a popular form of weight loss and physical fitness, often taking a commercial form.

- Tennis and jogging gained prominence and popularity in the 1970s, and significantly reduced the number of obese Americans.
- Judi Sheppard Missett largely helped create the market for commercial aerobics with her Jazzercise programme in the 1970s
- Richard Simmons hosted an aerobic exercise show on television, beginning in the 1980s, and continued with a variety of exercise videos.
- Billy Blanks's Tae Bo helped popularize cardio-boxing, workouts that used martial arts movements in the 1990s
- The Nia Technique, also called Neuromuscular Integrative Action, was developed in the 1980s as a form of "non-impact" aerobics (the original word is in the acronym). This is in contrast to popular "no pain no gain" attitudes, and attempted to combat the problem of impact injuries.

Anaerobic Exercise

Anaerobic exercise is exercise intense enough to trigger anaerobic metabolism. It is used by athletes in non-endurance sports to build power and by body builders to build muscle mass. Muscles trained under anaerobic conditions develop differently, leading to greater performance in short duration, high intensity activities, which last up to about 2 minutes.

Aerobic exercise, on the other hand, includes lower intensity activities performed for longer periods of time. Such activities like walking, running, swimming, and cycling require a great deal of oxygen to generate the energy needed for prolonged exercise.

There are two types of anaerobic energy systems, the ATP-CP energy system, which uses creatine phosphate as the main energy source, and the lactic acid (or anaerobic glycolysis) system that uses glucose (or glycogen) in the absence of oxygen. Events or activity that last up to about thirty seconds rely primarily on the former, phosphagen, system. Beyond this time aerobic and anaerobic glycolysis begin to predominate. Anaerobic glycolysis uses glucose inefficiently, and produces by-products such as lactic acid that are thought to be detrimental to muscle function; this limits activity based predominantly on anaerobic glycolysis to about 2 minutes. The effectiveness of anaerobic activity can be improved through training.

Lactate Threshold (LIP or Lactate Inflection Point)

The lactate threshold (LT) is the exercise intensity at which lactic acid starts to accumulate in the blood stream. This happens when it is produced faster than it can be removed (metabolized). This point is sometimes referred to as the anaerobic threshold (AT), or the onset of blood lactate accumulation (OBLA). When exercising below the LT intensity any lactate produced by the muscles is removed by the body without it building up. The lactate threshold is a useful measure for deciding exercise intensity for training and racing in endurance sports (e.g. long distance running, cycling, rowing, swimming, motocross, and cross country skiing), and can be increased greatly with training. The anaerobic threshold is considered to be somewhere between

90% and 95% of your maximum heart rate and interval training takes advantage of the body being able to temporarily exceed the lactate threshold, and then recover (reduce blood-lactate) while operating below the threshold and while still doing physical activity.

Fartlek and interval training are similar, the main difference being the relative intensities of the exercise, best illustrated in a real-world example: Fartlek training would involve constantly running, for a period time running just above the lactate threshold, and then running at just below it, while interval training would be running quite high above the threshold, but then slowing to a walk or slow jog during the rest periods.

Interval training can take the form of many different types of exercise and should closely replicate the movements found in the sport.

Fartlek would be used by people who are constantly moving, with occasional bouts of speed, such as soccer players, while interval training is more suited to sprinters, who exert maximum effort and then can stop exerting completely. With both styles of training, one can exert more effort before fatiguing and burn more calories than exercising at a constant pace (continuous training), but will emphasize training the anaerobic system rather than the aerobic system. Long duration training below the lactate threshold is recommended to primarily work the aerobic system.

Accurately measuring the lactate threshold involves taking blood samples (normally a pinprick to the finger, earlobe or thumb) during a ramp test where the exercise intensity is progressively increased. Measuring the threshold can also be performed non-invasively using gas-exchange (Respiratory quotient) methods, which requires a metabolic cart to measure air inspired and expired.

Although the lactate threshold is defined as the point when lactic acid starts to accumulate, some testers approximate this by using the point at which lactate reaches a concentration of 4 mM (at rest it is around 1 mM).

Difference between Yoga and Physical Exercise

Like regular exercise, yoga strengthens and tones the body. Regular exercise typically makes a body stronger and less flexible. Weight training for example, builds strength by breaking down and rebuilding muscle tissue. That bulky, muscle bound look and tighter muscle mass is a result of this breaking down and rebuilding of muscle. Yoga strengthens the body by toning the muscles and creates longer, leaner muscles due to the stretching. Yoga creates a body that is stronger and more flexible. Often the goal of regular exercise is to increase the heart rate.

While yoga can be practiced vigorously to increase heart rate, it can also be practiced in a way that reduces the heart rate and lowers blood pressure. Typically one exercises to a point of fatigue. At the end of a yoga practice, you feel as though you have had a workout, but are more relaxed and energized. Hatha yoga is not just a series of exercises, but a principle of exercise that involves concentration, breathing and movement.

Yoga offers many additional benefits as well. Bending, stretching and twisting the body massages and soothes the internal organs aiding digestion and elimination. Our hormones are brought into greater balance due to the toning of the endocrine system. The respiratory system is strengthened and the nervous system is soothed. Stress relief is also a major benefit of practicing yoga. In fact, all systems of the body are affected by a yoga practice. A qualified yoga teacher can advise you on the most appropriate yoga practice for you, regardless of age, health issues and fitness level.

Whether practicing vigorously with challenging poses or practicing gently with soothing poses, yoga is balanced action of the body, awareness of breath and steadiness of mind. This is yoga in action, union of the body/mind.

Regular exercise and yoga both help us to lead active, healthy lives. Yet, yoga is a life support system...a way of life that helps us to maintain a healthier body, a calmer mind and a more balanced and peaceful life.

The regular practice of Yoga is good for maintaining health compare to all other physical exercise, due to its extreme benefits as well as its superiority. The some of the main difference between the Yoga practices along with the physical exercises are listed as below.

Physical Exercise	Yoga
1. By the exercise body becomes stiff and inflexible.	1. By the practice of yoga the body become flexible
2. Exercises affect only muscles, not nerves.	2. Nerves are energised.
3.Does not impact the purification of Blood.	3. Yoga removes all impurities from the blood.
4. Unregulated breathing is observed after the practice.	4. Harmonized breathing is observed and breathing is regulated.
5. Digestion becomes weak as blood supply to other parts of the body increases.	5. Digestion improves by the regular practice of Yoga
6. Only external muscles get benifited.	6. Affects internal organs as well.
7. Only Physical body gets benifted.	7. All the bodies including the spiritual ones get benefited
9. Does not affect any energy centers.	9. With yoga this energy center of the body is protected.
10. Diseases are not eliminated through exercise.	10.Yoga is helpful to over come Diseases.
11. Only physical attributes are acquired.	11. Attributes like tolerance, self-control, self-confidence are automatically developed.
12. Integrity and behavioral changes are not achieved.	12. Through the practice of Yoga a man's behavior changes for the good.
13. After the practice Man gets tired.	13. Tiredness goes away through the practice of yoga. Man becomes energetic.
14. A lot of time and energy is wasted.	14. Time and energy are conserved. Yoga can be done in little time.
15. Old people cannot practice Exercises.	15.There is no Age limitation for yoga practice
16. Equipment and large spaces are needed.	16. No equipment is needed and yoga can be done in little space.
17. During travels exercise is not possible.	17. Yoga can be done during traveling.

Bibliography

Adams, Ronald C. : *Games, Sports and Exercises for the Physically Disabled*, Philadelphia, Lea & Febiger, 1991.

Auxter, D., Pyfer, J. and Huettig, C. H. : *Principles and Methods of Adapted Physical Education and Recreation*, St. Louis, MO, Mosby, 1993.

Barton, L. : *'Disability, Empowerment and Physical Education', Equality, Education and Physical Education*, London, Falmer, 1993.

Block, M. E. : *A Teacher's Guide to Including Students with Disabilities in Regular Physical Education*, Baltimore, MD, Paul H. Brookes Publishing Co., 1994.

Brettsneider, W.D. : *Psychological Outcomes and Social Benefits of Sport Involvement and Physical Activity: Implications for Physical Education,* ICSSPE, Berlin, 2001.

Buchik, N.T. : *Improving the Personal Fitness of Secondary Trainable Mentally Handicapped Students Through Aerobic Exercise*, M.S. Practicum Report, Nova University, 1990.

Buell, C. E. : *Physical Education for the Visually Handicapped*, Washington, D.C., AAHPER Press, 1973.

Cheatum, B.A. and Hammond, A.A. : *Physical Activities for Improving Children's Learning and Behavior: A Guide to Sensory Motor Development*, Windsor, OH, Human Kinetics, 2000.

Cosentino, Frank, and Maxwell L. Howell : *A History of Physical Education in Canada,* Toronto, General Publishing, 1971.

Craft, D. and Lieberman, L.J. : *'Visual Impairments and Deafness', in. Winnick*, IL, Human Kinetics Publishers, 2000.

Cratty, B. : *Adapted Physical Education in the Mainstream*, Denver, CO: Love, 1989.

Dauer, Victor P., and Robert P. Pangrazi: *Physical Education for Elementary School Children,* Minneapolis: Burges Publishing Company, 1983.

Davis, K. : *Adapted Physical Education for Students with Autism*, Springfield, IL: Charles C. Thomas, 1990.

Desira, Y. : *The Inclusion of Children with Physical Impairment in Physical Education in Girls' Secondary Schools*, B.Ed Thesis, Malta, 2002.

Dunn, J. M. : *Special Physical Education: Adapted, Individualized, Developmental*, Madison, WI, Brown and Benchmark Publishers, 1997.0

Fait, H. F. : *Adapted Physical Education*, Philadelphia, W.B. Saunders Company, 1960.

Geggus, R. : *Der Sportunterricht an Sonderschulen für Lernbehinderte, Examenarbeit,* Heidelberg, 1977.

Gerber, Ellen W.: *Innovators and Institutions in Physical Education.* Philadelphia: Lea and Febiger, 1971.

Hackensmith, Charles W.: *History of Physical Education.* New York: Harper and Row, 1966.

Haley, Bruce: *The Healthy Body and Victorian Culture.* Cambridge, MA: Harvard University Press, 1978.

Hardman, A. & Stensel, D. :*Physical Activity and Health: The Evidence Explained*, London, Routledge, 2003.

Hill, A.P., King, N.A, Byrne, N.M. : *Children, Obesity and Exercise: Prevention, Treatment and Management of Childhood Obesity*, Routledge, UK. 2007.

Hodge, S., Murata, N., Block, M., and Lieberman, L.J. : *Case Studies in Adapted Physical Education: Empowering Critical Thinking*, Scottsdale, AZ, Holcom Hathaway Publishers, 2003.

Jansma, P. and French, R. : *Special Physical Education: Physical Activity, Sports, and Recreation*, Englewood Cliffs, NJ: Prentice-Hall, 1994.

Knight, E. and Chedzoy, S. : *Physical Education in Primary Schools: Access for All*, London, David Fulton, 1998.

Lau, S. K. : *Physical Education for the Physically Handicapped*, Delhi, Khel Sahitya Kendra, 2001.

Lieberman, L. : *'Games and Activities for Individuals with Sensory Impairments', in Grosse,* Reston, VA, AAHPERD Publications, 1993.

Lieberman, L. : *'Including Everyone in Physical Education, & Peer Tutoring Strategies', in Physical Education Methods for Classroom Teachers,* Champaign, IL, Human Kinetics Publishers, 1999.

Moon, M.S. : *Making School and Community Recreation Fun for Everyone: Places and Ways to Integrate*, Baltimore, MD, Paul H Brookes, 1994.

Oja, P. & Borms, J. : *Health Enhancing Physical Activity. ICSSPE Perspectives*, Meyer & Meyer Sport, Germany, 2004.

Oliva, G. and Crider, L. : *Shape up 'n sign*, Laurel, MD, Author, 1991.

Portwood, M. : *Dyslexia and Physical Education*, London, David Fulton Publishers, 2003.

Scherer, H.-G., Bietz, J. and Herwig, H. : *Motorisches Handeln und Lernen bei Blindheit. Eine Projektskizze*, Unpublished manuscript, Marburg, 1991.

Schraag, M. : *Sport in der Lernbehindertenschule*, Berlin, Marhold, 1979.

Seaman, J. A. DePauw : *Making Connections From Theory to Practice in Adapted Physical Education*, Scottsdale, AZ: Holcomb Hathaway, 2003.

Seaman, J.A. : *Physical Best and Individuals with Disabilities*, AAHPERD, Reston, VA, 1995.

Shepard, R.J. : *Fitness in Special Populations*, Champaign, IL, Human Kinetics, 1990.

Sherborne, V. : *Developmental Movement for Children: Mainstream, Special Needs and Pre-School*, Cambridge, Cambridge University Press, 1990.

Sherrill, C. : *Adapted Physical Activity, Recreation and Sport: Cross Disciplinary and Lifespan*, Madison, WI, Brown and Benchmark, 1998.

Sherrill, C. : *Adapted Physical Education and Recreation*, Dubuque, IA: William C. Brown, 1994.

Sugden, D. and Wright, H. : *'Curricular entitlement and implementation for all children', in Armstrong,* London, Cassell, 1996.

Thomas, J.R. : *Exercise and Cognitive Function, in C. Bouchard et al. Physical Activity, Fitness and Health: International Proceedings and Consensus Statement*, Champagne, Illinois, Human Kinetics, 1994.

Van Dalen, Deobold, and Bruce L. Bennett: *A World History of Physical Education, Cultural, Philosophical, Comparative,* Englewood Cliffs, NJ: Prentice-Hall, 1971.

Vickermann, P. : *'Knowing your pupils and planning for different needs', in Capel, S. Learning to Teach Physical Education in the Secondary School*, London, Routledge, 1997.

Weiss, Gillian : *"An Essential Year for the Child: The Kindergarten in British Columbia," in J. Donald and David C. Jones, Schooling and Society in Twentieth Century British Columbia*, Calgary, Detselig, 1980.

Williams, I. : *'Is Physical Education Really for "Everyone"?', B.C. Journal of Special Education*, 1991.

Winnick, J.P. : *Adapted Physical Education and Sport*, Champaign, IL, Human Kinetics, 1990.

Wiseman, D.C. : *Physical Education for Exceptional Students: Theory to Practice*, Albany, NY, Delmar Publishers, 1994.

Wright. H. and Sugden, D. : *Physical Education for All: Developing Physical Education in the Curriculum for Pupils with Special Educational Needs*, London, David Fulton, 1999.

Index

N

O

P

R

S

□□□